VOTING ONLINE

MCGILL-QUEEN'S STUDIES IN URBAN GOVERNANCE

Series editors: Kristin Good and Martin Horak

In recent years there has been an explosion of interest in local politics and the governance of cities – both in Canada and around the world. Globally, the city has become a consequential site where instances of social conflict and of cooperation play out. Urban centres are increasingly understood as vital engines of innovation and prosperity and a growing body of interdisciplinary research on urban issues suggests that high-performing cities have become crucial to the success of nations, even in the global era. Yet at the same time, local and regional governments continue to struggle for political recognition and for the policy resources needed to manage cities, to effectively govern, and to achieve sustainable growth.

The purpose of the McGill-Queen's Studies in Urban Governance series is to highlight the growing importance of municipal issues, local governance, and the need for policy reform in urban spaces. The series aims to answer the question "why do cities matter?" while exploring relationships between levels of government and examining the changing dynamics of metropolitan and community development. By taking a four-pronged approach to the study of urban governance, the series encourages debate and discussion of: (1) actors, institutions, and how cities are governed; (2) policy issues and policy reform; (3) the city as case study; and (4) urban politics and policy through a comparative framework.

With a strong focus on governance, policy, and the role of the city, this series publishes books in a broad range of disciplines and viewpoints.

10 A Neighborhood Politics of Last Resort
Post-Katrina New Orleans and the Right to the City
Stephen Danley

11 Shaping the Metropolis
Institutions and Urbanization in the United States and Canada
Zack Taylor

12 China's Urban Future and the Quest for Stability
Edited by Rebecca Clothey and Richardson Dilworth

13 Big Moves
Global Agendas, Local Aspirations, and Urban Mobility in Canada
Anthony Perl, Matt Hern, and Jeffrey Kenworthy

14 The Right to an Age-Friendly City
Redistribution, Recognition, and Senior Citizen Rights in Urban Spaces
Meghan Joy

15 The Platform Economy and the Smart City
Technology and the Transformation of Urban Policy
Edited by Austin Zwick and Zachary Spicer

16 Political Engagement in Canadian City Elections
Edited by R. Michael McGregor and Laura B. Stephenson

17 Voting Online
Technology and Democracy in Municipal Elections
Nicole Goodman, Helen A. Hayes, R. Michael McGregor, Scott Pruysers, and Zachary Spicer

Voting Online

Technology and Democracy in Municipal Elections

Nicole Goodman

Helen A. Hayes

R. Michael McGregor

Scott Pruysers

Zachary Spicer

McGill-Queen's University Press
Montreal & Kingston • London • Chicago

ISBN 978-0-2280-2124-7 (cloth)
ISBN 978-0-2280-2125-4 (paper)
ISBN 978-0-2280-2178-0 (ePDF)
ISBN 978-0-2280-2179-7 (ePUB)

Legal deposit second quarter 2024
Bibliothèque nationale du Québec

Printed in Canada on acid-free paper that is 100% ancient forest free (100% post-consumer recycled), processed chlorine free

This book has been published with the help of a grant from the Canadian Federation for the Humanities and Social Sciences, through the Awards to Scholarly Publications Program, using funds provided by the Social Sciences and Humanities Research Council of Canada.

Funded by the Government of Canada | Financé par le gouvernement du Canada | Canada

Canada Council for the Arts | Conseil des arts du Canada

We acknowledge the support of the Canada Council for the Arts.
Nous remercions le Conseil des arts du Canada de son soutien.

McGill-Queen's University Press in Montreal is on land which long served as a site of meeting and exchange amongst Indigenous Peoples, including the Haudenosaunee and Anishinabeg nations. In Kingston it is situated on the territory of the Haudenosaunee and Anishinaabek. We acknowledge and thank the diverse Indigenous Peoples whose footsteps have marked these territories on which peoples of the world now gather.

Library and Archives Canada Cataloguing in Publication

Title: Voting online : technology and democracy in municipal elections / Nicole Goodman, Helen A. Hayes, R. Michael McGregor, Scott Pruysers, Zachary Spicer.
Names: Goodman, Nicole, author. | Hayes, Helen A., author. | McGregor, R. Michael, author. | Pruysers, Scott, 1985– author. | Spicer, Zachary, 1983– author.
Series: McGill-Queen's studies in urban governance ; 17.
Description: Series statement: McGill-Queen's studies in urban governance ; 17 | Includes bibliographical references and index.
Identifiers: Canadiana (print) 20230581323 | Canadiana (ebook) 2023058134X | ISBN 9780228021247 (cloth) | ISBN 9780228021254 (paper) | ISBN 9780228021780 (ePDF) | ISBN 9780228021797 (ePUB)
Subjects: LCSH: Internet voting—Ontario—Case studies. | LCSH: Local elections Ontario—Case studies. | LCSH: Voting—Ontario—Case studies. | LCGFT: Case studies
Classification: LCC JF1032.G66 2024 | DDC 324.6/502854678—dc23

This book was typeset in 10.5/13 Sabon.

Contents

Tables and Figures

TABLES

FIGURES

Acknowledgments

This book is the result of input and assistance from many. First and foremost, we wish to thank the electors, candidates, and election administrators who took the time to participate in our surveys and focus groups. We are also grateful to the Association of Municipal Managers, Clerks and Treasurers of Ontario (AMCTO) for supporting us to establish our focus groups and accessing the necessary contact lists to facilitate our administrator's survey. We thank AMCTO as well for hosting a workshop about the book's findings at their annual conference. Initial portions of this work were presented at the annual conferences of the Canadian Political Science Association, the American Political Science Association, and the International Conference for Electronic Voting. We thank the discussants and audience members at each for their engagement with our work. We would also like to extend our thanks to online voting vendors for providing information about the market and their products to ensure content accuracy.

Throughout the project, invaluable research assistance was provided by Noah Nickel, Carlie Pagliacci, and Amanda Tieber. Special thanks to Jason Roy for reviewing early chapters of the book, to Iulia Spycher-Krivosonova for her input, and to Aleksander Essex for fielding technical questions. We also owe a debt of gratitude to Sharon Janzen for her map-making services and Carla Caruana for her help with copyediting and indexing.

Finally, we are extremely thankful for the thorough and thoughtful work of the book's reviewers. Each provided us with much to consider as we revised the manuscript. We also wish to thank the helpful staff at McGill-Queen's University Press, in particular our tireless editor, Emily Andrew, who supported us throughout the entire publishing process.

This research was financially supported by the Social Sciences and Humanities Research Council of Canada (grants number 435-2018-1281, 435-2017-0993, and 430-2022-01059) and the Government of Ontario's Early Researcher Awards program (grant number ER17-13-035).

VOTING ONLINE

I

Studying Online Voting in Ontario Local Elections

INTRODUCTION

Most elections held around the world today are, in some capacity, digitized. In many instances, technological adoption has initially begun on the back-end, involving the administration of election processes like voter registration, changes to voter information collection and management, electronic voter lists and poll books, or election reporting (Krivonosova 2022). However, in a growing number of jurisdictions, Canada included, technology is being embraced in both vote casting and counting. In other words, we are increasingly witnessing the digitization of front-facing electoral processes (Garnett and James 2020; Goodman et al. 2010). Scholars of elections have used these developments as examples to justify their classification of our current time as "the age of cyber elections" (Garnett and James 2020).

Of possible ways to modernize or digitize elections, online voting presents both more excitement and worry than other reforms. In fact, when it comes to the potential hopes and pitfalls of voting in particular, online ballots have long been regarded as among the most noteworthy, given on the one hand their potential benefits for accessibility and participation (Norris 2001; Norris 2005) and, on the other, possible risks regarding the security and integrity of elections (Goodman and Smith 2016; Essex and Goodman 2020). Many have pointed to online voting as one possible method to arrest declining participation and improve voter access to the electoral process more generally (Alvarez et al. 2009; Gerlach and Gasser 2009; Goodman and Stokes 2020; Germann and Serdült 2017; Solvak and Vassil 2018; Trechsel and Vassil 2010; Vassil and Weber 2011).

These potential benefits have been heavily emphasized in discourse concerning electors who either cannot access or have difficulty attending physical polling stations, including people with disabilities, the elderly, military officials, students or citizens living abroad, and persons who are incarcerated (Dandoy and Kernalegenn 2021; Germann 2021; Goodman et al. 2010; Goodman and Smith 2017).

Online voting has also been shown to have potential benefits for the voting process itself. For instance, research has found that internet voting eliminates concerns with improperly marked ballots and makes vote counting immune to potential human error, such as over or under voting (Goodman 2017; Pammett and Goodman 2013; Benaloh et al. 2014; Essex 2016). Online voting has also been shown to lower some election costs, as the administration of online ballots is often outsourced to private companies, thereby requiring less oversight from municipal staff (Goodman et al. 2010). Others have argued, however, that the risks associated with online voting have never been greater given that "foreign enemies" are forthright about their willingness to threaten Western democracies through digital means (Essex and Goodman 2022; Jamieson 2018). Even with many of these concerns noted, the promise that online voting may improve elections and democracy has led to its precipitous uptake around the world, including in Ontario, Canada: the case that informs this book and which currently represents one the largest uses of online voting in the world.

Uptake in online voting has ebbed and flowed since the turn of the century, largely motivated by a growing belief that technology could be a solution to rectify or improve electoral participation and other emerging democratic problems. This attitude is often referred to as "tech-solutionism," which posits that digital technologies are necessarily better and more reliable than human beings at objectively and justly solving social and political problems (Broussard 2019, 156). Those who embrace this view claim that technology can increase productivity (Schwab 2016), redefine stakeholder trust in electoral processes (Shahaab et al. 2020), improve government services (Twizeyimana and Andersson 2019), and contribute to economic growth (Frey 2019). Proponents suggest that the extent to which society embraces technological innovation is a key determinant of progress (Jaffe 2021; Sejinowski 2018; Schwab 2016).

This "tech-solutionist" lens suggests that online voting may be the panacea to reverse or counter turnout declines in Western democracies, boost electoral legitimacy (Norris 2005) and, more broadly, act as a catalyst to positively impact political environments (Bridgmon and Milewicz 2004; Norris 2002; Small and Jansen 2020). These beliefs – and tech-solutionism more broadly – have, in part, informed the growing adoption of online voting in many jurisdictions, including in the United Kingdom in 2002, Canada and Switzerland in 2003, and Estonia in 2005. Motivation for implementation among municipal administrators in the province of Ontario have mirrored those internationally, with accessibility, convenience, and turnout being largely at the forefront (Goodman et al. 2010; Goodman 2014). Introducing election efficiencies, including simplifying election administration, and tabulating vote outcomes faster, have also been considerations, albeit to a lesser extent in Ontario (Duenas-Cid et al. 2021; Krimmer et al. 2021; Goodman and Smith 2016).

Ontario has the longest-standing online voting deployment in the world. It is therefore an ideal case to study and learn about the effects of online voting in local elections. Hundreds of towns and cities across the province have adopted online voting over the past two decades. As is the case in most provinces, municipalities in Ontario are responsible for the administration of their own elections. Accordingly, in each municipality, decision makers (either elected officials or unelected bureaucrats) must make important administrative choices regarding their local elections. This has resulted in a great deal of variation with respect to whether, when, and how online voting is used. These multiple dimensions of variation make Ontario an ideal case for an academic examination of internet voting. Additionally, despite the widespread adoption of online voting across Ontario and the fact that its use has been changing local elections and democracy for nearly two decades, the topic has received less academic study than one might expect.

Studies of online voting span a variety of academic fields. Computer scientists and engineers may be interested in its technical aspects, including security and secrecy, while economists and business scholars may wish to study its risks and benefits, especially concerning the inclusion of private entities (contractors who provide the electronic voting services) in the electoral process. In this book, we focus on the attitudes and behaviours of relevant political and public administration actors – electors (voters and non-voters), candidates, and administrators – towards online voting both independently and in comparison to one another. These analyses are long overdue; no scholarly book has been written on this topic in more than a decade, and none addresses these issues similarly or substantively. In fact, to our knowledge, this book represents the first scholarly study of this subject in Canada. We suspect that this is primarily because local governments and elections in Canada tend to receive a small fraction of the attention of their provincial and federal counterparts (Cutler and Matthews 2005; Taylor and Eidelman 2010; McGregor et al. 2021; Lucas and McGregor 2022).

To study the attitudes towards and perceptions of voters, candidates, and administrators, we draw upon original large-N surveys from each group. These datasets allow us to answer many questions about these actors, three of which recur throughout the book:

1 How consistent are orientations within groups, across groups, and across time? By considering data from multiple sources and at multiple points in time, we can map out the multiple dimensions in which attitudes and behaviour towards internet voting vary.
2 What accounts for variation in attitudes and behaviour? Here, we consider whether individual-level and contextual factors influence orientations towards internet voting; what accounts for the differences within and between groups?
3 Does internet voting have an effect on attitudes and behaviour? How does online voting affect the actors – both electors and elites – who are exposed to it?

Guided by these questions, this book represents an important step forward in the study of political behaviour in Canadian elections. It also contributes to the international literature on the topic. For example, only two books have been written addressing internet voting in the United States, both of which were published over a decade ago when internet voting was in its infancy (Alvarez and Hall 2003; Alvarez and Hall 2010). Since this time, there have been edited volumes containing chapters on Canada (Grofman et al. 2014), special issue journals that include an examination of online voting (Garnett and James 2020), and numerous journal articles that study topics surrounding internet voting in this country. Existing work covers topics such as turnout (Goodman and Stokes 2020), the manner in which online voting may attract or dissuade certain types of electors from participating (Couture et al. 2017; Goodman et al., 2018), case studies of individual cities (Goodman 2014), election administration (Goodman and Spicer 2019; Hayes et al. 2022), political parties (Goodman and Pruysers 2019), regulation (Essex and Goodman 2020) and security risk exposure (Essex and Goodman 2022).

Journal articles and individual chapters are, however, too brief to tackle these topics in a holistic manner. This book-length study provides thorough accounts of our case, discusses important theoretical considerations, describes our unique data sources, asks and answers several important and related research questions, and details the many implications of our findings. This book also contributes to more general literature on electoral institutions and institutional change. In Canada, this literature has focused overwhelmingly on reform of the electoral system. As this type of reform has yet to be widely embraced, most of this literature is normative and argues in favour of or in opposition to change (Milner 1999; Potter et al. 2017). A noteworthy bit of empirical, rather than normative, work on this subject is a piece by Anderson and Stephenson (2021) that considers the effect of the adoption of ranked choice voting in London (the city has since reverted to a single member plurality system). There is also some research into the effects of adding or extending advance or early voting opportunities (Blais et al. 2007; Garnett 2019).

Institutional research has also focused on fixed election dates (Alcantara and Roy 2014), including studies of their supposed benefits (Leuprecht and McHugh 2008; Dodek 2010) and election timing affecting incumbent performance (Roy and Alcantara 2012). Despite the introduction of online voting being arguably as significant of an institutional change as any of these others, little has been written on the topic. This is also the case despite discussions and examinations of online voting at all levels of government in Canada (ERRE 2016; Elections BC 2014; Elections Ontario 2018).

Although scholarly attention is increasingly being devoted to the views and perceptions of federal and provincial candidates in Canada (Cross and Pruysers 2019; Cross et al. 2020; Cross et al. 2022; Thomas and Bodet 2013; Sayers 1999; Stevens et al. 2018; Pruysers and Cross 2018), far less is known about municipal candidates.[1] As Goodman and Lucas (2016, 36) conclude, "our knowledge of Canadian municipal candidates is much more limited." This is particularly true regarding municipal candidates and online voting. Whereas surveys of federal candidates' attitudes towards online voting have been conducted during recent election cycles, we are unaware of any similar treatment for local candidates. Providing new insights regarding how local candidates view the adoption of online voting not only contributes to our understanding of how electronic elections shape democratic attitudes and campaign behaviours, but also begins to address the voter-candidate imbalance in municipal political behaviour literature more broadly.

In addition, we go further by also considering election administrators. If local candidates have been largely ignored, research regarding local administrators is non-existent. This, of course, is surprising given the fundamental role these individuals have during elections and the amount of agency they have to influence political life in local government (Goodman and Spicer 2019; Hayes et al. 2022). By combining original data from three different cohorts of political actors – electors, candidates, and administrators – this book makes a unique contribution to the field.

Finally, our research adds to the rapidly growing study of local elections in Canada, which, in the last decade, has examined candidates (Scott and Medeiros 2021; Breux et al. 2019; Kiss et al. 2020), electors (Lucas and McGregor 2021; McGregor et al. 2021; Moore et al. 2017; McGregor et al. 2016), and local political institutions (Anderson and Stephenson 2022). While these works have substantially added to an understudied and undertheorized research area, much less is known about municipalities than about any other order of government. This is perhaps surprising, given the many unique features of local elections in Canada, including the use of online voting.

In addition to the academic benefits that accrue from detailed studies of this nature, there are significant practical implications that stem from analyses of emerging and important social phenomena like internet voting. Those individuals making decisions about voting systems should do so armed with as much of an understanding of these systems and their effects as possible. Their decisions should be based not only upon normative considerations but also empirical observations; evidence should inform these debates. As many municipalities in Ontario – particularly the large ones – have yet to adopt online voting, the findings presented here have meaningful policy implications, especially as debates regarding the implementation of online voting continue in other provinces and at other orders of government.

The remainder of this chapter sets the scene for those that follow. First, we provide an overview of the different ways that elections are increasingly becoming "electronic" and define our use of the terms "internet voting" and "online voting" (which we use synonymously). Second, the chapter provides practical background information on the history of internet voting. In doing so, it offers an overview of the growth of this voting method both in Canada and abroad. Third, we justify our focus on Ontario, making the case that the province is valuable to the study of internet voting. The chapter also provides an overview of the existing social science literature on the subject (we engage more thoroughly with this literature in subsequent chapters). Finally, the chapter concludes with an overview of those to come and a detailed description of the data sources that we employ in our many and varied analyses.

WHAT IS ONLINE VOTING?

The focus of this book is remote online voting. Online voting is a form of "electronic" or "e-voting," which is a general term that encompasses a range of voting technologies that may or may not use the internet. In the broadest terms, electronic elections are those where aspects of the elections are digital in nature, including registration, voter strike-off, counting, or voting itself. Through its most recent recommendation (Rec(2017)5), the Council of Europe defines electronic voting as including technologies such as optical scan tabulators, direct-recording electronic voting machines, and online voting systems (Council of Europe 2017). Definitions from other international agencies similarly classify a spectrum of technologies under the e-voting umbrella, including information and communication technologies that facilitate "the recording, casting, or counting of votes in political elections and referendums" (International IDEA 2011, 6). Online or internet voting is a distinct type of e-voting; even the term online voting itself can serve as a label for different types and ways of voting that involve the internet.

There are two important distinctions to make when defining online voting in Ontario. Unlike in other countries where the term "online voting" may refer to a voting process whereby only the receipt of a ballot or its tabulation is carried out online, both of these aspects of Ontario's municipal online voting processes are carried out online. The United States Public Policy Council of the

Association of Computing Machinery, for example, refers to methods such as email and fax voting as forms of online voting since they involve the "transmission of ballots over the internet" (Greenhalgh et al. 2018). The specific type of online voting used in municipal elections in Ontario, however, relies on an internet connection for all aspects of the voting process – ballot receipt, completion, casting, and tabulation.

The second necessary distinction is that most online voting in Ontario is carried out remotely. Ballots are cast using devices connected to the internet from home, a workplace, or another location that is not supervised by election officials. In their seminal work on online voting, Alvarez and Hall (2004) denote four types of voting by internet. Two of these types involve casting a ballot on a computer or machine using an internet connection at a polling location – either at a voter's designated polling location (known as "polling place online voting") or any available poll location (known as "precinct online voting"). In a third type, online ballots can be cast from kiosks at specified locations that are not polling places but that are supervised by election officials. Finally, the fourth type, which we focus on in this book, is remote online voting, where votes are cast from outside of a polling place.

Some municipalities in Ontario do offer polling place online voting or precinct online voting, but these supervised options are administered in a more limited capacity than voting remotely online, and they are not our focus here. When we define online or internet voting throughout this book, we refer to remote online voting only. This type of online voting offers election officials the least control and introduces the most risk exposure but provides electors with the greatest possible accessibility and convenience (Goodman et al. 2010). Remote online voting is also the form of digitization that has the greatest potential impact upon the actors which are our focus here: electors and elites. Therefore, for the purposes of this book, we define online voting *as a voting system wherein the receipt, casting, and counting of ballots is conducted over the internet and can be facilitated remotely.*[2]

The above distinctions are important because carrying out a portion of a vote online, such as receiving a ballot online but then casting it manually or receiving it by mail and then casting it virtually, changes the costs of voting for electors and may not have the same impact on their inclination to participate, their attitudes toward the voting mode or their voting experience. For these reasons, and to understand the context of the findings in the book, it is important to outline the specific type of online voting predominately deployed in Ontario's municipal elections.

The detailed study of online voting is needed given its widespread adoption in Ontario and spread elsewhere in Canada. As we note in greater detail below, hundreds of municipalities in Ontario currently employ remote online voting and that number continues to increase each election cycle. Municipalities exhibit important variation across time (the system has been adopted slowly across the province since 2003) and location (though most municipalities now employ online voting, a sizable number still do not, including most of the province's largest cities). While variation also exists with respect to other forms of electoral digitization, from the point of view of electors, the most significant form of digitization is remote online voting.

ONLINE VOTING: TRENDS IN USE

International use

In response to technological advances and the hope that online voting might help remedy electoral ills (Norris, 2001), several jurisdictions have either enacted trials or have embarked on larger scale adoption of online voting overtime. Canada is one of the most active of these jurisdictions, by way of the early and continuing activity in local elections in Ontario. Among the first international uses of online voting in binding government elections include the United Kingdom in 2002, Canada and Switzerland in 2003 and Estonia in 2005 (Norris 2005; Goodman 2014; Alvarez et al. 2009; Serdült et al. 2015).[3] All of these initial elections were held at a subnational level. In 2007, Estonia became the first country in the world to employ online voting in a national election (Ehin et al. 2022). Since then, several jurisdictions have implemented the technology for a range of votes, from local to supranational elections. In addition to growing adoption, there is considerable variation in terms of implementation: some countries employ online voting for national elections and referenda, while others use it only for subnational contests. There is also variation with respect to the type of electors and share of the electorate who are eligible to cast their ballots online.

While the list of jurisdictions that have trialed or adopted online voting is growing, the list of countries that continue to use it is still relatively short. According to International IDEA's Internet and Communication Technologies in Elections Database (2023), at the time of writing fifteen countries have active online voting programs or trials including Armenia, Australia, Canada, Ecuador, Estonia, France, Mexico, New Zealand, Oman, Pakistan, Panama, Russia, South Korea, Switzerland, and the United Arab Emirates. In other instances, the use of online voting has been temporary, in some cases lasting no longer than a few election cycles (e.g., Norway), whereas others (e.g., the Åland Islands, Finland) were halted before completion (Krivonosova 2022). The most frequent rationale for discontinuation is concerns relating to security or technical vulnerabilities (Duenas-Cid et al. 2020; Essex and Goodman 2022; Segaard et al. 2016).

Even in locations where online voting is well established, use tends to remain a topic of discussion, with many jurisdictions either refining their existing approach (e.g., Estonia and Switzerland) or reconsidering the use of online voting altogether (e.g., the United Kingdom and Norway) (Averia 2022). Switzerland highlights this point well. The country used online voting from 2003 to 2019 in fifteen cantons, but paused deployment from 2019 to 2023 to allow time to refine the online voting system and address security concerns (Federal Chancellery 2022). The Swiss Federal Council announced in March 2023 that several cantons could resume use of online voting on a limited basis (Federal Chancellery 2023). Norway has also gone back and forth with their use of online voting systems. After deploying online voting in select municipalities in 2011 and for parliamentary elections in 2013, the country dropped the system due to security concerns (Segaard et al. 2016). Yet in 2018 and 2022, several small counties brought back the voting mode for referendums (Smartmatic 2022). In local elections in Ontario, a small number of municipalities that once used online voting have subsequently halted their use of the system. The City of Guelph provides an example of this phenomenon (and one which we consider in more detail later in this book): in 2014, this mid-sized city in southwestern Ontario used online voting but then reverted to traditional paper ballots for the 2018 election. Put plainly, past use of online voting does not guarantee future use.

Online voting systems are used for many types of votes. Online voting is used in some jurisdictions for national but not subnational elections (e.g., the Netherlands and Armenia), where elsewhere such systems are used at both levels (e.g., Australia, Estonia, Norway, and Panama). It is even more commonly the case, however, that internet voting is used exclusively for subnational elections (e.g., Finland, New Zealand, the United Kingdom, and Canada). There are also cases where online voting is used for supranational elections (e.g., for European Parliament votes in Estonia), as well as for referenda (e.g., Armenia, Norway, Russia, and the United Kingdom). There is significant variation, therefore, in the way countries adopt and deploy online voting. By our estimation, however, subnational elections are the most common foci of online voting.

A final noteworthy feature of the adoption of online voting systems is that it is commonly the case that only select groups of electors are eligible to cast ballots online. While this most often involves military or overseas voters, it also includes electors from certain areas or a certain percentage of the population[4] while the remainder of voters in a given jurisdiction often use traditional paper ballots, cast in-person. In some places, citizens abroad are the only ones who can cast votes electronically (e.g., France, Mexico, and Panama). In others, military members and diplomatic staff are allowed but others are not (Armenia and the United States). Still, in other locales, limitations have been or are geographically based, with voting methods varying by location (e.g., Switzerland and Canada).

In sum, the history of international online voting use has three notable features. First, despite increasing adoption, only a small minority of countries have used, or currently use, online voting. Second, in those countries where online voting is used, it is mostly deployed at the subnational level. Third, only in very few cases is online voting offered to the full electorate.

Despite the lack of consistency of online voting deployment, both across time and geography, it remains an important and high-profile voting reform that is regularly debated and trialed around the world. Pressure for election agencies to offer regular and accessible elections has only intensified since the outbreak of the COVID-19 pandemic. Jurisdictions everywhere, regardless of their experience with internet voting, can benefit from a detailed scholarly examination of this phenomenon. As Ontario has the longest standing record of consecutive use of online voting, this setting has the potential to provide new insights and lessons of relevance to debates about online voting around the world.

Table 1.1 | Online voting use in Canada

Jurisdiction	Year(s) adopted	Type	Eligibility
Ontario	2003–current	Municipal elections	Full electorate in select municipalities
Nova Scotia	2008–current	Municipal elections	Full electorate in select municipalities
PEI	2016	Non-binding plebiscite on electoral reform	Full electorate
Northwest Territories	2019–current	Territorial election	Absentee voters
Yukon	2022–current	School board elections	All eligible voters
First Nations	2011–current	Elections, referendums, ratification/ agreement votes, community polls	Full electorate in select First Nations
Inuit	2017–current	Elections and other votes	Full electorate
Métis	2016–current	Elections, ratification votes, plebiscites	Full electorate

Canadian Developments

While we have seen a range of election and voting technologies used in Canada, the bulk of online voting occurs in local governments in the province of Ontario. Over the past two decades, online voting has become a mainstay in Ontario's local elections, and more than half of the province's municipalities employ remote online voting as of 2022. While also used by most municipalities for local elections in Nova Scotia and on a smaller scale in provincial and territorial elections for select voters in regular elections or in the context of smaller or non-binding votes, Ontario is the epicentre of remote online voting activity in Canada. Table 1.1 illustrates the instances of online voting use in elections and votes of Canadian governments, indicating the periods in which online voting has been in place, the type of elections it is used for, and who is eligible to vote online.

The breadth and frequency of online voting use in Ontario is a key reason why this setting is the focus of this book (though we later outline in more detail other reasons why Ontario is an important case study). Online voting is no longer just a municipal project in Canada; it has also long been used by Indigenous governments and other organizations, such as labour unions, and is being adopted and used by provincial and territorial election agencies with a notable increase in interest since the emergence of COVID-19 (Elections Nova Scotia 2022; Elections Quebec 2022). As interest and use grows, lessons learned about electors and elites in Ontario's local elections can provide important insights into electronic elections elsewhere in the country.

Despite growing use among other governments in Canada, trends in this country mirror those witnessed internationally, in the sense that internet voting is predominately used in community-level elections – at the municipal level and in Indigenous communities. While provincial and territorial governments are slowly starting to adopt or at least consider the adoption of online voting, they nevertheless use it in much more limited ways than what we see in many Ontario municipal elections. The use of online voting in these locations tends to either be focused on specific groups of voters (e.g., absentee voters in the Northwest Territories or absentee voters in the Canadian armed forces overseas in Nova Scotia) or in contests that many would consider to be relatively unimportant, for instance in a non-binding referendum or school board elections (e.g., PEI and the Yukon). These governments have not committed to online voting to the same extent as many Ontario municipalities. The federal government has yet to use internet voting, although its implementation was researched as part of Elections Canada's 2008–13 Strategic Plan and discussed by the Special Committee on Electoral Reform (Goodman et al. 2010; ERRE 2016; Goodman 2017).

Nevertheless, overall, the use of online voting is clearly trending upwards in Canada. The Northwest Territories and Yukon plan to use online voting in future elections and expand trials already conducted, and Prince Edward Island passed an amendment to its

Election Act to allow online voting in future binding votes. Both Elections Nova Scotia and Elections Quebec recently released separate requests for proposals to tender online voting services. The Elections Nova Scotia request will support online voting in its 2025 provincial election for absentee voters, with a focus on members of the military and voters with accessibility needs (Elections Nova Scotia 2022). While the Elections Quebec request does not indicate a firm commitment to use the voting mode, it is part of information gathering for possible future adoption (Elections Quebec 2022).

Online voting has also been widely used, and uptake continues to grow, among First Nations, Inuit, and Métis governments and organizations across Canada. These groups have a long history of use, implementing online voting for ratification and agreement votes, elections, referendums, community polls, and annual general meetings since 2011 (Budd et al. 2019; Gabel and Goodman 2021). To date, more than 150 First Nations have adopted online voting to improve participation of citizens living on and off-reserve lands, promote self-determination, better connect community, and modernize governance (Gabel et al. 2016; Budd et al. 2019). Uptake among First Nations has also seen growth due to the COVID-19 pandemic, with more than 170 online votes being facilitated between the beginning of the pandemic and 2021 (Budd et al. 2021).

In addition to these other contexts, online voting continues to grow at the municipal level, both in Ontario and in other provinces. As part of a research project, several scholars organized a citizens' assembly in the City of Longueuil in June 2023 to consider four voting reforms, including online voting (Longueuil 2023). Elections Quebec was a partner of the project. There has also been discussion of possible use in municipalities in British Columbia and Alberta (Kamenova and Goodman 2015). Coupled with the fact that online voting continues to be adopted at a rapid rate by municipalities in Ontario and Nova Scotia, these patterns suggest that municipalities continue to be primary loci of online voting in Canada.

Finally, it is worth noting that online voting use extends to other organizations, including unions, political parties, universities, and private sector companies (Goodman 2014). The voting mode has been regularly used for two decades to support a variety of union votes and political party races for leadership as well as internal matters like unity agreements, annual general meetings, council and executive elections, leadership reviews, delegate votes, and by-law amendments (Goodman and Pruysers 2019). Online voting has been used by provincial and federal parties of all stripes.[5] Though these groups and organizations fall outside of the purview of this work, it is doubtless that they will be able to learn lessons from the experiences of Ontario municipalities.

WHY ONTARIO?

Ontario's position as the epicentre of online voting activity in Canada makes it an attractive environment in which to study the voting reform. While the sheer number of municipalities using online voting would make the province a suitable case for anyone interested in the study of internet voting, there are other unique characteristics of Ontario that help justify this focus. These include the lengthy history of use of online voting in the province, the great variation in the point in time that online voting was adopted, and the fact that there are several variations in the types of systems adopted. All these dimensions of difference are possible due to the permissive nature of government legislation and regulation. As a result, Ontario's municipalities have a great deal of latitude with respect to how they administer their elections. We discuss this matter in greater detail in chapter 2, but for now, the key point is that this setting has not only a high number of cases (municipalities) to study but also numerous dimensions of variation that are beneficial for academic inquiry.

As already noted, hundreds of Ontario municipalities employ online voting, and the province has one of the longest-standing and continued uses of online voting in the world. These factors combine to provide a rich context for research. Starting with just twelve municipalities in 2003, uptake has increased with each election cycle. By 2018, 177 municipalities used online voting (Cardillo et al. 2019). This number increased, by our count, to 231 municipalities in the 2022 election, representing 56 per cent of the 414 municipalities that run elections in the province of Ontario.[6] These cities and towns include roughly 42 per cent of the province's electors – note that these percentages differ because it is generally municipalities with smaller populations that have been more inclined to adopt online voting systems (refer to appendix 1.1 for a full list of municipalities that adopted online voting in 2018 and 2022). All other things equal, a high number of cases for study is always preferred

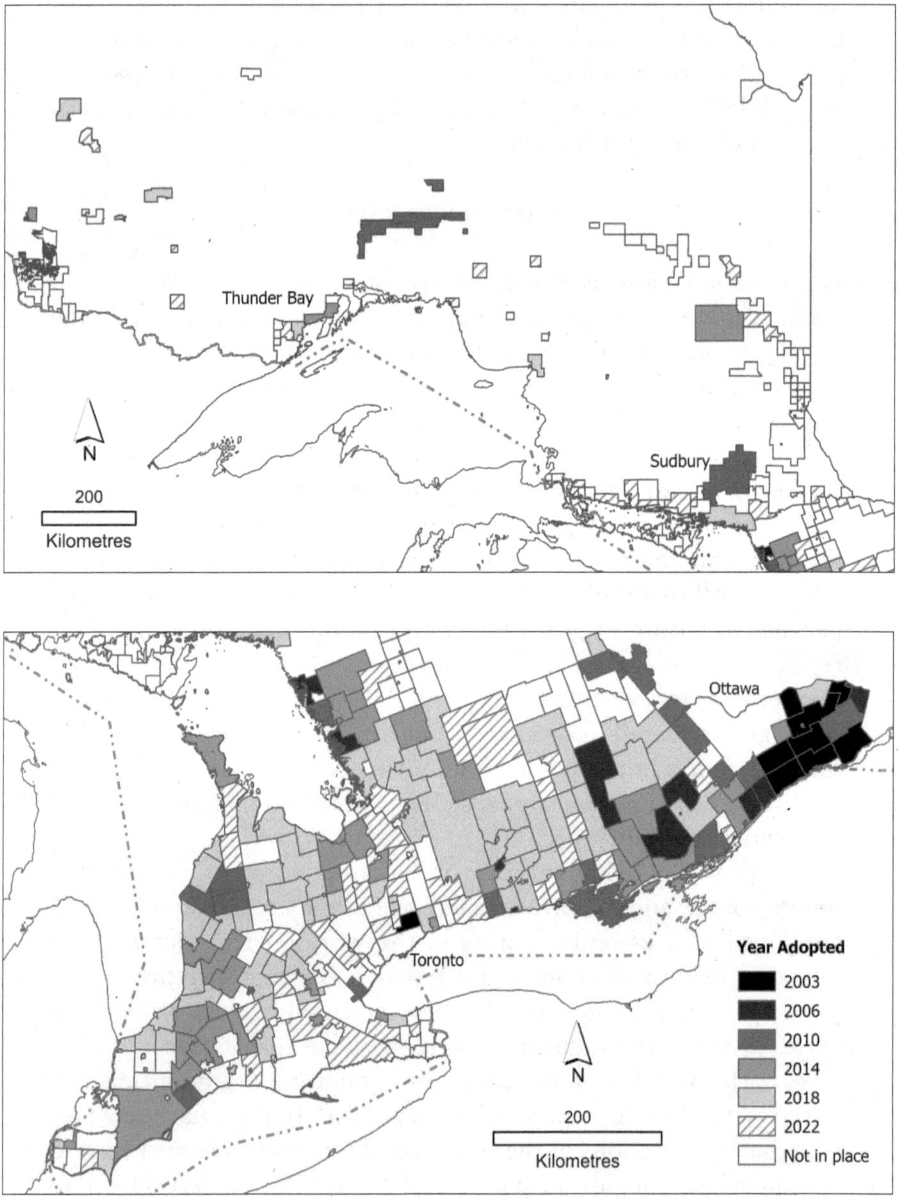

Figures 1.1a and 1.1b | Online voting adoption in Ontario municipalities, 2003–22

by social scientists, as a large sample size aids in one's ability to generalize based upon conclusions and to consider a high number of dimensions of difference.

Figure 1.1 presents two maps that graphically depict the history and state of online voting adoption in Ontario. The maps indicate where internet voting has been used, as well as the point in time at which it was adopted in different locations. They show just how much of the territory of the province is covered by cities and towns that run online elections. The reader will notice that the system is in use in most of the land area in the south of the province. We note that, in some instances, online voting has been introduced and then subsequently removed. Such municipalities are shaded in the figure according to their date of adoption. The reader should also note the large swathe of land in the north of the province which is unincorporated territory and thus not part of a municipality. This land is unshaded here.[7]

Yet another reason why Ontario is an invaluable case for study is the fact that the province provides examples of a wide range of variations of the system. Because municipalities have the latitude to set their own election rules, there is variation with respect to the period during which online voting is used (during the pre-election period and on election day), the methods used to authenticate voters, how the votes are stored and verified, and the complementary voting modes that are offered or not. We return to this matter in greater detail in chapter 2. For now, it is sufficient to state that, due to the vast number of cases and variation provided by Ontario's municipalities, the province is an ideal place in which to study how electors and elites view and respond to online voting.

ONLINE VOTING: WHAT WE ALREADY KNOW

Though online voting has been increasingly adopted in Canada and around the world and has been in place for decades, social science research on the topic remains modest and has tended to focus on three broad questions: how does online voting affect turnout; who votes online; and how has online voting been implemented in specific cases? The answers to these questions depend upon location, time, and, in the case of the former two questions, the research methods employed to study such outcomes (Alvarez et al. 2009; Ladner and Pianzola 2010; LeRoux et al. 2020; Fivaz and Nedig

2010; Blais 2006; Couture et al. 2017; Powell et al. 2012; Germann 2021; Trechsel 2008; Serdült et al. 2015; Solvak and Vassil 2021; Vassil and Weber 2011).

Within this scholarship, the potential for increased voter turnout is most frequently used to support calls for the implementation of online voting (Goodman et al. 2010; Goodman 2014). Whether online voting contributes to increased voter turnout, however, is up for scholarly debate. Turnout is declining across the advanced industrialized world (Putnam 2000; Gray and Caul 2000; Wattenberg 2002; Blais et al. 2004) and levels in Canadian local elections are far below the rates witnessed at federal and provincial elections (Moore and McGregor 2017; Breux et al. 2017; Hajnal and Lewis 2003; Breux et al. 2017). Given that democratic outcomes are often viewed as being more legitimate as turnout rates increase and that voters are sensitive to deficits in representation (Blais et al. 2017), the groups considered in this book – electors, candidates, and administrators – have an interest in knowing if and how online voting might influence turnout.

There are plenty of reasons to expect that the introduction of a new voting mode might affect patterns of participation. On the one hand, by allowing potential voters to cast their ballots without physically visiting an election office or polling station and hence lowering the perceived "costs" of voting (Blais 2000), one might expect that rates of participation would increase, or, at the very least, that trends towards declining turnout would be tempered (Alvarez and Hall 2004; Petitpas et al. 2021). By making voting quicker and easier, electors with an internet voting option could be less inclined to use inconvenience or "busyness" as an excuse for not voting. The option of voting online also addresses many of the issues of everyday life that can limit attendance at the ballot box, such as inclement weather, illness, or mobility issues, and being away from the community (Goodman 2014; Goodman and Pyman 2016). By making voting more convenient and reducing the barriers to casting a ballot, one might expect that more electors would vote. This finding is common in studies of convenience voting reforms such as voting by mail (Gronke et al. 2008).

On the other hand, new voting methods might not necessarily provide a boost in turnout. For some, voting online may not be perceived as a way of reducing the costs of voting. Most Canadians find it very easy to vote in person; that is, the effort required to cast their ballot is minimal (Blais et al. 2019). There is also evidence that this aspect of cost (the time required to actually vote) plays only a very little part in turnout decisions (Blais and Daoust 2020). They may, therefore, see little to no benefit in this regard from voting online. In fact, the time required to learn how to use a new online voting system may conceivably *increase* the cost of voting.

A lack of trust in online systems may also cause some electors to lose faith in, and detach from, the electoral process (Carter and Bélanger 2005; Carter and Campbell 2011; Culnane et al. 2017; Essex and Goodman 2022). This reasoning contrasts with evidence, however, that online voting may reduce the number of mistakes that voters make when casting ballots (Hall 2015; Goodman et al. 2010) and many public policies to ensure electoral integrity, regardless of voting method (Alvarez et al. 2022; Cardillo et al. 2019; Goodman and Essex 2020). The literature on the security and technical aspects of online voting is multi-disciplinary, mainly addressed by computer scientists and software engineers (Springall et al. 2014; Culnane et al. 2017; Clark et al. 2007; Culnane et al. 2019; Essex and Goodman 2022; Cardillo et al. 2019; Cardillo and Essex 2018; Essex 2016). These studies are of relevance to social scientists as the perceived security of online voting systems has significant potential to affect levels of support for their use and the public policies that govern their operation.

Research on the technological aspects of online voting, especially in the social sciences, also considers electors' digital proficiencies and the level of technical knowledge required to cast a ballot online. Much of this work focuses on the "digital disenfranchisement" of those with lower levels of so-called tech literacy who may be discouraged from, or even unable to, vote online (Carter and Bélanger 2012; Licht et al. 2021; Goodman et al. 2018). These effects are particularly pronounced in elections where paper ballot voting is not offered as an option – meaning that electors must cast their ballot online or not vote at all. There is evidence from such contexts which shows that, even if aggregate levels of participation are unchanged, the composition of the electorate may change, with the less technologically savvy members of society dropping out of the voting pool (Goodman et al. 2018).

Though contemplating the relationship between online voting and turnout is not a goal of this book, we can provide some data to that effect here. A rudimentary analysis of data from Ontario municipalities from 2014 and 2018 (the year that most of the data used in this

Table 1.2 | Voter turnout by year and presence of online voting

	2014		2018	
	No online voting	Online voting	No online voting	Online voting
Average turnout (%)	44.7	44.9	42.9	43.6
Standard deviation (% points)	7.5	7.0	7.4	7.5
N	188	64	132	120

book were collected) fails to provide compelling evidence that the introduction of online voting has had a positive effect upon turnout. Compiling data on turnout rates for all Ontario's municipalities for both the 2014 and 2018 elections allowed us to compare participation rates across time, as well as between municipalities. To maximize the comparability of the cities in our sample, we limited our analysis to those cities that held elections, without acclamations at the "top-of-the-ticket" race, in either year (as acclamations have a sizable dampening effect upon turnout). This leaves us with a total of 252 municipalities. Among these cases, the average level of turnout was 44.74 per cent in 2014 and 43.26 per cent in 2018, for an average decline of 1.48 percentage points.

Table 1.2 shows the rates of turnout for cities that used online voting and those that did not, in 2014 and 2018. This allows us to compare turnout in the two types of cities at two individual points in time. The table shows that cities with online voting do have slightly higher turnout but that these differences are negligible at best. Turnout in cities with internet voting was 0.2 percentage points higher in 2014 and 0.7 points higher in 2018. These gaps do little to suggest that online voting is the panacea for voter turnout, despite what some of its proponents suggest.

Table 1.3 looks at changes in turnout, between 2014 and 2018, based upon the voting method used. We group municipalities into

Table 1.3 | Changes in voter turnout, by presence of online voting

	No online voting either year	Online voting both years	Online voting added in 2018	Online voting removed in 2018
Change in turnout (% points)	-1.9	0.0	-2.0	-6.1
Standard deviation (% points)	8.0	4.6	7.0	4.0
N	130	62	58	2

four categories, including those that had no change in voting methods across years (using online voting neither year or both) and those that changed methods across time (those that adopted online voting in 2018 and those that abandoned it). Though very few municipalities in our sample abandoned online voting (just two), we include these results for comprehensiveness.

Table 1.3 paints a muddy but nevertheless slightly more positive picture of the relationship between online voting and turnout. The only type of municipality where turnout did not decline was in those places that used online voting in both elections. This lack of decline can be contrasted, however, with a nearly two-point decrease in municipalities that did not employ internet voting in either year. This figure is nearly identical to the change in turnout in cities that adopted online voting in 2018 – if online voting has such a positive effect upon turnout, one would expect this to be the highest value in the table. Still, a decline of two points is less than the decrease of more than six points in the two cities that removed online voting. Overall, despite this data being limited and only covering two election years, neither table suggests a convincing positive relationship between online voting and turnout.

Observant readers will note, however, that the preceding analyses are devoid of causal language. Studying the effects of institutional changes is notoriously difficult, and cross-tabs of the nature shown in tables 1.2 and 1.3 cannot be used to make causal claims. At first glance, the most obvious method for studying the effects of institutional change is to compare an outcome variable of interest (such as turnout) from before and after an institutional change (such as the introduction of online voting) is made (this is what table 1.3 shows). Such an approach is fraught, however, given that any number of factors, other than institutional change, can cause outcome changes between and during elections. We know, for example, that the presence of incumbents and the competitiveness of races significantly influences turnout in local elections (Anderson et al. 2020; Trounstine 2012). Likewise, local elections in the province do not have an insignificant number of acclaimed races. Whether these occur in mayoral, council, or school board races, acclamations have a significant dampening effect on turnout. Any number of other unobserved differences between cities might also influence changes over time. These factors, and many more, can change between elections, so a sufficient assessment cannot be made from simply comparing before-and-after turnout rates.

Just as an across-time analysis of this nature is flawed, so too is a between-cases analysis, which compares turnout between locations with and without the institutional feature under study. One could simply compare turnout rates in cities with online voting to cities without it, as we have done for 2014 and 2018 (see table 1.2). Even when limiting such analysis to cities that are comparable in as many ways as possible (for example, controlling for things like incumbency, competitiveness, and acclamation), such comparisons are not nearly robust enough to be trustworthy. There are simply too many factors that might differ between cities to make any valid claims about the causal effects of institutional changes. It is also highly likely that decisions to implement online voting (or not) are influenced by electors themselves. We expect that cities that do switch voting methods often do so, at least partially, based upon feedback from engaged electors, requesting such a change. In more formal terms, we expect that the decision to adopt online voting is endogenous to electors' engagement with local politics, of which turnout is just one form. Despite these challenges, our goal is not to study turnout, and we leave this matter for other scholars to continue to debate. Future work should do a deeper dive to examine this question in the context of Ontario and Canada.

The second major question considered by scholars of internet voting is the matter of who votes online. These analyses are necessarily limited to those contexts where online voting is offered as a complementary option to other available methods (the question is moot if only one voting method is available). Unsurprisingly, answers to this question are somewhat lower profile than research on participation rates, given that the study of turnout is one of the central preoccupations of political behaviour researchers. Still, a variety of scholars have undertaken research into who votes how, and they have done so in many contexts (Alvarez et al. 2009; Serdült et al. 2015; Trechsel 2007; Vassil et al. 2016; Blais and Loewen 2011; Budd et al. 2019; Goodman et al. 2018; Goodman 2014). We take up this question in chapter 4, where we find that older voters, those with a high income, homeowners, white voters, and those on the ideological left tend to vote online. These results are not entirely consistent with those observed elsewhere, illustrating that the answer to "who votes how" is context dependent.

This research can provide insight into the factors that influence electors' choices and preferences associated with voting. For example, electors may prefer to vote in-person, despite having an online option available to them, because they feel more confident in the security and accuracy of traditional voting processes (Fisher and Savani 2022; Krimmer et al. 2021; Loeber 2018; Segaard et al. 2016). Others, however, may prefer to vote online because of its convenience and accessibility or because they are accustomed to digitization in other aspects of their lives (Alvarez et al. 2009; Vassil et al. 2016; Petitpas et al. 2021; Mellon et al. 2016). Interestingly, research likewise suggests that online voters are "faithful" to the method once they have been exposed to it (Alvarez et al. 2009; Germann and Serdült 2014; Mendez and Serdült 2017), suggesting that exposure to online voting may influence its adoption overtime. Understanding the rationale behind voter choices may help administrators make informed decisions about whether to employ online voting methods and, if so, whether to accompany those methods with others, including telephone voting, mail-in ballots, and traditional in-person voting.

The third major strand in the literature on online voting focuses on how online voting has been adopted in different contexts. This work, which tends to be in the form of case studies, sheds light on how online voting is organized and deployed in various jurisdictions, issues and frameworks associated with its governance, and how its development has evolved over time (Alvarez et al. 2009; Ehin et al. 2022; Serdült et al. 2016; Solvak and Vassil 2016; Trechsel et al. 2008; Goodman et al. 2010; Goodman and Pammett 2014; Goodman and Spicer 2019). Notable country cases include Estonia (Alvarez et al. 2009; Ehin et al. 2022; Solvak and Vassil 2016; Trechsel et al. 2008), Switzerland (Serdült et al. 2016; Gasser and Gerlach 2011) and Canada (Goodman et al. 2010; Goodman and Pammett 2014; Goodman and Spicer 2019). This work highlights successful cases but also instances where online voting has failed and the considerations that contributed to the halting of projects (Duenas-Cid et al. 2020; Loeber 2014). Such research provides important context for scholars studying online voting and for practitioners considering or planning to implement online ballots by pointing to strategies in adoption and issues that needed to be overcome. Such context is also helpful for those looking to understand how online voting trials and programs have taken shape worldwide and what unique factors those models embody that we could learn from. In the second chapter, which provides context for the remainder of the book, we address how online voting is organized in Ontario municipalities, some of the issues associated with its governance, and how it has developed over time, providing the most up-to-date assessment on its evolution in the province.

With this landscape in mind, the goal of the present work is to consider a variety of unconsidered research questions about online voting. Here we take up some previously ignored or understudied questions. We turn next to a more detailed discussion of our research questions.

BOOK OVERVIEW

This book adds to the existing social science research on internet voting in several noteworthy ways. It considers a variety of research questions that have yet to be considered in Canada or elsewhere and does so using several new types of data. Whereas existing research into online voting tends to be focused upon a single source of data (usually from a survey of electors), our analyses draw upon data from a range of actors of relevance to online voting: electors, candidates (successful and otherwise), and municipal administrators who are responsible for overseeing elections. In this section we provide an overview of the research questions that are the focus of this book and the data we draw upon to answer them.

NEW QUESTIONS

In addition to using data from a particularly wide variety of sources (which we describe in more detail below), this work addresses numerous previously unconsidered questions about the orientations towards and effects of online voting. Though the literature on internet voting is expanding, there remains a great deal to learn about the topic. Developing a detailed understanding of this phenomenon is of vital practical importance, given that online voting is growing rapidly around the world and that, even in places where online voting is not used, it is often widely discussed by decision makers.

The second chapter provides an overview of the local government ecosystem in Ontario, offering important background information and context needed to situate the latter chapters. The second chapter describes in greater detail the scope and scale of online voting developments in Ontario. In addition to more fully detailing the unique features of our case, we outline why online voting adoption has taken shape the way it has and characterize specific phases of development. Specifically, we point to a variety of government and market forces that have shaped the online voting environment, explain how online voting is implemented and the main deployment approaches, and outline past and current trends in uptake. This information helps the reader to understand the context in which electors, candidates, and electoral administrators are operating. Information in this chapter is based upon publicly available government information, existing academic literature, and interviews and focus groups with municipal officials.

We begin our first data driven chapter (chapter 3) by considering some of the attitudinal effects of online voting. As noted above, the existing literature on such effects is focused overwhelmingly upon turnout. Instead, we consider whether the introduction of online voting influences satisfaction with local democracy. The introduction of the voting method may be viewed positively by some who believe that it makes voting easier and more accessible. Conversely, security concerns about the adoption of online voting may lead some electors to lose faith in local political institutions and democracy. This chapter also examines whether the implementation of online voting in municipal elections influences attitudes towards the potential adoption of the voting mode at provincial and federal levels in Canada. Though internet voting is used by hundreds of municipalities in Ontario and Nova Scotia, it has yet to be used in federal or provincial elections in the province (though a small number of provinces and territories have recently adopted the system for various voting opportunities). Our results from a survey experiment suggest that, though the introduction of online voting has a positive effect upon satisfaction with local democracy, this does not translate into increased support for use of the voting method at other levels of government.

The fourth chapter uses survey data from both electors and candidates for local office. It starts by addressing a critical question: who votes online? In places where there is a choice in voting method – online or in person – voters must decide how to cast their ballot. This decision also speaks indirectly to some of the motivations for adopting online voting in the first place. Does the implementation of a new voting method have the potential to increase participation rates by providing voters with an additional voting channel? If so, is the method more attractive to some types of electors than others? Chapter 4 goes a step further, however, to consider whether candidates or electors understand who casts their ballot in which manner. Debates over the adoption of online voting are no doubt influenced by perceptions of who might cast an online ballot and if there is any benefit to be had by adopting online voting (or not). The data reveal that many sociodemographic indicators (including age, income, homeownership, and race) as well as ideology are related to voting method. Neither candidates nor electors themselves, however, have a good understanding of these patterns.

The fifth chapter digs deeper into the attitudes and behaviour of candidates themselves. It identifies the types of candidates who are supportive or opposed to the use of online voting in their municipalities and considers why this might be. Among candidates who operate in a setting where online voting is present, the chapter also considers if and how campaigning is affected. We find several individual-level characteristics to be correlated with support for online voting, including ideology, age, and personality. Incumbent status also matters under specific circumstances. The findings for ideology and incumbency are of particular note, since candidates as a whole seem to believe that incumbents and candidates of the left benefit from the use of online voting. Finally, we see that just half of the candidates surveyed campaigned differently in response to the presence of online voting than they might have otherwise.

Among those candidates who campaigned differently, the two primary responses were to campaign more online and to devote time to providing information on how to vote online.

In the final data chapter (chapter 6), we shift our focus to election administrators. These public servants have unique insights and power into local decisions on which voting methods are adopted. We surveyed hundreds of administrators in 2022 from around the province, in municipalities of all sizes, asking them what motivates them when contemplating the adoption of online voting. As public servants, it is also important to consider whether the views of these individuals are aligned with the people they serve. We therefore compare administrator attitudes to those of electors and candidates. In this same vein, we consider the perceptions of administrators regarding public support for online voting. Finally, this chapter considers the views of administrators with respect to two major events that had the potential to seriously affect the uptake of online voting in Ontario: COVID-19 and a technical incident that affected forty-three municipalities that used online voting in 2018.

In our conclusion (chapter 7), we consider what our findings tell us about online voting in Ontario. What do the answers to our new research questions tell us about how the most important stakeholders in the electoral process view and engage with internet voting? The answers to these questions have important implications for the future of online voting in this country. As part of this, we reflect on municipal administrators' visions of the future of electronic elections in Ontario. We end the book by proposing a series of new questions for scholarly consideration, with the aim of building upon our ever-expanding knowledge of the phenomenon of internet voting, both in the context of Ontario and more generally. The book concludes with a short epilogue that discusses some noteworthy features of the 2022 elections and briefly speculates about what these events mean for the future of online voting in Ontario.

NEW DATA

The chapters that follow draw upon data from a variety of sources including surveys of eligible voters, candidates for office, and the administrators who oversee local elections (see table 1.4, below for a snapshot of the data that inform this book). These three groups are all important actors in our local democracies, and the study of each

Table 1.4 | Our data

Data source	Time in field	N	Survey items
Survey of electors	26 Oct–9 Dec 2018	N=4,728	Qs cover political attitudes, behaviour, socio-demographic items
Survey of candidates	3 Sept–4 Dec 2018	N=538	Qs cover political attitudes, opinions (designed to compare with elector survey), socio-demographic items
Survey of administrators	21 April–27 May 2022	N=281	Qs cover 2018 shock, COVID, battery of attitudes, history of use, etc.
Administrator focus group	22 April 2022	N=6 participants from 5 municipalities	Qs had four themes: state of e-voting, the 2018 tech incident, COVID, and the future of municipal elections
Administrator interviews	12 May–2 August 2022	N=30	Qs about additional insight on tech incident and COVID, and the future of municipal election administration

provides important insights that help us to better understand how online voting functions and is viewed in this province. In addition to considering the groups independently, we also draw comparisons between them, where possible, to see how in-sync (or not) the different types of actors are. The combination of these varied sources of data allows us to paint a detailed and unique picture of how online voting functions and is viewed in Ontario. Altogether, 5,781 respondents completed our surveys. We owe an enormous debt of gratitude to them all for taking the time to provide us with their views.

The first data source we employ is a survey of eligible Ontario electors, collected just after the 2018 municipal elections. Electors are the "demos" (the people) which form the basis of all democracies. The power and legitimacy of Canadian governments of all levels flow from the collective will of the people, as demonstrated on election day. Surveying electors (which includes both voters and non-voters) is therefore of the utmost importance for the study of any election or electoral method.

Data from the elector survey were collected between 26 October and 9 December 2018 (election day was 22 October 2018). A total of 4,960 participants completed the questionnaire. Respondents were recruited from twenty municipalities that employ or have employed online voting in the past, including Ajax, Belleville, Bradford West Gwillimbury, Brantford, Burlington, Cambridge, Chatham-Kent, Guelph, Innisfil, Kawartha Lakes, Kingston, Markham, Newmarket, Pickering, Quinte West, Sarnia, St Thomas, Sudbury, Thunder Bay, and Timmins. The fact that the survey is focused on municipalities that have experience with online voting is an important feature of our study. It influences the types of research questions we consider, and our results must be viewed with this focus in mind. Though we cannot compare electors in places with online voting to those without, such comparisons would be limited at best given the vast number of other factors that might influence potential outcome variables of interest. Our focus is instead upon conducting a very large-N study with the maximum number of respondents possible (given funding limitations) from cities and towns where online voting is, or has been, a feature of elections.

Forum Research Inc. was responsible for recruitment (completed via phone and random digit dialing to both landlines and cell phones and involving a live operator who collected email addresses) and administration of the survey, which was carried out online. The survey consists of approximately sixty questions focused on the themes of municipal politics, online voting, general political orientations, and sociodemographic characteristics. Many survey questions are standard in political surveys, while many were designed specifically for the purposes of this book, allowing us to consider several novel research questions. We provide greater detail on the specific survey questions we employ in subsequent chapters.

The second major data source we draw upon is a survey of candidates for 2018 municipal office. As central actors in our local democracy, the views of candidates are of vital importance to understanding how online voting affects municipal politics and elections in Ontario. Candidates must work within the institutional frameworks of their systems, but they will not all react to such frameworks in the same way. Moreover, if successful, candidates make decisions regarding electoral rules (such as the adoption of online voting) as elected municipal councillors. Their views and actions in response to the use of online voting are thus a central component of our study.

Candidate names and email addresses were scraped from official websites for the same twenty cities included in the elector survey. A total of 964 valid survey invitations were sent via email, with multiple reminders, and the survey was administered using the Qualtrics interface. Two waves of surveys were fielded, with 56 per cent of recipients completing at least one wave of the survey. The pre-election survey was open from 7 September to 21 October, with an N of 538. The post-election survey was fielded between 30 October and 4 December, with an N of 330. Respondents include many winners and losers, incumbents and challengers, and candidates for all positions, including for mayor (reeve), council, and school board as well as, where applicable, regional council, regional chair, and deputy mayor. Candidates were asked a variety of questions about their views and behaviour, including many questions that were also asked to electors. They were also asked questions unique to their role as candidates, including their perceptions of the views and behaviours of electors and of the effect that online voting has upon candidacy.

The third and final survey dataset that we employ is a survey of local election officials responsible for election governance in the province. Each municipality makes its own independent decision about what types of voting systems to employ and, according to survey respondents themselves (as we note in chapter 6), administrators have a central role in this decision. The purpose of the administrator survey is to measure the attitudes, perceptions, and actions of local election administrators regarding online voting.

To identify potential survey respondents, we obtained a contact list from the Association of Municipal Managers, Clerks, and Treasurers of Ontario (AMCTO). AMCTO provided 676 valid email addresses for administrators across Ontario's 444 municipalities. A total of 281 respondents completed the survey, from 217 municipalities, for a response rate of 41 per cent. Surveys were programmed and distributed via the Qualtrics interface and included questions regarding the rationale for online voting adoption (or rejection), perceived benefits and challenges of online voting, as well as a series of other attitudinal and demographic items. The survey was administered between 21 April and 27 May 2022. Though these data were obtained four years later than the other survey datasets, they allow us to consider administrator attitudes towards events that occurred at and since the 2018 election, including COVID-19. We also ask questions about how administrators perceived the attitudes of electors in 2018 and how they have changed since then.

Finally, to inform the framing of the book and ensure we adequately captured the environment and evolution of online voting adoption in Ontario, we sought additional explanatory insight to the administrator survey by way of a focus group and thirty interviews with municipal administrators from across the province carried out between April and August of 2022. The focus group was carried out with AMCTO's Election Working Group. The Election Working Group is composed of municipal officials across Ontario who are responsible for the administration of local elections and meet regularly to share strategies and best practices. The group was conducted over a two-hour period and addressed four major themes: the state of online voting in Ontario municipalities with a focus on developments in participant cities, a 2018 technical incident, the COVID-19 pandemic, and their perceptions of the extent to which the future of Ontario's local elections is digital. Six officials from five municipalities took part. These municipalities differed in size,[8] types of voting modes employed, and thoughts on online voting. Two of the cities represented had not used online voting and had no interest in doing so in future, one had not used online voting but hoped to adopt it soon, and the remaining two cities had used it in the past and had plans to continue with implementation.

A total of thirty semi-structured interviews were conducted with local administrators that opted to take part via the administrator survey discussed above. Interviews were conducted virtually via Zoom between May and August of 2022 and were approximately thirty minutes in duration. Interviewees were selected as evenly as possible from three groups: municipalities that used online voting in 2018 and 2022, municipalities that did not use online voting in 2018 or 2022, and, finally, municipalities that did not offer online voting in 2018 but adopted the voting reform in 2022.[9] The goal of this split was to get a deeper sense of administrators' varied attitudes towards online voting, specific concerns about adoption, especially given technical issues in recent years, how COVID-19 affected uptake of online voting, if at all, and thoughts on the (digital) future of Ontario's municipal elections. While we draw upon these interviews to provide additional context and understanding to our empirical findings, we also return to them in the conclusion where we discuss the future of electronic elections in Ontario.

2

The Rise of Online Voting in Ontario

INTRODUCTION

The scale and scope of online voting use in Ontario, combined with the high degree of variation in online voting deployment that exists across municipalities, makes the province an ideal case to examine the potential impact that internet voting has on the political attitudes and behaviours of electors and elites. Before we can conduct such analyses (chapters 3 to 6), however, it is important to understand the intricacies of internet voting growth in Canada and in Ontario in particular.

Informed by interviews undertaken with municipal elections administrators, as well as academic literature on internet voting in the province, this chapter provides a brief examination of online voting development in Ontario between 2003 and 2022. In doing so, we provide an overview of Ontario's local government sector and point to some of the defining structural factors that have shaped online voting development and deployment in the province. This includes an examination of the government and market forces that have contributed to the high rates of online voting uptake in Ontario. We also consider the diffusion of online voting in Ontario among local governments and explore four distinct "phases" of online voting adoption (innovators, early adopters, early majority, and late majority).

The chapter addresses the following question: why and how has online voting grown in Ontario? In answering this, our discussion provides important background and sets the stage for our analyses of how internet voting shapes the voter, candidate, and administrator attitudes explored in subsequent chapters. We begin with an overview of government forces, considering the permissible and decentralized nature of election administration on the one hand and the lack of regulation and oversight on the other. We then move to a discussion of market forces, both supply and demand, that have interacted with local autonomy to produce a significant uptake in online voting. We end by describing the diffusion of online voting in Ontario, exploring adoption trends between 2003 and 2022. This history helps us understand the context in which electors and elites view and engage with online voting in the province.

GOVERNMENT FORCES

As "creatures of the provinces" lacking formal constitutional standing of their own, Canadian municipalities are largely subject to the whims of their respective provincial governments. One area where local governments have a great deal of autonomy, however, is in the administration of elections. In Ontario, municipal governments have taken great advantage of this autonomy and a combination of permissive provincial legislation and an absence of provincial regulation have created the ideal environment for the growth of and experimentation with internet voting.

Legislative Permissiveness

The first factor that has contributed to the growth of online voting in Ontario is the set of legislative rules governing what is and is not permissible. All provinces in Canada have at least one piece of legislation outlining the structure, authority, and purpose of municipal governments within their jurisdiction. In Ontario, that legislation is the Municipal Act, 2001. This legislation sets the boundaries of municipal power and describes the responsibility of local officials for a range of service areas (including transportation and waste management), supplies the scope of local governance responsibilities, and gives direction on how council functions. While the Municipal Act outlines the powers and responsibilities of elected municipal representatives, it gives only cursory mention to the electoral process itself. Most of that guidance is contained in Ontario's Municipal Elections Act, 1996 (hereafter referred to as the "act"), which sets out the rules, timing, and procedures governing municipal elections across the province. This act is firm in many ways, including several mandatory elements. For instance, it prescribes the timing of the writ period and ensures it is uniform across all municipalities in the province. It also provides precise conditions regarding who can vote and seek elected office. Going further, the act outlines specific procedures to follow to qualify the voters list or register those without a fixed address and lays out instructions for candidates to follow during the writ period. It provides a range of penalties for contravening these guidelines and describes in detail the forms that need to be completed and submitted before and after a person's candidacy. In many areas, therefore, the act leaves little room for interpretation by either candidates or election administrators.

Other sections, however, provide a great deal of flexibility for the discretion of local decision makers. For instance, Section 42(3) of the act provides for the use of alternative voting methods during municipal elections if the council of the municipality has approved the use of such methods. This section can be interpreted broadly to mean any voting methods that do not require a voter to attend a voting location in person, thereby permitting the use of a range of ballot options, including mail-in ballots, telephone voting, or online voting.[1] The act, however, does not provide guidance on unsupervised voting methods beyond the ability to use them. In response to this legislative void, municipalities have developed their own processes for administering and governing remote voting methods, including remote internet voting.

The absence of a legislative framework has created a patchwork of adoption across the province (Goodman and Pammett, 2014; Goodman and Smith 2016) in terms of the types of voting modes used, the models or approaches used to deploy the voting technology and any processes or protocols needed to govern its administration. Some local governments opt to use in-person paper ballots only, while others offer a combination of paper ballots, online voting, telephone voting, and/or mail-in ballots. The act also allows the use of vote-counting equipment, such as voting machines, voting recorders, and/or optical scan tabulators, which further adds to the variation in local elections across the province. Each variation or combination of voting modes is entirely permissible under provincial legislation.

The act has, in part, helped foster an environment that some refer to as the "wild west" of online voting (Renaud 2021). While this has been less than ideal for fostering uniformity in election administration across the municipal sector, it has created an excellent environment in which to learn about the effects of online voting, especially given that municipalities with varied socio-demographic, geographic, and rural/urban profiles use the technology but also take different approaches to adopting and deploying it. The Municipal Act, 2001 and the Municipal Elections Act, 1996 have opened the door for Ontario's municipalities to use internet voting and for the subsequent academic study of such systems.

The Absence of Regulation

In addition to the legislative rules permitting alternative voting methods, there are other policy forces at play. Among the most important of these are the lack of standards or regulations for municipal online voting use, which make it easier for cities to experiment with online voting methods. The regulatory landscape in Ontario lays out general authority and responsibilities for municipalities. Once drafted and implemented, product standards for online voting would outline uniform practices, processes, and technical criteria for online voting systems used in municipal elections in Canada.

Despite nearly two decades of online voting deployment in Ontario, regulations to govern and standardize its deployment have yet to come into force (Essex and Goodman 2020). While some regulatory efforts are underway, only one set of regulations have officially passed at the time of writing – the Northwest Territories' Electronic Voting Regulations, which were signed into force in June 2023. For the most part, election authorities in Canada have pointed to American standards such as the Voluntary Voting System Guidelines 1.0 and 2.0 (United States Election Assistance Commission 2005; United States Election Assistance Commission 2021). These standards, however, apply to tabulators, which are a type of voting hardware. They do not apply to voting software or systems. While newer certification requirements in the United States do apply to the software of e-poll book systems, they do not cover voting technology software nor online voting itself (United States Election Assistance Commission, 2023). In Canada, this regulatory absence has allowed municipalities to operate electronic elections as they see fit and for vendors to do the same. For example, while some municipalities conduct extensive independent testing prior to deployment, others rely on vendors for information about what type of tests to carry out.

Likewise, vendors are not subject to any prescribed testing or uniform practices beyond what is requested by individual cities. An example of this variation can be seen in the ways that voters are (or are not) authenticated before they can access an online ballot. Some municipalities require registration before voting as an additional layer of authentication, while others simply ask for a unique PIN code and a second credential to confirm a voter's identity, such as year or full date of birth. In some cases, albeit few, municipalities do not even require voters to submit a second credential for authentication. In these instances, voters can access and cast their ballots by submitting the PIN displayed on their voter card.[2] The absence of strong standards allows for considerable latitude in developing and deploying online voting in the province. When combined with permissive legislative rules regarding the use of alternative voting methods, and no mention of any legislative requirements regarding unsupervised voting, the lack of online voting regulation allows municipalities to adopt online voting systems without a set of commonplace baseline standards. Likewise, it has allowed for the adoption of online voting systems with weaker authentication and verification capabilities than are used elsewhere.

While a lack of standards may have helped municipal uptake of online voting in some instances, there is also reason to believe that the absence of regulation may prevent a subset of municipalities from moving forward with adoption, particularly in places where decision makers are more risk averse and want assurances of certain technical specifications before moving forward. While regulations for municipal use of online voting systems remain absent, they are currently in development (CIO Strategy Council, 2021). Even though standards have not yet been formally adopted, awareness of the commencement of the standards process has already influenced some online voting uptake in Ontario. These sentiments were revealed in a series of interviews with municipal administrators carried out in the summer of 2022. For example, some municipalities that had doubts about online voting reported that they were more comfortable proceeding because standard development was underway. Other administrators who had concerns about adopting online voting in the 2018 and/or 2022 elections expressed the potential for increased comfort with online voting adoption should standards be in place before the 2026 municipal elections. Finally, some local officials have become actively involved in the standard development process, by either sitting on the technical or drafting committees and proactively seeking out best practices as part of the process. Thus, while regulations are sometimes viewed as a hindrance to technological adoption, their presence should reduce risk exposure, potentially contributing to increased perceptions of legitimacy and therefore advancing the next phase of adoption.

THE MARKET FOR ONLINE VOTING

In addition to government forces, market forces have also played an important role in the adoption of online voting in Ontario. Beginning with the demand side, there is consistent evidence that online voting is a popular initiative. Poll after poll shows that there is a clear demand for online voting in Canadian elections from ordinary electors. Elections Canada (2017), for example, reports that approximately 75 per cent of Canadians support the use of online voting for federal elections. Likewise, a 2016 EKOS poll finds that 77 per cent would be either very or somewhat likely to make use of online voting if it were an option.[3] Along these lines, the Mydemocracy initiative, a survey of more than 300,000 individuals, found that 72 per cent of participants believed that online voting would increase turnout in Canadian elections (Vox Pop 2017).

Electors, however, are not the only stakeholders interested in the potential turn towards online voting. Political elites – administrators and candidates – tend to be supportive of the digitalization of elections, too. As will be discussed in the fifth chapter, three quarters of recent federal election candidates support online elector registration, and a sizeable portion (ranging from 35 per cent to 44 per cent depending on the election year) support the adoption of online voting. Municipal candidates express even greater support, with upwards of 80 per cent of our sample agreeing that online voting should be available during local elections. Thus, while support tends to be higher among members of the public, elites are also quite supportive. Taken together, there is a clear demand for online voting from the perspective of both electors and elites.

The high demand for online voting systems has been accompanied by an increase in the number and type of vendors, which has significantly increased the availability of various online voting technologies. As a result of increased technical scrutiny among some municipalities since the 2018 municipal election and pressures among others to offer electronic voting as a result of the COVID-19 pandemic, new vendors have emerged with different types of technology intended to enhance the security of the vote, while others are finally bringing services to Ontario that were already deployed in other jurisdictions.[4] In 2022, seven vendors offered online voting services in the province (compared to four that had market share in 2018).[5] These vendors offer a variety of price points and types of services (internet, telephone, and mail-in ballots), authentication procedures, security measures, and options to cast a ballot including in-person or remotely.

The diversity in vendor offerings has resulted in three different security approaches to online voting. Companies that use "generic" security employ traditional web applications wherein votes are cast via a web browser and then collected and stored in a database. Vendors offering this service have traditionally occupied the market share of online elections in Ontario and continue to do so despite the availability of new technologies and approaches. Other providers market themselves as being more security-focused and use blockchain security technology to transfer data.[6] A third approach offers verifiable voting, which involves allowing voters to verify certain aspects of the vote. In some cases, this includes end-to-end verifiable online voting, which offers the highest level of security and is considered the gold standard among computer scientists (Panja and Roy 2021) because it allows voters to confirm that their ballot was both cast and counted correctly (Benaloh et al. 2014; Goodman 2017). The emergence of new vendors and online voting approaches are indicative of the market responding to growth in demand, both in Ontario and elsewhere.

When combined, permissive legislation, a lack of regulatory obstacles, and a market with strong demand and growing supply have cultivated an environment in Ontario wherein the adoption and usage of online voting methods has flourished. Figure 2.1 shows how online voting has grown in Ontario since 2003. The 2022 elections represent the first time that a majority of municipalities (56 per cent) offered the voting method.[7] The growth of online voting has been monotonic and non-linear; each election has seen more municipalities adopt online voting than the last.

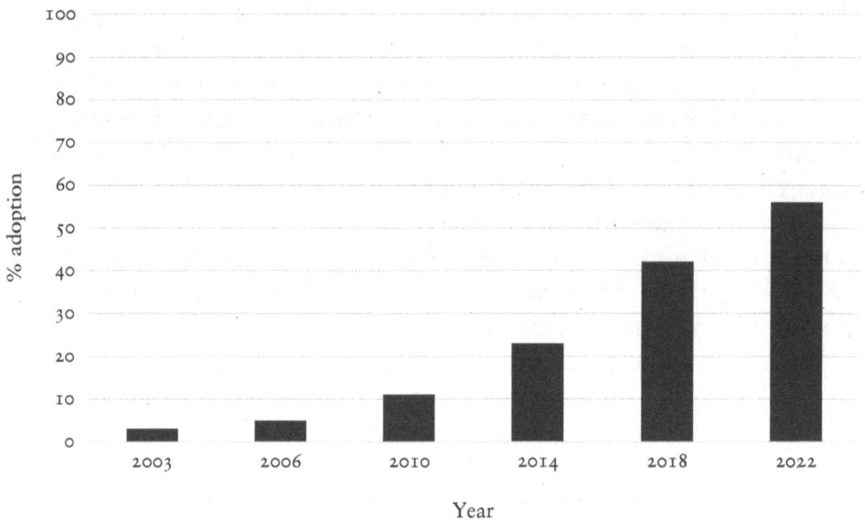

Figure 2.1 | Percentage of municipalities offering online voting (Ontario 2003–22)

Before moving on, we need to note that internet voting is spreading not only across municipalities but also within municipalities that have multiple voting options in place. That is, in those locations where both online and paper voting is allowed, voters are increasingly turning to the online option. In 2014, thirty-eight municipalities had both electronic and paper options and, in these places, an average of 46 per cent of votes were cast online. By 2018, forty-four municipalities had both options, and an average of 57 per cent of votes were submitted electronically (2022 data are not yet fully available).[8] This aggregate-level increase is not the result of a change in municipalities that use online voting. In those municipalities that had these same voting options in both years (several cities made changes to voting methods between these times), we see the same pattern. In the twenty-eight municipalities which, by our account, used multiple voting options in both years and for which data are available, turnout rose from 46 per cent to 55 per cent. Online voting seems, therefore, to be diffusing to new towns and cities but also to new voters.

DIFFUSION OF INNOVATION: UNDERSTANDING ONLINE VOTING UPTAKE IN ONTARIO

Thus far we have outlined some of the prominent features (permissible legislation, a lack of clear standards or regulatory framework, and market forces) that have created an environment for online voting methods to thrive in Ontario. With that context in mind, we now discuss the stages of growth of online voting in the province. When making decisions regarding what type of voting methods to use, municipal decision makers do not act in an informational vacuum. Given the widespread experimentation that has occurred in Ontario, policy learning across local governments has significantly influenced online voting development (Goodman and Smith 2016). Through regular meetings, working groups, and other information sharing practices across municipalities, early innovator municipalities have paved the way for increased online voting adoption by using specific approaches to its deployment (Goodman and Spicer 2019). In the remainder of this chapter, we draw upon theories of policy diffusion (Shipen and Volden 2008; Messenger and Giraldi 2009) to map out the growth of online voting in Ontario. In doing so, our goal is to identify specific phases of municipal adoption of online voting technologies. Policy diffusion theories have often been used to explain online voting diffusion amongst individual voters (Vassil et al. 2016) and diffusion of electoral methods across levels of government including between international electoral systems (Bol et al. 2015; Linos 2011). But, it has not been widely used as a lens through which to view patterns of online voting adoption across municipal governments within the same province.

Theories of policy diffusion suggest that ideas for new programs, services, or innovations[9] spread within a social system, becoming widely accepted via their "adoption," defined either by date, degree, or magnitude by individuals and groups (Berry and Berry 2018). Adoption is affected by the extent to which relevant resources are made available or allocated to the adopter, both by propagators of the innovations and the society at large, as well as the adopters' ability to utilize these resources. Learning from the experiences of other earlier adopters is also a key driver of decisions to embrace an innovation. According to Rogers (2003), there are five main groups of actors in the diffusion of technologies. These include:

- *Innovators*: those with high risk tolerance and the desire to develop or contribute to the development of new ideas.
- *Early adopters*: opinion leaders that embrace change opportunities.
- *Early majority*: those that adopt new ideas before the typical person but require more information about technology and its efficacy before adoption.
- *Late majority*: those that only adopt a technology once it has been widely adopted and proven elsewhere.
- *Laggards*: those that are the last in a social system to adopt an innovation.

These categories are derived from characteristics of the pattern of adoption as well as the relative "innovativeness" of the various adopters. Innovativeness in this sense relates to how quickly a new technology was adopted (Rogers 2003). Innovators are the first to adopt (accounting for approximately the first 2.5 per cent), followed by early adopters (the next 13.5 per cent), early majority (the next 34 per cent), late majority (the next 34 per cent), and finally the laggards (the final 16 per cent). Figure 2.2 highlights this distribution of relative adoption.[10] In Ontario's case, the 2022 municipal elections saw approximately 56 per cent of municipalities from across the province use online voting, suggesting that we have now moved through the first three phases of development (innovators, early adopters, and early majority) and may be moving into a new phase of adoption where online voting is the norm, rather than the exception.

Though our focus is more on the trajectory of the growth of online voting rather than on the type of municipalities that adopt it, theory suggests that organizational size is usually one of the most prominent characteristics that influences the adoption of innovations (Brown 1981). Larger organizations have advantages over smaller ones insofar as they have greater ability to raise capital, bear the cost of the innovation, and take on the risk of failure (Brown 1981). They are also more likely to afford the managerial and technical specialists that are often needed to evaluate and implement the innovation. One might, therefore, infer that adoption takes place first by larger organizations and is consequently followed by smaller ones after a successful trial. In fact, in Ontario, smaller municipalities have been equally if not more willing to take the leap and innovate with online voting despite not having the resources or capital to necessarily vet

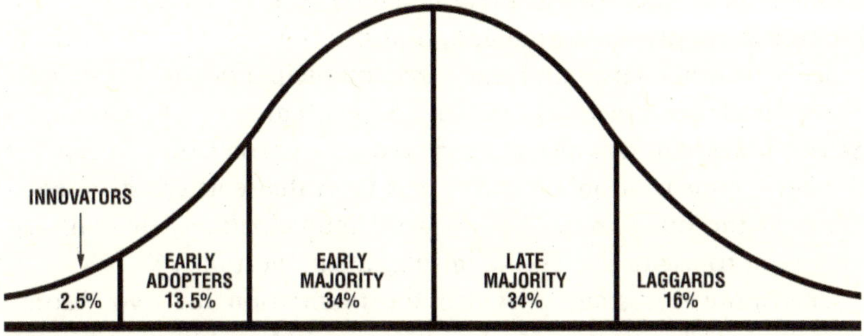

Figure 2.2 | Rogers (2003): Adopter categorization on the basis of innovativeness

potential vendors to the same extent as larger cities. Such a pattern suggests that online voting is atypical in the adoption of innovation. This may be because there are many small municipalities (70 per cent of Ontario municipalities have fewer than 10,000 electors), and it may also have to do with the costs associated with running elections of various types. Though high-cost innovations tend to be adopted by larger organizations first, evidence suggests that such a pattern might not hold true for low-cost innovations (Meyers and Marquis 1969). Vendors can very often provide services that are of a comparable cost to a traditional in-person election, if not less given that fewer (or no) poll workers and facilities are required.

In the remainder of the chapter, we document the rate of growth of online voting in Ontario, placing municipalities into the various categories identified by Rogers (2003).

Innovators, 2003

Focused on improving turnout and accessibility in local elections, eleven small townships[11] and one large municipality, the City of Markham, were the first adopters of online voting systems in Ontario in 2003 (Goodman et al. 2010; Goodman 2014). These twelve cases, while only accounting for 3 per cent of municipalities across the province, have played a crucial role in the diffusion of online voting practices across Ontario. Despite being just one of the twelve "innovators," Markham is often considered the original adopter of online voting, predominantly due to its size but also because its approach to the adoption of internet voting influenced models in other large and mid-sized municipalities in subsequent years – both in Ontario and in Nova Scotia (Pammett and Goodman 2013). Markham was also active in creating partnerships to support the development of online voting and to evaluate its effectiveness.[12] Some of the other initial "innovator" municipalities, by contrast, opted not to use online voting in subsequent elections.[13]

This innovator stage provided the foundation for two distinct models that characterize the innovator and early adoption phases: one from the City of Markham and the other model used by the eleven smaller municipalities (Goodman and Spicer 2019). The two models differed on the basis of three characteristics: the length of the online voting period, the types of voting modes used and the voting authentication process (either one or two steps, the latter which required online registration prior to voting).[14] Over time, municipalities across the province have taken different approaches to rolling out online voting based upon these initial experiences (Goodman et al. 2010; Goodman and Spicer 2019). The lessons learned from these innovators greatly informed the next phase of diffusion: the early adopter stage.

Early Adopters, 2006–10

News of the successful implementation of online voting methods in the 2003 election encouraged modest uptake among cities and towns in the two subsequent elections. Twenty municipalities offered online voting in 2006 (5 per cent of Ontario municipalities) and forty-four (11 per cent of Ontario municipalities) did so in 2010. This span of time can be considered the "early adopter" phase of diffusion. Online voting technology was still relatively new, and growth during this period was slow. According to Rogers' model, the municipalities adopting online voting during this phase can be characterized as those willing to take risk and embrace opportunities for change. They may have adopted the voting reform in the hopes of seeing some of the potential benefits of online voting such as enhanced accessibility, boosted turnout, and a revitalization of local democracy (Goodman et al. 2010; Goodman 2014), but the technology was still risky insofar as it had not been widely tested across the province.

Most municipalities deploying online voting during the "early adopter" phase were small, with electorates fewer than 25,000 people. Such municipalities were often rural as well (though exceptions to this pattern include Peterborough in 2006 and Belleville and Burlington in 2010). For the most part, two approaches continued to characterize this period. Some smaller municipalities offered online voting throughout the full election (during the advance voting period and on election day), used one-step authentication to identify voters, and eliminated paper voting entirely. In the second, which was generally employed by municipalities with electorates greater than 25,000, online voting was offered in the advance polling period only, required registration as a second step to cast an online ballot (making it a two-step authentication process), and maintained a paper ballot option.

Early Majority, 2014–18

The third phase of online voting diffusion among the "early majority" saw uptake climb to ninety-seven municipalities in 2014 (23 per cent of Ontario municipalities) and 177 in 2018 (42 per cent of Ontario municipalities).[15] As noted, members of the early majority group are more willing to embrace new opportunities than most of their counterparts, but they require additional information about the technology and its effectiveness before they are willing to bring it on board. By 2014, online voting had been employed in Ontario for more than a decade, and municipalities had a long record to reflect upon when deciding whether to adopt the voting mode. As the number of successful trials grew and as an increasing number of municipalities learned about the potential benefits of online voting for voters and administrators, more began to make the leap to introduce the voting reform. This period saw the fastest growth of online voting ever in the province, with nearly four times as many municipalities using online voting in 2018 than in 2010.

During this period, municipalities continued to experiment with the ways they employed online voting. The early majority phase saw the greatest growth in the number of municipalities using online voting, but it also marked a shift in the two earlier models that had become commonplace. Municipalities became more inclined to drop registration as a requirement and extend the option of advance voting through the full election period, and to drop in-person voting. Though not all municipalities made these changes, the trend toward online voting adoption grew during this period. Further changes to online voting deployment allowed municipalities that had not yet adopted the voting reform to learn more from the experiences of cities that had employed different versions of the system.

Late Majority, 2022

The 2022 elections can also be characterized as the beginning of the "late majority" phase. This election saw a total of 231 municipalities decide to offer online voting. For Rogers, the "late majority" phase comes to pass once a technology has been sufficiently adopted and proven, such that even more conservative and risk-averse users will adopt it. Though the system experienced some high-profile challenges in 2018 (we discuss the effects of these challenges upon the adoption of online voting in chapter 6), with online voting in place for five election cycles covering a nineteen-year period, decision makers now had a great deal of information about how internet voting functions in local elections in Ontario. By 2022, a majority of Ontario's municipalities (56 per cent) made use of online voting.

The move to the late majority stage of online voting diffusion in Ontario has been accompanied by even more experimentation among municipalities and includes some notable shifts. For one, uptake of telephone voting has slowed and been scaled back or removed in many municipalities. Municipalities in our interviews confirmed that it is relatively difficult for administrators to deploy, and electors' use of telephone voting is usually extremely low compared to other voting modes. Most municipalities that continue to offer telephone voting do so because of weak digital infrastructure and/or poor connectivity as a way to ensure all voters have equal access to the ballot box.[16] Although it is too early to tell, these small shifts could further shape this late majority phase of online voting development in Ontario. If risk exposure can be further mitigated and security concerns properly addressed, it is likely that we will see continued growth of online voting in the province.

CONCLUSION

Ontario is a unique case, both within Canada and internationally, when it comes to online voting adoption. This uniqueness stems from the staggering number of municipalities that employ online voting, the fact that these municipalities use, or have used, many variations of the system, and that remote internet voting has been employed here for two decades. This chapter has explored some of the government and market forces that have made such a high level of adoption and variation possible. On the legislative front, the Municipal Elections Act, 1996 provides a great deal of flexibility for municipalities to implement alternative voting methods. The permissibility of the language in the act has allowed municipalities to adopt methods such as mail, phone, and online ballots. The absence of standards or a regulatory framework for online voting systems at the municipal level has also given cities maximum leeway in which to experiment with different methods and vendors little incentive to standardize their offerings. Meanwhile, the policy learning process has allowed for collaboration and consultation across the province. Finally, the market – both in terms of supply and demand – has also been supportive. On the demand side, a clear majority of both electors and political elites want online voting options. As for supply, several vendors offer online voting services with a range of options, both in terms of cost, the types of services provided, and security processes and mechanisms. When taken together, these factors have created an environment where online voting has flourished.

The second part of the chapter mapped out the various phases of adoption, beginning in 2003 with just twelve municipalities. The 2022 municipal elections ushered in the start of the "late majority" phase where, for the first time ever, a majority (56 per cent) of the local governments in Ontario that are responsible for running elections made use of online voting methods. Municipalities also have a great deal of experience experimenting with variations of the system. It is within this context of widespread growth and ample experience with experimentation that the results of our following chapters are to be understood. In the chapters that follow, we explore public and elite attitudes towards online voting, keeping in mind that attitudes are shaped by this experience but also that they will affect the future of online voting in Ontario.

3

The Effects of Online Voting

INTRODUCTION

Western industrialized democracies have witnessed considerable transformation in recent decades. Subject to what has been labelled the "democratic deficit" (Gidengil et al. 2004; Norris 2011; Warren 2009), many democratic states face declining rates of civic engagement (Putnam 2000), falling levels of trust in government and political institutions more generally (Chanley et al. 2000; Blendon et al. 1997; Citrin et al. 1975), weakening partisan attachments (Dalton and Wattenberg 2000; Clarke and Stewart 1998), and low satisfaction with democracy, especially among "losers" whose favoured candidates or parties are not successful (Anderson et al. 2005; Blais and Gelineau 2007; Cross and Pruysers 2019). One trend in particular – declining levels of voter turnout (Gray and Caul 2000; Wattenberg 2002) – has received considerable scholarly attention (Blais et al. 2004; Heath 2007; McGregor et al. 2020; Flickinger and Studlar 1992; Pammett and LeDuc 2003; Patterson 2005).

As voter turnout declines around the world, several possible solutions have been offered to mitigate these apathetic tendencies (Blais and Rubenson 2013). A growing body of research has considered whether institutional changes such as early voting (Gronke et al. 2007; Blais et al. 2007), relaxed voter registration requirements (Grimmer et al. 2018), and more convenient methods of voting such as mail-in-ballots (Thompson et al. 2020) can address and foster greater electoral participation. Likewise, digital voting modes have become more popular over the last several decades. Online voting, in particular, has received much attention for its potential to lower voting costs, improve the voter experience (Goodman 2014), and increase turnout (Hall 2015). Despite hopes that the speed, ease, and convenience of online voting might halt and even perhaps reverse turnout decline, the available evidence fails to demonstrate that internet voting is a magic bullet solution (Germann and Serdült 2017; Solvak and Vassil 2017). Pammett and Goodman (2013, 12), for instance, write that with respect to internet voting any "hoped-for 'turnout effect' has been elusive; in some cases it was minor and in others non-existent."

While turnout is undoubtedly important, far less research has considered other effects associated with the introduction of internet voting. In this context, what other outcome variables should be studied? Aside from research on feelings toward and adoption of internet voting by different types of voters (which we discuss in chapter 4) what other effects might exist? For example, does the introduction of this controversial method of voting affect democratic malaise or attitudes about democracy itself? The purpose of this chapter, therefore, is to consider some of the other possible consequences of online voting beyond turnout. In doing so, we ask two questions. First, does online voting affect satisfaction with democracy? Consistent with initial expectations for turnout, the accessibility and convenience of online voting might also be associated with greater democratic satisfaction. Second, does experience with online voting at the municipal level affect attitudes towards its adoption at other levels of government in Canada? Federalism offers political actors across jurisdictions the ability to experiment with a variety of reforms, raising questions about whether attitudes towards those reforms might be "contagious" across levels. Such a question is important to consider, given that discussions of internet voting are ubiquitous during elections at all levels (particularly since the onset of the COVID-19 pandemic). Public servants and politicians alike would benefit from understanding the factors that shape support for the adoption of online voting.

Given that cities are responsible for determining how local elections are administered, there is considerable variation in online voting adoption in Ontario. Drawing from survey data, we divided our approximately 4,300 survey responses into four major groups of cities: (a) recent adopters of online voting, (b) long-time users, (c) cities that use online voting without a paper ballot option, and (d) those that used online voting but switched back to paper ballots in subsequent elections. This approach allows us to consider effects on political attitudes in a variety of different scenarios depending on respondents' expected level of experience with online voting.

The adoption of online voting, however, is not completely exogenous to local political attitudes. After all, public opinion may have conceivably shaped decisions about the adoption of online voting in the first place. A simple comparison of attitudes between city groupings is therefore insufficient to draw inferences about the effects of the implementation of online voting. To account for this, we conducted a survey experiment that provided varied information to respondents prior to asking them questions about attitudes towards democracy and internet voting. Respondents in the treatment groups for each of the aforementioned city types were provided with information on the status of online voting in their city (including whether it is used and for how long). Respondents in the control groups, by contrast, were not provided with any such information. This "within-group" approach allows us to properly isolate the effect that changing voting methods has upon our attitudes of interest.

Data reveal that the implementation of online voting has a positive effect upon satisfaction with local municipal democracy. Its elimination as an option, however, has no effect. Our results suggest a very different pattern with respect to opinions of whether online voting should be adopted at other levels of government; the introduction of online voting has no effect on opinions of whether online voting should be in place at any level of government. The elimination of online voting, however, decreases support for such an option at all three levels of government. These somewhat paradoxical findings suggest that, while online voting can be a useful tool for increasing support for democracy, this support fails to extend to the diffusion of online voting in "higher" orders of government.

BACKGROUND

Summarizing the democratic deficit, Norris (2004, 4) writes that citizens "have gradually become more distrustful of politicians, detached from parties, and doubtful about public sector institutions" (Dalton and Wattenberg 2000; Blendon et al. 1997; Savoie 2019; Carty 2010). As Cross (2008) suggests, however, these developments are not entirely new. More than thirty years ago, the Spicer Commission,[1] for example, highlighted sustained public dissatisfaction with democratic politics:

> One of the strongest messages the forum received from participants was that they have lost their faith in both the political process and their political leaders. They do not feel that their governments, especially at the federal level, reflect the will of the people, and they do not feel that citizens have the means at the moment to correct this. (Citizens' Forum 1991, 135)

Declining voter turnout is a key element of the democratic malaise that characterizes contemporary democratic life. This decline is now a well-documented trend among established Western democracies (Gray and Caul 2000; Wattenberg 2002; Blais et al. 2004).[2] Canada, of course, is no exception. Turnout for federal elections has dropped more than ten percentage points from an average of 77 per cent during elections in the 1960s to 65 per cent in elections during the 2010s (Elections Canada 2022). This story, however, is even worse at the municipal level, where turnout is usually below 50 per cent.

As a crucial element of democratic life, much has been written about factors associated with low voter turnout, including potential reforms to stave off further decline. The structure and machinery of elections has been long thought to influence rates of participation and to shape voter attitudes and behaviours more broadly. A consistent, albeit unsurprising finding, for example, is that compulsory voting increases turnout, often by 10 to 16 percentage points (Jackman 1987; Franklin 2004). Additionally, correlations between electoral system and voter participation have been well studied and there is good reason to expect higher turnout under proportional representation than majoritarian and plurality systems. Writing about psychological effects, Stockemer (2017, 704) notes that proportional representation may entice "voters to turn out, because the addition of a few more votes could allow parties to win a seat or gain an [additional] seat." Conversely, under a first-past-the-post system, especially one with a regionally dominant party or parties, the outcome of an election in a district (or cluster of districts) may be a forgone conclusion for individual voters (Cross 2008). Such a scenario is (theoretically) expected to suppress turnout because the utility of voting is necessarily diminished given that one additional vote will have little effect on electoral outcomes.

However, while many early studies found relationships between electoral system and turnout (Blais and Carty 1990; Blais and Dobrzynska 2008), this debate is far from settled. Blais (2006, 121), for example, writes that he is "not convinced" by prior findings in part because institutions "matter less than we are prone to believe." Likewise, Stockemer (2017, 704), reviewing more than 130 studies, concludes that "proportional representation has no influence on macro-level electoral participation." As such, many scholars have recently turned their attention to other voting reforms, focusing on the mode in which citizens can cast their ballot, rather than the electoral system itself.

While promising, the adoption of other convenience voting reforms such as an advanced voting period (Gronke et al. 2007) and mail-in ballots (Kousser and Mullin 2007; Thompson et al. 2020) have been found to have a modest impact on turnout.[3] Nevertheless, the introduction of online voting has long been viewed as a potential solution to turnout decline (Norris 2004; Alvarez and Hall 2004). As Petitpas et al. (2021, 1) explain, "simplifying the voting process and offering new, easy-to-use voting modes, such as internet voting, was expected to foster political participation or at least to put a halt to further turnout decline."

However, evidence that the introduction of online voting increases turnout is weak, at best. Some studies have found no relationship between internet voting and turnout (Boschler 2010; Germann and Serdült 2017); others have found modest positive effects (Dandoy and Kernalegenn 2021; Germann 2021; Goodman and Stokes 2020; Spada et al. 2016; Trechsel and Vassil 2010) or larger results (Solop 2001); and some have been inconclusive (Henry 2003). Part of this variation in results has to do with the context of the cases themselves but also issues with research design and limitations of data. As Germann (2021, 2) points out "it is also not always clear to what extent findings from existing studies can be trusted because many suffer from obvious methodological issues, such as reliance on self-reported impact measures." In general, however, although the effect of internet voting on turnout "remains an open question," there is a growing consensus that the voting mode is not the magic bullet solution to counter turnout declines, at least in the aggregate (Germann 2021, 2; Goodman and Stokes, 2020; Petitpas et al., 2021).

For some sub-groups of the population, however, results are more positive. Germann (2021), examining Switzerland, and Dandoy and Kernalegenn (2021), exploring France, for example, find that internet voting can increase turnout among expatriates. There is also evidence to suggest that internet voting can foster turnout among select groups of abstainers and occasional or less committed voters (Couture et al. 2017; Goodman 2014; Petitpas et al. 2021).

Considering internet voting's seemingly modest impact on turnout, it is worth considering whether it might shape other political attitudes and behaviours. Though turnout is commonly, and somewhat mistakenly, used as a singular justification for the adoption of online voting, other attitudes are important, including public evaluations of the quality of democracy. Surprisingly, the literature on the effects of internet voting on attitudes and behaviours beyond voting/turnout is modest. One strand of research considers the effects of adopting internet voting on levels of elector trust in technology and to government agencies that deploy such technologies (Warkentin et al. 2018; Madise and Martens 2005; Pomares et al. 2014). Other contributions have looked at acceptance of internet voting (Delis et al. 2014), voter confidence (Alvarez et al. 2011), and the relationship between party preferences and orientations toward online voting (Musiał-Karg and Kapsa 2020). In Canada, examinations of online voter attitudes have been mostly relegated to public facing reports (Goodman and Pyman 2016; Goodman and Harvey 2022). These latter assessments have relied on self-selected data of online voters and not representative samples.

Overall, research about the relationship between internet voting and trust in broader democratic institutions is sparse and inadequate to draw conclusive evidence. In fact, other work suggests that the acceptance of internet voting may instead be a function of "risk acceptance" based on the evaluation of the costs versus benefits of technology usage, rather than on trust of the technological systems or governments employing them (Babayan et al. 2021). The goal of this chapter is to address the general lack of research into the effects of internet voting on attitudes and behaviours beyond turnout.

Recent evidence suggests that internet voting does not affect specific outcomes including the representativeness of selected candidates. In elections where internet voting has been used, women candidates have not been elected at higher rates nor are they more likely to step forward as candidates (Wigginton and Stockemer 2021). This lack of representational benefit coupled with technological and security concerns (Park et al. 2021; Essex and Goodman 2022) suggests that the adoption of internet voting could negatively impact democratic outcomes. At the same time, however, there are theoretical reasons for expecting that the introduction of internet voting might boost satisfaction with democracy, including the perception that voting might be simpler or more accessible, even if voters do not necessarily take advantage of the method. Conversely, for those individuals who live in a city that has abandoned internet voting, we might also expect to see effects upon attitudes towards democracy. Does the removal of an internet voting option negatively affect satisfaction with democracy? Might concerns about the safety of internet voting systems lead electors to become more satisfied with democracy when online voting is eliminated as an option? We view these questions as exploratory without specific expectations.

The administration of Canadian municipal elections may also affect peoples' attitudes towards internet voting across other levels of government (provincial and/or federal). Acknowledging this possibility, however, requires questioning whether experiences with online voting in local elections affects attitudes about whether such a system should be adopted in "higher" order elections as well. Studies of internet voting diffusion tend to focus on individual users of internet voting, studying how and why those users adopt internet voting over time (Vassil et al. 2016; Miner 2011). This research does not necessarily look at diffusion across countries or even within a single country.[4] Given that internet voting is currently limited to municipal elections in Canada, we consider whether there is the possibility for multi-level policy diffusion in the form of support for internet voting across orders of government.

More generally, there is evidence that questions of electoral reform and the adoption of new electoral mechanisms do not occur in a vacuum. Bol et al. (2015) find that national legislatures are more likely to engage in electoral reform when "peer countries" have made similar choices. Krook (2006), for example, writes about the diffusion of electoral quotas in this context. Pruysers and Stewart (2018, 745) likewise note that "the very nature of federalism means that there will be multiple arenas of electoral competition, many more political parties, and therefore more opportunities for experimentation." This sentiment is echoed by Courtney (2010, 132) who writes that federalism allows for "test-tube" experimentation. In Canada, electoral innovation is often tested in the provincial arena. Cross et al. (2016), for example, highlight how provincial parties were the first to broaden their leadership elections, allowing party members to vote in person and by mail or telephone, often long before federal parties caught up (Goodman and Pruysers 2019). This provincial "first mover" trend also extends to electoral reform. Several provinces have seriously considered the adoption of new electoral systems for provincial elections – provinces such as British Columbia, Ontario, and Prince Edward Island have all held (unsuccessful) referendums on electoral reform.[5] In contrast, the federal government has done relatively little to meaningfully explore reform.[6] In terms of the adoption of online voting, there has obviously been a great deal of diffusion across Canadian municipalities. We know little, however, about how public support for diffusion across levels is shaped.

In fact, there is good evidence that public policy in general can be diffused across levels in a multi-level system. Exploring policy diffusion in Canada, Foucault and Monpetit (2013, 210) find "territorial clusters of attention." Here the authors note that policy diffusion in Canada often has a horizontal dimension with certain provinces, especially the western ones, clustering together. Likewise, writing about the policy diffusion of Canada's public healthcare system, Boyd (2021, 3) writes, "within a decade, a policy experiment in what was at the time one of the country's smaller and poorer provinces became a national program that is now a fixture in the Canadian policy landscape, and a cultural institution in the country." All of this suggests that policy and reform are not static: there is often a multi-level component. At the same time, however, the municipal arena is often, if not always, left out of this discussion. Even though thousands of municipalities in Canada offer an exceptionally ripe context for policy experimentation (or perhaps because of it), Canadian scholars tend to focus overwhelmingly on provincial and federal levels. To address this gap, we consider whether municipal electors support the adoption of internet voting for "higher" orders of government and whether this is influenced by their experience with internet voting at the municipal level.

THE CASES

All cities included in the dataset have at some point offered an online voting option in their elections. Although heavily regulated by provincial legislation, municipalities are nevertheless responsible for making decisions on voting methods (see chapter 2). Even though the government of Ontario has revoked the ability of municipalities to employ alternative voting systems (ranked ballots, in particular), municipal councils retain the ability to determine how votes will be cast in their elections.[7] As already noted, there is a great deal of variation in internet voting adoption in Ontario. Some cities have provided such an option for many prior election cycles, others are more recent adopters, and hundreds of municipalities still do not provide an online voting option. Among those that do employ online voting, there is a further dimension of variation to consider: whether paper ballots are concurrently used with the internet voting option.

We employ these forms of variation to determine how various online voting options affect (a) satisfaction with local democracy and (b) opinions of whether online voting should be available at any other level of government in Canada. Does experience with online voting make one more or less satisfied with democracy? Does it affect confidence in such a system, thus influencing support for its use at other levels of government? It is conceivably the case that different types of experience with internet voting elections might lead to different outcomes on these dimensions.

Cities are therefore categorized based on when internet voting was implemented and whether it is used concurrently with a paper option. In total, there are four city groups in our sample. The first group includes cities where online voting was adopted in 2018 and a traditional paper ballot option was retained (Bradford West Gwillimbury, Kawartha Lakes, Pickering, Sarnia, St Thomas, and Thunder Bay). The second group of cities are those where internet voting has been an option alongside paper ballots for at least two elections (Brantford, Cambridge, Chatham-Kent, Kingston, Timmins, Quinte West, Belleville, Burlington, and Markham). Comparing these groups allows us to determine if any observed outcomes might take effect immediately or if they take longer to build up. The third group of cities are those that do not offer a paper voting option (Ajax, Sudbury, Newmarket, and Innisfil). Finally, the fourth group contains only one city: Guelph. This is the only city in Ontario that employed online voting in 2014 but not in 2018. As this group includes only one city, we oversampled in Guelph (13.4 per cent of respondents in our dataset are from this one city alone). The inclusion of such a case in our experiment allows us to determine the effects of removing an online voting option upon our outcome attitudes of interest.

THE EXPERIMENT

Studying the effects of the implementation of online voting in municipalities is challenging, as is studying any major institutional change. To do so, one might compare residents' opinions of internet voting in municipalities that do and do not use the technology, to see if residents in these two groups differ on the outcome variables of interest. This approach, however, is fraught with risk, as residents' opinions may be influenced by other factors that differ between municipalities (i.e., not solely factors related to the use or non-use of online voting technologies). Moreover, the public's opinions of online voting might influence municipalities' decisions about whether to adopt online voting in the first place. As such, we cannot be sure that patterns observed using an "across-city" approach only result from the choices of voting modes available to the electors in the first place.

Another potential option for studying the effects of online voting is to study municipalities across time. More specifically, attitudes could be measured prior to and after the implementation of online voting. This "within-city" approach is beneficial in that existing differences between municipalities no longer pose a problem for drawing causal conclusions. A new issue arises here, though, considering that events other than changes in voting methods, including candidate changes, political scandals, and other important social and political events might influence and shape residents' attitudes. Considering this, it is clearly difficult, if not impossible, to control adequately for all factors. Therefore, the same problem arises with the "within-city" and "across-city" approaches: the inability to attribute causation to a single factor.

To avoid these issues, we answer our research questions by way of a survey experiment, using informational primes. In the experiment, half of the respondents in each city group are supplied with factually correct information on the status of internet voting in their city, while the other half are not. We then compare responses from individuals in the two groups to see if the messages influence attitudes. This method allows us to avoid the problems of using "across-city" or "within-city" approaches.

Our analysis is based upon the elector survey (mentioned in chapter 1) that includes responses from more than 4,000 respondents from twenty cities. The survey consists of questions about municipal politics, online voting, general political orientations, and sociodemographic characteristics. Importantly, it also includes questions on satisfaction with local democracy, as well as opinions of whether internet voting should be employed at the local, provincial, and federal levels. These questions, which serve as the basis of our outcome variables, were all asked as part of the same question battery. See appendix 3.I for a complete list of survey questions.

The latter questions, about opinions of whether internet voting should be used at the three levels of government, are straightforward and simple to interpret for respondents and researchers alike. The question about satisfaction, however, can potentially be interpreted in different ways, and care must be taken when employing such a concept. Early work on support for political systems (Easton 1965) differentiated between specific support (of the government of the day) and diffuse support (more general opinions towards the basic political arrangements of politics and democracy in a polity). More recent work suggests that measures of democratic satisfaction, in fact, tap into both factors and that democratic satisfaction "fall[s] between more diffuse support for political community and regime principles and more specific support for regime institutions and political actors" (Kostelka and Blais 2018, 370), thus capturing "citizens' evaluations of how the democratic system as a whole, works in practice" (Nadeau et al. 2021, 6). Fortunately, the experimental nature of this study allows us to, in effect, control for the "specific" components of these assessments; as respondents are assigned randomly to a treatment group, we expect that the average evaluations of the current regime are equal across groups and that the differences in results we observed are upon diffuse considerations (which includes voting method).

Prior to being asked questions about satisfaction and their opinions of internet voting (as part of an agree/disagree battery), respondents were assigned to one of two experimental groups. Members of the control group were simply asked the extent to which they agree with a series of statements about satisfaction with democracy and whether internet voting should be employed at the various orders of government. Members of the treatment group were presented with a short informational preamble, which informed/reminded electors of the actual status of internet voting in their city. The text of these pre-ambles was as follows:

Group 1 (Internet voting just added): In 2018, internet voting was added as a voting option for municipal elections in [city name]. Residents could vote either ONLINE or IN PERSON by paper ballot.

Group 2 (Internet voting present for at least two elections): Internet voting has been an option for municipal elections in [city name] since 2014/2010. In 2018, residents could vote either ONLINE or IN PERSON by paper ballot.

Group 3 (Online only, no in-person option): In 2018, municipal elections in [city name] were run completely online. Residents COULD vote ONLINE, but they COULD NOT vote IN PERSON by paper ballot.

Group 4 (Internet voting eliminated): In 2018, municipal elections in [city name] were run using paper voting IN PERSON at the polls only. In the 2014 local elections, residents were able to vote either ONLINE or IN PERSON by paper ballot, but the online option was taken away in 2018.

The purpose of this informational experiment is to determine if being reminded and/or informed of the city's experience with internet voting has an effect upon any of the outcome variables. These informational preambles serve two purposes. The first is educational: local elections are notoriously low information affairs, and most electors pay less attention to local level politics than to either provincial or federal politics (McGregor et al. 2021). Though we expect that our survey respondents are more informed about local politics than the average elector,[8] it is still plausible that some participants were unaware of the status and/or history of the use of internet voting in their city. We expect, therefore, that the messages serve an educative purpose to some respondents in the treatment groups. Regardless of pre-existing knowledge of respondents, the second purpose of the experimental messages is to prime respondents in the treatment group so that the topic of internet voting becomes a more central consideration when answering attitudinal questions (Zaller 1992). We expect that such primes will increase the likelihood that orientations towards internet voting, and the information provided in the primes about internet voting in the respondent's specific municipality, will be factored into answers to questions about democratic satisfaction and whether internet voting should be applied at the various orders of government in Canada. We likewise make the assumption that the survey preambles have effects on respondents that are indicative of the effects of implementing or removing an internet voting option on electors. We do not make claims of the magnitude of effects, given that experiments of this nature are unable to do so. However, we suggest that any directional effects observed are externally valid.

An experiment of this nature, as explained above, is the best way to identify effects using cross-sectional data.[9] One cannot simply compare the attitudes of respondents in the four city groups. Rather, the best way to identify effects is to compare individuals within city groups. Only if we find that the experimental and treatment groups differ from one another, for each category of city, can we be confident in our assessment that internet voting affects attitudes.[10] Experiments of this nature are always associated with concerns about external validity – that is, the question of whether results of such studies travel to the "real world." While we recognize this concern, we remain convinced that this approach is the best one for answering our research questions. In contrast to some online experiments about fictional elections or candidates, respondents in our treatment groups are presented with factually accurate information about their municipalities, and they are asked about real elections and democracies. While such an approach may lead to imprecise estimates of the magnitude of effects, we see no reason why directional effect would not extend to the "real world."

Before presenting the results of our survey, we must note that our city groups are not mutually exclusive. Some cities that do not have a paper ballot option (group three) adopted their system in 2018, while some did so previously. Among cities without a paper voting option, therefore, we do not attempt to draw conclusions about the period of use of this approach (since our informational prime made no mention of this). Similarly, the city groups are non-exhaustive; we do not include respondents from any of the hundreds of Ontario municipalities without internet voting, though there is certainly value in conducting a study of this nature in such cities in the future. Nevertheless, our cases allow us to draw conclusions in several dimensions. Firstly, we can evaluate whether the implementation of online voting has effects after just one election cycle or if two are required (groups one and two). Secondly, we can determine if the elimination of paper ballots temper any potential effects from the use of online voting (group three). Finally, the inclusion of Guelph (which has eliminated online voting) allows us to determine if the elimination of online voting has any effects (group four). The survey data therefore provide a thorough consideration of the effects of online voting across Ontario in municipal elections.

RESULTS

Satisfaction with Democracy

Prior to presenting the experimental results, we consider the sample as a whole. Respondents were asked the extent to which they agreed with the following statement: "I am satisfied with the quality of democracy in [city name]." Overall, results were positive. A total of 79.7 per cent agreed (28.5 per cent strongly and 51.2 per cent somewhat), while just 20.3 per cent disagreed (6.4 per cent strongly and 13.9 per cent somewhat) (N=4,329).[11] Though our data do not allow us to speak to the reasons for this general positive sentiment, these figures do paint a fairly rosy picture of assessments of local democracy in Ontario.[12] Interested readers can refer to appendix 3.III for a detailed assessment of the correlates of democratic satisfaction.

Rather than focusing on aggregate levels of support for local democracy, however, we are interested in how the adoption of online voting affects these evaluations. Figure 3.1 shows the distribution of responses to the satisfaction question for each city group, by experimental treatment. We evaluate the treatment effects by way of chi-squared tests (p-values for these tests are reported in the figure). Recall that the groups are as follows: Group one: internet voting just added; Group two: internet voting present for at least two elections; Group three: online voting only, no in-person option; and Group four: internet voting eliminated.

Figure 3.1 shows a clear pattern: the informational messages in groups one, two, and three (where internet voting is in place) had a positive effect upon satisfaction with local democracy. This effect is present regardless of when online voting was implemented (groups one versus two) and, somewhat surprisingly, whether paper ballots remain an option or not ($p<0.1$ in group three). Though all

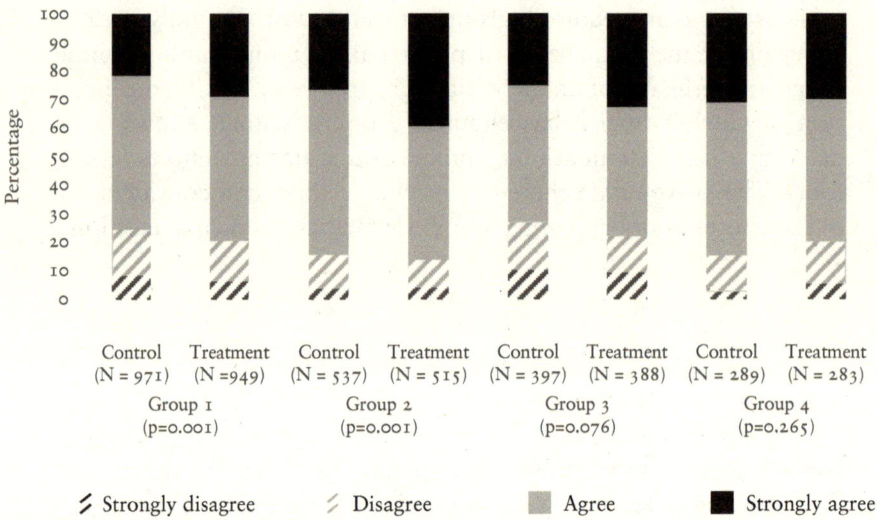

Figure 3.1 | Satisfaction with local democracy, by experimental treatment

treatments saw a reduction in the rate of "disagree" responses (both strongly and otherwise), the effect here seems largely to increase the rate of "strongly agree" responses and a similar reduction of "agree" responses. In short, being told/reminded that online voting was in place increased the likelihood of individuals being highly satisfied with local democracy.

Perhaps surprisingly, given the consistency of the findings in groups one, two, and three, being told about the removal of internet voting has no observable effect in figure 3.1. There is no statistically significant effect of the treatment among respondents in group four. Even after respondents were told of the removal of the online voting option, this does not seem to have negatively affected evaluations of the quality of democracy among respondents in this group. Though the sample size of this group is smaller than it is for the others (making it more difficult to find statistically significant results), a visual comparison of the control and treatment results for this group make it clear that there is very little difference between the treatment and control categories in this group. These data suggest, therefore, that the introduction of online voting has a positive effect upon citizen satisfaction, but there is no evidence that its removal has a negative impact.

Opinions of Online Voting

Next, we consider the effects of the information treatments on levels of support for using online voting in municipal, provincial, and federal elections. This analysis allows us to consider the effects of experience with online voting at the local level on support at other levels of government. We do so through three figures illustrated below.

Some important trends emerge from these data separate from the experimental results. First, there is strong support in our sample for the use of online voting at all three levels of government. There was agreement (either somewhat or strongly) from 86.6 per cent of respondents that online voting should be in place in at least one level of government, while 77.8 per cent agreed that it should be used in elections at all three levels. We do not wish to imply, however, that these figures are necessarily indicative of support across all of Ontario. Given that our data were collected online and only from cities having experience with internet voting, we expect that the sample is more supportive of online voting than the general population. Nevertheless, these figures must be encouraging to proponents of online voting. Appendix 3.III contains a detailed analysis of the correlates of support for the use of online voting at the three levels of government.

One other noteworthy trend emerges from these data: there is slightly more support for online voting at the local level than there is provincially or federally. Among the sample, 84.6 per cent (57.7 per cent strongly and 26.7 per cent somewhat) agreed that online voting should be used at the municipal level. The comparable figures for the provincial and federal levels are 81.1 per cent (55.0 per cent strongly and 26.0 per cent somewhat agree) and 80.0 per cent (54.5 per cent strongly and 25.5 per cent somewhat agree). Put another way, 5.6 per cent of respondents who agreed that online voting should be used in local elections did not think this should be the case provincially, and 7.2 per cent did not think it should be used in federal elections. Regardless of the reason for these differences, the finding is instructive. Even when electors have experience in an election where internet voting is offered and even when they support

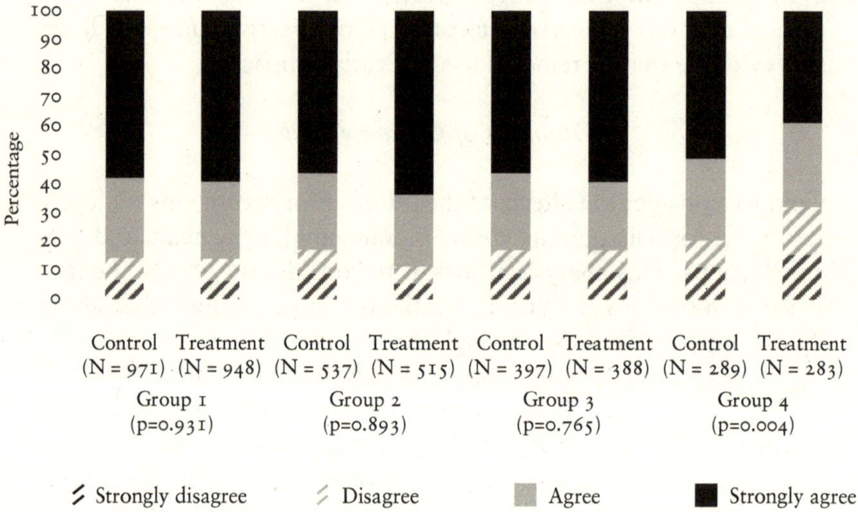

Figure 3.2 | Attitudes towards the adoption of online voting at municipal level, by experimental treatment

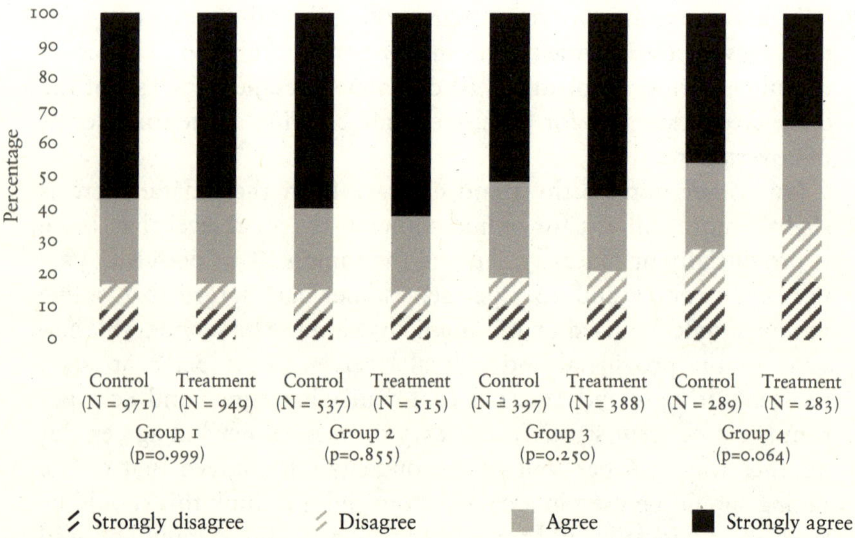

Figure 3.3 | Attitudes towards the adoption of online voting at provincial level, by experimental treatment

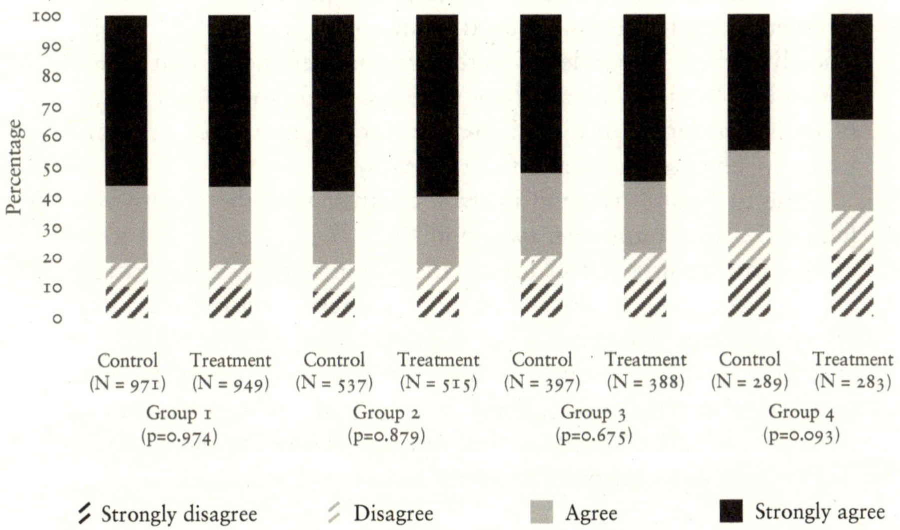

Figure 3.4 | Attitudes towards the adoption of online voting at federal level, by experimental treatment

it, they do not universally take the view that the system should be employed in other elections.

More important than the aggregate values, however, are the results of the experiment. Figures 3.2 to 3.4 show results in the same format as figure 3.1, but the outcome variables are now opinions of the adoption of online voting at the municipal, provincial, and federal level respectively. We show the distribution of each variable by experimental group, as well as chi-squared results to indicate whether the effects of the experimental treatments were statistically significant.

Figures 3.2 to 3.4 show two consistent trends. Firstly, the treatment has no effect upon the attitudes of respondents in groups one, two, and three. In other words, being told about the implementation of internet voting has no effect upon attitudes towards whether internet voting should be in place at any level of government. The consistency of null findings across groups and levels is striking. There are no noteworthy differences between any of these groups or across levels. The second major finding from these figures is that the treatment did have an effect on respondents in group four, where internet voting had been removed as an option for 2018. More specifically, when respondents were informed/reminded that online voting had been eliminated, they were less likely to support the use of online voting at any level ($p<0.01$ for the municipal level and $p<0.1$ for the provincial and federal levels).

These two patterns stand in stark contrast with the results from figure 3.2. In groups one, two, and three the informational treatment had a positive effect upon satisfaction with local democracy but no effect upon opinions of employing internet voting at any level of government. The trend is the opposite in group four. There, the treatment had no effect upon satisfaction but a negative effect upon support for internet voting. These very different findings suggest that the implementation or removal of internet voting can have varying effects upon different types of attitudes.

CONCLUSION

Municipalities have become the laboratories of electoral reform in Canada. The vast number of local governments, coupled with the significant degrees of variation between them, suggests that there are many important lessons to be learned from local governments through comparative studies like ours. Ontario's municipalities vary greatly in terms of size and composition but also in terms of their structures (district magnitude and single versus two-tiered systems) and electoral system (ranked ballots were employed by London in 2018, while Kingston and Cambridge held plebiscites on whether to adopt the system for future elections). Of relevance to the current work, Ontario's municipalities exhibit a great deal of variation in terms of voting rules and methods. Since cities have the autonomy to set many of their own rules for administering elections (see chapter 2), there is a great deal of variation on electoral procedure, including in setting advance polling dates and determining voting modes. In-person, mail, telephone, and internet voting options are all available at various locales in the province. By far the most used and controversial of these non-traditional methods has, of course, been internet voting.

As noted earlier, many scholars have considered the question of whether online voting affects turnout patterns. Very little has been written, however, about other potential effects that such a significant institutional change might have upon the electorate. Our goal here is to move past the turnout question to focus on how adopting or abandoning online voting affects (a) satisfaction with democracy and (b) opinions of online voting. We find that both types of attitudes are influenced, depending upon whether cities have implemented or removed an internet voting option.

In our sample, levels of satisfaction with democracy and support for internet voting are both high. Though these findings are unsurprising given the online nature of our opt-in survey, they should not be ignored. This is particularly true with respect to levels of support for online voting. Among this politically active and engaged segment of the population, support for experimentation with a new voting method, at all three levels of government, is extremely high. Regardless of the exact share of the population that is supportive of this voting system, however, it behooves policy makers at all levels to have serious conversations about the voting options to be presented to Canadians.

More important than point estimates of our outcome variables, however, are questions about the type of effects that the experimental treatments (that serve as a proxy for the effects of actual institutional changes) have upon these attitudes. We believe that these messages serve to educate and prime respondents so that voting methods are a "top-of-mind" consideration when responding to our attitudinal questions of interest. The treatments thus allow us to identify directional effects that mimic the effects of "real-world" changes to voting methods.

The data also suggest that the introduction of internet voting seems to improve evaluations of local democracy. This finding shows that institutional reform can improve evaluations of local democracy, reducing the malaise that accompanies the democratic deficit. At the same time, however, we see no evidence that the use of internet voting at the local level serves as a "gateway" for internet voting in either provincial or federal elections. Even though levels of satisfaction increase when online voting is implemented, there is no corresponding increase in support for the use of online voting. Such a finding is somewhat paradoxical: online voting provides a boost to democratic satisfaction, even if it does not boost support for use of the system, in any setting. This null finding should be particularly striking to those who assume that electoral reform might naturally diffuse across levels once electors have experience with a new system at the local level.

These results also point to two final questions warranting consideration. First, further research is required to confirm the findings from group four, where online voting was eliminated. Is there something specific about Guelph's decision to abandon online voting that might have contributed to our findings? To our knowledge, there was no scandal that led to the change. While there was not a particularly large outcry against online voting, there were residents that lobbied for its disbandment and brought in a cyber-security expert to provide testimony to council the night of the vote. After a heated debate, council voted to drop internet voting seven against six. Despite this debate, however, we see no obvious confounding variable that might account for our findings and therefore expect that our results should likely be similar in other cities. However, since this group only included one city, Guelph, respondents were oversampled, and thus, conclusions must be drawn with caution.

A second important question that arises from these results is the matter of whether those individuals who voted online might have responded differently to the experimental treatment than those who did not. This chapter has shown that online voters differ in multiple dimensions from other voters, and therefore, it is conceivable that the effects of implementing online voting upon the population might have similar, patterned effects. If, for example, the results in the above figures are driven by online voters, then this would suggest that the effects of living in a city where internet voting was adopted or abandoned would be contingent upon one's personal voting method. Fortunately, we can answer this question using our data. Differences between internet and other voters can be tested by creating a series of simple regression models where the experimental treatment can be interacted with reported voting method. We did so here – running one model for each group, for each outcome variable, for a total of sixteen models (results not shown but available from the authors).[13] In none of the models was the interaction term significant, suggesting that there is no discernible difference between online voters and those who cast their ballots using other methods.[14] These null findings suggest that the effects of implementing or removing online voting are population-wide, rather than being dependent upon the voting methods of individual voters.

The study of the consequences of introducing internet voting is a subfield still in its infancy. Though turnout is overwhelmingly the focus of researchers, this chapter points to other types of effects that changes to electoral mode options can have upon electors. In the next chapters we turn to consider how candidates and election administrators respond to and navigate an environment where online voting is a consideration.

4

Who Votes Online? Perception versus Reality

INTRODUCTION

Deciding how citizens will cast their ballot in an election is not always straightforward and involves questions about ballot structure, district magnitude, and voting formula. Increasingly, debates surrounding electoral reform involve discussions about the adoption of new technologies, including internet voting. Like most other public policy issues, decisions regarding voting reform, including the adoption of internet voting, generally rest with political elites (Boix 1999; Colomer 2004; Norris 1995; Pilon 2013).[1] This, however, raises an important concern: elected representatives tend to be decision makers regarding the rules of the vote despite the fact that such institutional changes can have a direct – and substantial – effect on the types of voters that visit the polls and, in turn, the likelihood that certain candidates will be elected or re-elected (Katz 2005; De Winter 2005; Morelli 2004).[2] The behaviour and preferences of many elected officials during these debates is without a doubt coloured, at least in part, by their expectation of how certain institutional changes will affect their chances of re-election (Bol 2016; Renwick et al. 2009; Lagassé 2017).

How might the adoption of internet voting affect incumbent re-election, and do candidates have a good understanding of these dynamics? The literature suggests that the adoption and use of internet voting has potential implications for the kinds of individuals who are likely to vote (Alvarez et al. 2009; Goodman 2010) and the level of turnout in an election (Trechsel et al. 2010). Perceptions about who votes online matter, as these considerations inform elites' decisions to implement such administrative reforms (or to maintain the status quo). From a theoretical perspective, this line of thinking is supported by rational choice theories of partisan interests where political elites make decisions about reforms based on anticipated optimal rewards (Boix 1999; Colomer 2004; Norris 2011). Simply put, candidates and elected representatives who believe, correctly or not, that their base of supporters will not vote online will likely be more skeptical of enacting online voting reforms, especially if such reforms are tied to the elimination of traditional paper ballots. Likewise, in settings where online voting is already an option offered alongside traditional, in-person voting, candidate expectations about who votes online may have implications for campaign strategies and dynamics. Decisions on outreach strategies (virtual versus in person), messaging around turnout, and informational campaigns about how to navigate online voting technology might all be considered by candidates, and these considerations might in turn be weighed in light of the type of supporter that one expects or hopes to attract, either in ideological or sociodemographic terms.

Who candidates think will vote online therefore matters. Despite the potential impact that these perceptions might have, we know next to nothing about how candidates understand this dimension of the electorate's behaviour. Which factors, if any, do candidates for office associate with online voting? Are their assessments correct? Do they know more than the electors that they wish to represent? In this chapter, we address and answer these questions. But, before evaluating candidate perceptions (and their accuracy, for that matter), we must first develop a profile of electors who actually vote online. Thus, this chapter begins with a dive into voters' sociodemographic characteristics. We then move to a comparison of the characteristics of an online voter with relevant candidate and elector perceptions of those characteristics. Finally, we consider the accuracy of these assessments and discuss which kinds of candidates appear to be the most knowledgeable on the subject. Overall, then, this chapter addresses the following three research questions: (1) what is the profile of an online voter in Ontario (age, sex, ideology, etc.)?; (2) do candidates and electors have accurate perceptions about who votes online?; and, (3) which candidates are the most knowledgeable on the subject?

In developing our profile of an online voter, we find age, homeownership, ideology, race, and income as being related to the propensity to cast one's ballot online. Among other important findings, our analysis adds to growing Canadian literature revealing a rather counterintuitive finding: older voters engage in online voting at higher rates than younger ones (Goodman 2014; Goodman and Pyman 2016). Turning to perceptions, we find that neither candidates nor electors are particularly adept at identifying who decides to vote online. Candidates, for example, incorrectly perceive online voters to be younger and more diverse than they actually are. Candidates also do not appear to have an informational advantage over voters. Finally, when considering whether the characteristics of candidates themselves are related to knowledge of the relationship, we see that the characteristics of candidates seem to matter very little for understanding how voters cast their ballots.

BACKGROUND

Who Votes Online?

The first part of this chapter explores who votes online. Previous research examining who votes online in Canada has been limited to self-selected exit poll data and access to voter data in select municipalities. These studies show that online voters are often older, more educated, enjoy higher incomes, are less likely to live in urban areas, and often report less committed voting records compared to their paper voter counterparts (Goodman 2014; Goodman and Pyman 2016). Specifically, the literature suggests that the "average" online voter is fifty-three years of age, reports having attended "some university," has an annual household income from $80,000 to $99,000, and says that they vote "some of the time." Meanwhile, those who choose to continue to vote by paper have a mean age of forty-four years, have completed some technical or community college, report a median household income between $60,000 to $79,000, and say they vote "all of the time." Voters from these two groups express a relatively similar interest in politics (Goodman and Pyman 2016). Despite having a good sense of the types of electors that choose to vote online, earlier contributions do not consider factors such as homeownership, immigrant status or race, and the extent to which ideology may be a factor in the selection of voting modes. The latter of these is a particularly important consideration given that online voting may draw less committed voters into the voting process (Goodman 2014) and increase turnout (Goodman and Stokes 2020).

Internationally, many studies have focused on understanding who votes online (Trechsel and Vassil 2010; Serdült et al. 2015; Bock Segaard et al. 2014; Sciarini et al. 2013; Mendez and Serdült 2017; Vassil et al. 2016). The most comprehensive summary of this research reviews twenty-two empirical studies that examine socio-demographic variables in the context of online voting (Serdült et al. 2015). Despite some competing results among the different countries considered – Switzerland, Estonia, the United Kingdom, Norway, the United States, and Canada – the authors draw the conclusion that the typical online voter is younger, male, well-educated, and has an above average household income. Interestingly, most Canadian results show opposite patterns than in European countries, particularly for age. We seek here to further develop the profile of an online voter in Ontario local elections.

Digital literacy is another consideration of scholars interested in online voter characteristics (Van Deursen and Van Dijk 2011; Meyers et al. 2013; Goodman et al. 2018). Bélanger and Carter (2010) conceptualize digital literacy in reference to the "digital divide": the distinction between tech-literate and -illiterate electors. This divide is thought to be a key predictor of voting method choice (online versus paper), and our data confirm this to be true. Our survey asked respondents how they would describe their ability to use the internet (options were "poor," "fair," "good," and "very good"). Not surprisingly, given the online nature of our sample, respondents were overwhelmingly skewed towards the top end of the variable (fewer than 10 per cent of respondents had poor or fair abilities). Online voters were more likely to have a high level of skill (65.5 per cent reported being "very good" on the internet). We note, however, that even a sizable majority (59.0 per cent) of paper voters had "very good" skills (though, a chi-square analysis reveals that the difference between the groups is significant at $p<0.01$, N = 1,606).

We do not probe this variable further here, for both methodological and theoretical reasons. Methodologically, our recruitment lends itself to the creation of a sample with a high rate of digital literacy. Respondents completed our survey online, after opening it through a link sent via email. Though this process is minimally onerous for most people, such an approach no doubt excludes individuals who might be discouraged from participating in such a process (such individuals can reasonably be expected to be particularly willing to vote online if given the option). Theoretically, our focus here is on sociodemographic, rather than attitudinal or behavioural, characteristics. We are simply interested in who votes how (rather than why). Still, given the prevalence of research on the topic, we thought it important to include this brief note.

Candidate and Voter Perceptions

The second part of this chapter considers whether candidates are knowledgeable about voters and the voting modes to which certain voters are attracted. Classic contributions to theories of representation in political science point to a disjunction in politicians' beliefs about voters (Kingdon 1967; Miller and Stokes 1963). Political elites have often been shown to be "poorly informed" on public opinion (Uslaner and Weber 1978) and it is not uncommon for elected representatives to misunderstand constituent preferences on important issues (Brockman and Skovron 2018). Indeed, writing about the accuracy of elite perceptions, Brand (1969) describes it as "scandalously low." Reviewing several recent field experiments, Brockman and Skovron (2013, 7) write that "information about constituents' views materially changes how legislators vote, which in turn implies that politicians in their natural state do not have routine access to good information about their constituents' views." Such misperceptions have also been documented among legislative staff (Hertel-Fernandez et al. 2019). Politicians, therefore, routinely rely on their (often incorrect) beliefs and perceptions to make important decisions about public policy, campaign tactics, and their general approach to politics (Ekengren and Oscarsson 2011). If politicians do not accurately perceive what their constituents want, it is probable that political elites' perceptions of voters are lacking in other areas: notably, their understanding of which voters might be attracted to certain voting arrangements or methods.

If elites have low levels of knowledge about voters and voter preferences, how knowledgeable are voters on these issues? Evidence suggests that voters, at least in the aggregate, have the wisdom of the crowd. A growing literature, for instance, reveals that in the aggregate, voters are generally well equipped to predict election results (Temporao et al. 2019; Murr 2011; Lewis-Beck and Stegmaier 2011). At the individual level, however, the story is quite different: voters have trouble identifying local electoral dynamics (Blais and Turgeon 2004) and tend to have relatively low levels of general political knowledge (Delli Carpini and Keeter 1996; Pruysers and Blais 2014). Anderson et al. (2020), for example, find that relatively few electors can identify which challenger poses the strongest threat to a sitting incumbent. Like candidates, it is not clear that individual voters would have a good sense of who votes online either.

We might, therefore, expect both candidates for office and electors to have a low level of knowledge about the types of individuals who vote online versus in person. This contention, however, has yet to be tested, despite online voting becoming increasingly popular and debates over its implementation more common.

DATA AND METHODS

This chapter uses the elector and candidate survey data described in the first chapter. Here, however, we specifically focus our attention on fifteen municipalities that employ a mixture of both internet and paper voting.[3] With regards to the elector data, we draw upon a variety of questions about political attitudes, behaviour, and sociodemographic characteristics.[4] Importantly, elector respondents were asked about the method of voting (online or otherwise) that they used. Sociodemographic data are used in the first part of our analysis, below, where we consider whether voting mode is related to our sociodemographic indicators of interest. Women are compared to men, older voters to younger ones, those with a university degree to those without,[5] those with above median household incomes to those below, homeowners to renters, immigrants to Canadian born voters, visible minority to white voters,[6] and voters that self-identify as left- and right-leaning.[7] These variables were chosen for inclusion in the survey since they are commonly associated with local vote choice in Canada (McGregor et al. 2016; Lucas and McGregor 2022). The survey of electors also included a battery of questions where respondents were presented with a table listing the pairs of groups above. Respondents were asked which group they perceived as being more likely to vote online in municipal elections. For each pairing, respondents could choose one group, or state that they anticipated no difference. We compare these data to actual voting patterns to determine the extent to which electors accurately understand the voting habits of their counterparts.

The second dataset we draw upon in this chapter is our candidate survey. We limit our focus to candidates from the same fifteen cities. In total, 276 candidates completed the survey for the analysis used in this chapter, representing 37 per cent of the total candidate pool in these municipalities. Participants include those seeking the office of mayor (6.5 per cent), city councillor (58.2 per cent), school board trustee (33.3 per cent), regional chair (0.5 per cent), and regional councillor (1.5 per cent) – we note that very few municipalities in Ontario have regional councils. As the surveys of electors and candidates were designed with comparison in mind, candidate respondents were asked the same set of questions regarding their assessment of the voting methods preferred by the various socio-demographic groups described above.[8] This allows us to compare elector and candidate responses.

RESULTS

Who Votes Online?

In the fifteen cities considered here, online voting was the method of choice for a majority of voters, a finding that is consistent with previous studies (Goodman and Stokes 2018). A total of 62.1 per cent of participant voters cast their ballots online. At the city level, this figure ranges from 30.5 per cent in the City of Cambridge to 80.8 per cent in the City of Markham. The average rate of online voting was 54.5 per cent and standard deviation was 17.1 per cent. A sizable portion of the electorate therefore chose to participate in this manner.[9]

Is this mode of participation associated with politically salient factors? To answer this question, figure 4.1 plots the marginal effect of belonging to eight demographic groups of interest, as compared to the appropriate comparator group (all variables are binary). The outcome variable is a dummy, where 1 represents an online vote (versus in-person voting). Results show marginal effects of each variable upon the likelihood of voting online. Effects are estimated following bivariate logistic regression models (this is the manner in which questions are presented to electors and candidates), with fixed effects for city (N=15).[10] Whiskers show 95 per cent confidence intervals.

Five of the eight explanatory factors display a statistically significant relationship to method of voting. Younger voters[11] and racialized electors are each about 20 percentage points less likely to vote online than older voters and white electors. Homeownership

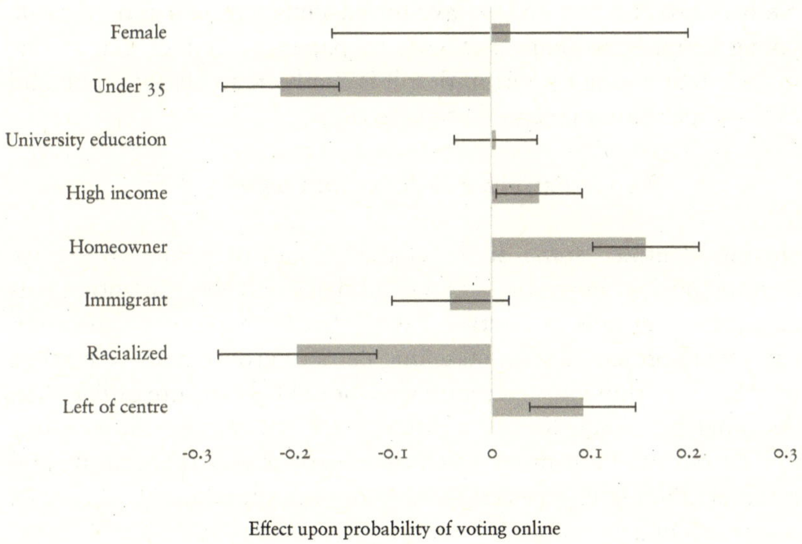

Figure 4.1 | Online voting by group

makes one roughly sixteen points more likely to vote online, while identifying as left-of-centre is associated with an effect of nine percentage points, as compared to right-of-centre voters.[12] High income also has a modest estimated effect, at five points.

Figure 4.1 therefore paints a profile of a coalition of online voters in Ontario municipal elections that seems familiar to scholars of political behaviour. Online voters tend to be older than thirty-five, white, have an above average income, and are homeowners. In vote choice models, these factors are typically associated with support for conservative candidates or parties in municipal elections (Lucas and McGregor 2022). The outlier in figure 4.1, however, is the ideology variable. Self-identified left-of-centre voters are, in fact, more likely to vote online than by paper ballot. Moreover, several other factors often related to vote choice are not related to voting method, including gender, education, and immigrant status. Figure 4.1 therefore identifies several factors associated with method of voting. It also suggests that these factors are not clearly the same as those often associated with vote choice. It is noteworthy that the finding about young people being less likely to vote online is not new. Studies in Canada (Goodman 2016), Norway (Segaard et al. 2016), and the

Netherlands (Loeber 2018) have found similar results and attribute young people's inclination to vote by paper to the fact that as one of their first voting opportunities, it is symbolic to attend a poll and cast a paper ballot (Segaard et al. 2016).

Who Is Perceived as Being an Online Voter?

Having identified some of the characteristics of online voters, we turn to consider how voters and candidates perceive the voting patterns of our groups of interest. Recall that both electors and candidates were presented with matching pairs of groups and were asked whether they thought one group was more likely to vote online than the other or if there were no difference.[13] We can use these results to determine the extent to which these perceptions are accurate and whether candidates or electors have an understanding of who votes online in Ontario municipal elections.

The columns in table 4.1 report a variety of data that allow us to make these assessments. First, we include the frequency distribution for assessments of each sociodemographic characteristic for electors and candidates. In these columns, we shade the "correct" answer, as indicated by the results in figure 4.1. In the next column, we report the p-values from chi-squared tests to determine the confidence with which we can declare that the distribution of responses from candidates differs from electors. On the right side of the table, we evaluate whether elector or candidate assessments were "correct" by simply evaluating whether the modal response matches actual voting patterns. In the final column, we consider whether one group (candidates or electors) had a better understanding of these patterns than the other (only reporting differences that are significant at $p<0.10$). In this one table, therefore, we can consider the extent to which assessments are correct and how electors compare to candidates in this regard.

Overall, neither electors nor candidates have a solid grasp of who votes online (table 4.1).[14] Electors as a whole made a correct assessment with respect to three of eight factors: gender, education, and immigrant status. Candidates were correct in only four dimensions: gender, education, income, and immigrant status. Both groups were therefore correct with regards to gender, education, and immigrant status. In all three of these instances, however, the correct answer is "the same," which happens to be the modal response for most

Table 4.1 | Perceptions of online voting by group

		Electors (%) (*N*=2,322)	Candidates (%) (*N*=201)	Difference (p-value)	Electors "correct"?	Candidates "correct"?	Is one group "more" correct?
Female	Less	11.70	13.90	0.138	Yes	Yes	No
	Same	76.10	67.20				
	More	12.20	18.90				
Under 35	Less	12.40	5.50	0.001	No	No	Electors
	Same	29.10	20.90				
	More	58.50	73.60				
University educated	Less	4.40	1.50				
	Same	66.70	58.70	0.008	Yes	Yes	Electors
	More	28.90	39.80				
High income	Less	6.70	7.00	0.000	No	Yes	Candidates
	Same	66.70	44.80				
	More	28.90	48.30				
Home owner	Less	4.50	2.50	0.153	No	No	No
	Same	73.70	68.70				
	More	21.80	28.90				
Immigrant	Less	31.30	39.80	0.054	Yes	Yes	Electors
	Same	60.20	55.70				
	More	8.50	4.50				
Racialized	Less	17.40	21.40	0.075	No	No	Candidates
	Same	76.80	76.10				
	More	5.80	2.50				
Left-of-centre	Less	4.80	4.00	0.488	No	No	No
	Same	88.30	85.60				
	More	6.90	10.50				

categories, from both electors and candidates. The fact that both electors and candidates are correct here might therefore be an artefact of some overall tendency among both groups to assume a lack of differences between groups. The "correct" findings here do little, therefore, to suggest that either group has a particularly solid grasp of who votes online.

In fact, neither electors nor candidates were very good at identifying differences between groups, where such differences exist. Few respondents from either group recognized that young people or immigrants were unlikely to vote online or that homeowners are more likely to do so. For only one variable was one of the groups able to correctly identify a difference: candidates on income (and even then, only a minority of respondents are able to do so). Looking at age, by contrast, both groups of respondents expected a difference that was in fact the opposite of reality. On the whole, therefore, it cannot be said that either electors or candidates have a good understanding of who votes online in municipal elections.

We also find no clear evidence that either group has a better understanding of who is more drawn to vote online than the other. Electors were more likely to make correct assessments on the basis of age, education, and immigrant status, while candidates were more correct when asked about income and race (the latter at $p<0.1$). Such a finding is consistent with the individual-level data regarding the average number of "correct" responses from the two groups; the average number of "correct" responses for the eight types of individuals discussed above is 2.99 (out of 8) for electors and 2.96 for candidates (this difference is statistically insignificant). The lack of a clear pattern in this respect is perhaps a bit surprising, as one might expect "elites" such as candidates to have a comparatively high level of knowledge about the electorate.

What Type of Candidate Knows Who Votes Online?

We end our analysis with an examination of which candidates are the most knowledgeable on the subject of how voters cast their ballots. Do incumbents, for instance, understand their constituents' voting behaviours better than challengers? Such knowledge might conceivably aid in shaping a campaign strategy, whereby certain types of voters are targeted through various means (online or in person). Similarly, candidates may aid their supporters of different types by providing

Table 4.2 Candidate characteristics and understanding how voters cast ballots

	No/Low	Yes/High	Difference
Female	3.07 (N=128)	2.83 (N=66)	-0.24
Over 50	2.89 (N=75)	3.08 (N=103)	0.18
University education	2.89 (N=95)	3.08 (N=95)	0.19
High income	2.82 (N=87)	3.13 (N=76)	0.32**
Immigrant	3.00 (N=156)	2.92 (N=36)	-0.08
Racialized	2.97 (N=152)	2.97 (N=36)	0.00
Left wing (versus right)	2.98 (N=55)	3.17 (N=46)	0.19
Left wing (versus centre)	2.87 (N=82)	3.17 (N=46)	0.30
Right wing (versus centre)	2.88 (N=82)	2.98 (N=55)	0.10

*p<0.10, **:p<0.05, ***:p<0.01

information on how to vote online. There are a number of ways in which this knowledge might conceivably shape a campaign and affect the electoral chances of candidates. All other things equal, we expect that knowledge of this nature can only serve to aid in one's campaign.

To determine whether certain types of candidates have a better understanding of voting method, we can consider the number of "correct" responses to the questions about the voting method of various types of electors. We compare various types of candidates on this measure to determine if levels of knowledge are associated with candidate characteristics. We consider the same characteristics as was the case in table 4.1 (with the exception of home ownership, which candidates were not asked). In short, if certain types of candidates have an informational advantage, then they may also have an electoral advantage. These results are shown in table 4.2. The table shows the estimated mean number of "correct" responses for each kind of candidate, as well as the difference in the estimated means, with an indication of whether such differences are statistically significant or not (determined through t-tests). Note that the "Yes/High" column refers to the characteristic listed in the left-most column. We include three rows for ideology to report pairwise comparisons for all three ideological positions (left, centre, and right).

Table 4.2 reveals that only one candidate characteristic, income, is associated with an accurate understanding of the voting method of various types of voters. More specifically, candidates with a household income above the median score higher on the aggregate measure of correctly understanding voting patterns. Putting this into context, however, this gap is quite small. The difference is equal to roughly one-third of one of the eight elector characteristics that candidates were asked about.

On top of the factors listed in table 4.2, we also tested two other characteristics: incumbent status and position sought (mayor vs councillor vs regional councillor vs trustee). In neither dimension did any group have a knowledge advantage according to our measure; none of the differences were statistically significant. Coupled with the null findings for the other factors considered in table 4.2, we see that very little separates candidates in terms of their understanding of the voting methods employed by electors. Understanding of the relationship between voter characteristics and voting is (almost) uniformly low among candidates.

CONCLUSION

The large sample size of the elector dataset used here allows us to identify with a large degree of certainty the type of individual that votes online in Canadian municipal elections. For those who have the option to vote either online or in person, internet voters tend to be older, wealthier, homeowners, white, and left of centre. Gender, education, and immigrant status have no relationship with voting method. This points to a rather unusual coalition of voters, at least in terms of what we are used to seeing in vote choice models.

Leveraging our unique candidate data that included the same questions asked of electors, we see that neither group has particularly accurate perceptions of who it is that votes online and that neither group is much better than the other in this regard. This null finding is noteworthy as it suggests that elites (candidates) do not have a better understanding of the behaviour of the electorate than do ordinary electors. We also see that, among candidates, income is the only characteristic associated with an understanding of patterns of voting methods and, even then, the difference is quite modest. Together, these findings would seem to suggest that candidates are generally on equal footing and that no kind of candidate (at least in the dimensions considered here) has a particularly acute informational advantage over their competitors.

One possible explanation for the general lack of understanding on the part of candidates and voters may be that the types of electors that are attracted to online voting are changing over time. Changes in the composition of the portion of the electorate that votes online have been observed in other country studies, notably in Estonia (Vassil et al. 2016). Data from the City of Markham – the only municipality that has collected exit survey data from online voters in five municipal elections since it first adopted the voting mode in 2003 – show that online voting respondents have become older and more educated over time (Goodman 2019). The characteristics of those attracted to online voting could well have shifted in other ways over the years, especially with respect to digital access and skillset, which has greatly expanded over the past two decades.

Finally, the findings in this chapter have important implications for debates of online voting implementation in new settings. Though online voting is an option in hundreds of Canadian municipalities, this still represents but a small fraction of the thousands of local jurisdictions that exist in Canada. There is no doubt that debates over the introduction of online voting in cities where it has not been trialed are coloured, either explicitly or otherwise, by calculations regarding the effect that the introduction of a new voting method may have on the success of certain types of candidates (Goodman and Spicer 2019). It is not a stretch to imagine a right-of-centre city councillor, for example, being cautious of introducing internet voting if they expect that the method might be taken up by individuals that might not support them (see chapter 5). Our results suggest that these calculations are not as straightforward as one might expect and that they may, in fact, be based upon incorrect assumptions. Two factors, in particular, are noteworthy. First, our data provide compelling evidence that voters under the age of thirty-five are considerably less likely (twenty points) to vote online than their older counterparts. Yet, both electors and candidates expect young voters to be more likely to cast their ballots online, perhaps because they are "digital natives" (Palfrey and Gasser 2011). Next, even though an overwhelming majority of candidates and electors expect voting method to be unrelated to ideology, this is not the case, as self-described left-of-centre voters are more likely to cast an online ballot than conservative voters. Our data show that, in many instances, politicians who base their support for online voting upon calculations regarding the chances of re-election are doing so under faulty assumptions.

5

Candidates and Online Voting

INTRODUCTION

While there is growing literature about who supports and makes use of internet voting from the perspective of ordinary electors (Goodman 2014; Goodman and Pyman 2016; Serdült et al. 2015; Trechsel and Vassil 2010), research regarding the views of politicians – either unsuccessful candidates or successfully elected officials – is much more limited.[1] Although there is emerging discourse on how municipal candidates conduct their campaigns, especially online via social media (Han et al. 2020; Raynauld and Greenberg 2014; Hagar 2010; Dumitrica 2010; Wagner 2016), there has been scant consideration of municipal candidates' views on the adoption of online voting and only cursory mention regarding how this new voting system affects their campaign (Goodman 2014; Tieber 2020) or election strategies. This is somewhat surprising given that municipal politics is the only arena in Canada in which electronic elections have taken place. Do, for instance, municipal candidates support the use of online voting for local elections? Who do they think will benefit from its adoption? Do they tailor their campaign strategies to respond to the use of online voting?

To fill this void in the literature, we address three specific research questions: First, what types of candidates support the adoption of online voting for municipal elections? Here we are interested in uncovering the general profile of municipal candidates who are more or less supportive of online voting. To explore this question and to ensure we can establish a broad profile, we consider three categories of factors: political, personal (sociodemographic), and personality.

Second, who do candidates perceive as the beneficiaries of online voting in municipal elections? In other words, is online voting viewed as a net neutral change to election administration or are some types of candidates viewed as benefiting from the change more than others? Third, how does online voting impact how candidates conduct their election campaigns? Do candidates campaign differently because of the presence of online voting? If so, how are they affected?

Throughout our analysis we pay particular attention to two candidate characteristics: ideology and incumbent status. We focus on these specific factors for at least two reasons. First, incumbency is tremendously important at the local level, much more so than provincially or federally (Kushner et al. 1997; Lucas 2019; Trounstine 2011). The incumbency advantage routinely results in a re-election rate of more than 90 per cent at the municipal level in Canada (CBC 2017). As Moore et al. (2015, 88) put it, "incumbents are king" in municipal politics. Given their strong position and desire for re-election, it stands to reason that incumbents may have unique views about making changes to the system that made them successful in the first place. Similarly, as individuals who are in the position to inform policy on the adoption of internet voting, their views are particularly relevant.

The role of ideology, by contrast, is less clear at the municipal level. On the one hand, municipal elections in Canada are (mostly) non-partisan affairs (Good 2017) and Ontario is no exception, as all elections in the province are contested by independents. Many argue that the non-partisan context of municipal elections and assemblies coupled with the low-information nature of local politics (Spicer et al. 2017; Taylor and McEleney 2017) results in voters relying on heuristics and candidates engaging in managerial claims more so than ideological ones (Peterson 1981; Oliver 2012). The result is that municipal politics is often portrayed as being non-ideological, especially when compared to other electoral arenas. Debate on this subject, however, continues. Lucas and McGregor (2021), for example, provide evidence that municipal politics is anything but non-ideological. In fact, their analysis on vote choice in some of the country's largest cities reveals that ideology plays a crucial role in the voting calculus of electors, even more so than standard sociodemographic explanations.[2] Given the ongoing debate, we are particularly interested in whether ideology matters or not when it comes to internet voting.

To examine candidate attitudes towards online voting, we draw upon a survey of candidates contesting the 2018 municipal elections in Ontario, from cities that employed online voting (this is the same dataset used in chapter 3). We find that candidates in our sample are overwhelmingly supportive of the use of internet voting in local elections. We also see that perceptions of who benefits from the use of online voting depends upon the characteristics of candidates. Finally, we observe that a small majority of candidates campaigned differently because their municipalities employ online voting. All the while, we consider the relevance of ideology and incumbent status to these attitudes and behaviours. Our analysis reveals several previously unknown findings about how candidates view and respond to online voting in Ontario local elections.

BACKGROUND

In this section we review the limited literature on candidate attitudes towards online voting and outline our theoretical expectations. Note, however, that we do not treat all three of our research questions the same. In particular, we put forward specific expectations for our first two questions (who supports online voting, and who are the perceived beneficiaries) while we view research question three (campaign impact) as more exploratory in nature.

Who Supports Online Voting?

As discussions about online voting become more mainstream, we might expect municipal candidates to have relatively high levels of support for the voting mode. Evidence from the federal level reveals that candidates are not inherently skeptical of the modernization of elections. Surveys of federal election candidates, commissioned by Elections Canada after recent elections, highlights this fact. In 2008 and 2011, for instance, candidates overwhelmingly supported the adoption and use of online elector registration (74 per cent in 2008 and 75 per cent in 2011). Support for internet voting, however, has been somewhat more tempered – hovering around the 50 per cent mark (46 per cent in 2008, 51 per cent in 2011, and 54 per cent in 2015; Phoenix Strategic Perspectives 2009; 2011; Ekos 2016). Perhaps due to technical issues with online voting in the 2018 Ontario municipal elections, support for internet voting among federal candidates dropped significantly in 2019, with just one in three candidates (35 per cent) expressing their support (Ekos 2020).[3] While there has been some research into the opinion of federal candidates, very little has been written on what municipal candidates think about the subject (Tieber 2020). As municipal elections are the only ones in Canada that have used internet voting over a prolonged period, we might expect candidates to be more comfortable with the technology and therefore more supportive of its usage (particularly in our sample, which is drawn completely from cities that use online voting). However, support for internet voting, like any public policy issue, is unlikely to be universal. Who, then, supports the adoption of online voting?

Our first set of explanatory factors consider the political characteristics of candidates. Here we expect incumbents who have already contested an election with online voting to be more supportive of the method. The logic here is simple: these individuals have already proven they can win an election using online voting and as a result they should be less concerned that internet voting will harm their chances of re-election.[4] At the same time, a competing hypothesis could be made regarding challengers. As incumbents have a monumental advantage in local elections, challengers might view any disruption to the status quo as beneficial. While the jury is still out on all the effects of online voting, the popular portrayal of internet voting is that it increases turnout and brings new cohorts of voters to the polls. The possibility of a shifting electorate may be viewed more positively by challengers hoping to unseat a stable incumbent.

In addition to incumbent status, we expect candidates on the right of the political spectrum to be less supportive of online voting. As individuals age, they tend to become more likely to vote for parties on the right (Tilley and Evans 2014). Older voters, however, are often thought to have fewer technological skills and are therefore at risk of being left behind in the digital divide (Goodman et al. 2018). Even though older voters make use of online voting in Canada at high rates, there is a clear perception that online voting is for younger voters (see chapter 4). If right wing candidates believe that older voters will be disenfranchised because of online voting or that younger progressive voters will turn out at higher rates than before, it stands to reason that they may be wary of adopting online voting. Also, recall that in chapter 4 we revealed that both voters and candidates believe that left-wing voters are slightly more likely to vote online. This too should dampen right-wing candidate support for online voting.

Our second set of explanatory factors consider the sociodemographic characteristics of candidates. Here we do not have a strong set of hypotheses, though we do put forward some tentative theoretical expectations. Like challengers generally, we might expect candidates from historically marginalized groups that have been locked out of elected office (women, ethnic minorities, etc.) to view the adoption of internet voting positively as it has the potential to disrupt the status quo.[5] Likewise, we might expect older candidates to view online voting more skeptically given the relationship between age and digital literacy and skills.

Our final set of explanatory factors consider the personality traits of candidates. Personality refers to a set of traits that are present in each individual from an early age, are deeply rooted, and tend to be remarkably stable over time (McCrae and Costa 2003; Larsen and Buss 2014). As Feist and Feist (2009, 4) explain, "personality is a pattern of relatively permanent traits and unique characteristics that give both consistency and individuality to a person's behavior." Among the most common models of personality is the Five Factor Model or the "Big Five." This model includes the general personality traits of openness, conscientiousness, extraversion, agreeableness, and neuroticism. Individual differences in personality have been shown to be related to a variety of political outcomes like participation (Mondak 2010; Chen et al. 2021), civic duty (Blais and Galais 2016; Blais and Labbé St-Vincent 2011; Pruysers et al. 2019), ideology/vote choice (Barbaranelli et al. 2007; Blais et al. 2022; Osborne et al. 2021), vote switching (Pruysers and Blais 2023), political ambition (Blais et al. 2019; Dynes et al. 2019), and political attitudes more generally (Pruysers 2021; 2020).[6]

We suspect that individual differences in personality will also relate to attitudes towards online voting. In particular, candidates scoring higher on the trait of openness should be more favourable while individuals higher in neuroticism should be less supportive. Open individuals are characterized as being inquisitive, willing to take risks, seek out new experiences, and are appreciative of art, knowledge, and new ideas. Given their appreciation for new and unconventional ideas and their willingness to take risks, candidates who score higher on openness should be more supportive of the adoption of new voting technologies. Neurotic individuals, by contrast, are characterized by a lack of emotional stability. These individuals are prone to negative emotions such as fear, anxiety, and vulnerability. Given that internet voting has not been without controversy – security problems and technical glitches are common (Jones 2021; Park et al. 2021)[7] – candidates who score higher on neuroticism should be less supportive of the adoption of internet voting due to its inherent risk compared to traditional paper balloting.

Who Benefits?

Our second question considers the perceived benefits of online voting. Specifically, which candidates would benefit from the adoption of online voting the most? The question of perceived benefits is likely connected to the question of support. After all, candidates are often portrayed as rational, self-interested, and election maximizing (Downs 1957). If a voting method is perceived to benefit them, they should be supportive and vice-versa. In this regard, the same reasons we expect right wing candidates to oppose online voting inform our rationale for why right-wing candidates should be the perceived losers of online voting. Concerns about their older voters' ability to navigate the digital voting technology, concerns about the mobilization of younger progressive voters into the electorate, and concerns about right-wing voter suppression more generally should all result in a perception that left-wing candidates will benefit more from the adoption of online voting. As for incumbents and challengers, we suspect that challengers will be the perceived beneficiaries of online voting. Incumbents already have such incredible advantages municipally that the change to online voting is not likely to move the needle for them. For challengers, by contrast, any change that could broaden the electorate is likely to be viewed as favouring their chances. For this reason, we expect a perception that challengers are the beneficiaries of online voting.

DATA AND ANALYSIS

All analysis in this chapter is based on our candidate survey, which consisted of pre- and post-election waves. Data for this chapter draws upon more than 300 municipal candidates that completed both waves (since questions from both waves are required).[8] Our analysis proceeds in three stages. First, we consider the correlates of candidate support for the use of online voting in municipal elections. Here we consider three types of candidate characteristics: political factors (including incumbency, ideology, and the position candidates are seeking), personal factors (the sociodemographic characteristics of the candidates), and personality (using the Big Five personality traits). As was shown in chapter 3, support for online voting can hinge upon whether the system was just adopted, whether it has been in place for at least one previous election, or if it has been abandoned by a municipality. We therefore include fixed effects in these models to account for the history of online voting in the municipalities under study. This analysis provides a detailed understanding of what type of candidates are more or less supportive of the use of online voting.

Building upon these results, we turn to discuss perceptions of who it is that benefits from the use of online voting. The controversial method has many detractors, and here we wish to determine if candidates perceive that certain types of candidates are advantaged or disadvantaged when online voting is used. More specifically, we ask whether incumbents, challengers, or individuals from different positions on the political spectrum are perceived as being privileged if online voting is used in local elections. Importantly, these opinions are separate from what the actual effects may be (identifying such effects would be extremely difficult to accomplish and lies outside of the purview of this chapter). Our focus here is upon the perceptions that candidates themselves have.

Finally, we answer the question of how the use of online voting affects campaigning and whether different types of candidates (based upon incumbency and ideology) campaign differently in response to the use of online voting. Again, we compare challengers to incumbents, and left-wing, centrist, and right-wing candidates to determine if they campaign differently in response to the use of online voting. We then examine some open-ended responses to identify the primary ways in which online voting does affect campaigning, among those who are affected.

These analyses provide us with a detailed understanding of who the proponents of online voting are, whether certain types of candidates are perceived as having an advantage, and if online voting changes the manner in which candidates campaign.

RESULTS

What Type of Candidate Supports Online Voting?

Overall, our data reveal that there is a great deal of support for online voting among candidates for local political office in Ontario. Candidates in our sample were asked the extent to which they agreed with the following statement: "Internet voting should be available in Municipal elections." Only 16.7 per cent disagreed (12.0 per cent strongly and 4.7 per cent somewhat), while a full 80.1 per cent of respondents agreed (57.4 per cent strongly and 22.8 per cent somewhat). A mere 3.1 per cent of respondents had no opinion (total N = 348). There is therefore widespread support among local candidates in Ontario for the use of this non-traditional voting method. Note that the survey question wording for this and all other variables employed in this chapter can be found in appendix 5.I.

The question we seek to answer here, however, is what type of candidates support online voting (or not)? Even though most candidates favour the use of online voting, a sizable number do not. Like any important political variables, there is value in understanding the correlates of these opinions, particularly since candidates (if successfully elected) often have the power to determine what types of voting methods will be used in future elections. To this end, we consider how three types of variables are related to attitudes towards the use of online voting in local elections. First, we consider a series of political characteristics. Here, we include the variables most central to this chapter: incumbent status (coded as a dummy using information collected by research assistants) and ideology (a standard interval-level left right variable, ranging from 0 to 1). We also include the type of position the candidate is seeking (all coded as dummies, with mayoral candidates as the baseline category). For this analysis we include a second model, where we interact incumbent status with dummy variables that indicate whether online voting was in place in 2014 in the candidate's city, whether it was just adopted for 2018, or if it was used in 2014 but abandoned in 2018 (readers may remember that this applies to one city in our sample: Guelph).[9] The reason for this is simple: we expect that incumbents elected (or acclaimed) under an online voting system might hold different attitudes towards the continued use of online voting than those who were elected under a system without online voting (and vice-versa).

We include fixed effects for these temporal variables in all models but include the interaction only with incumbency. Note that the baseline category for these variables are respondents from cities that did not have online voting in 2014 but adopted it for 2018.

The second set of models includes a series of standard socio-demographic characteristics. These factors are consistently known to be related to a variety of political attitudes. We have no particular expectations from this part of the analysis. Nevertheless, we view this as an interesting opportunity to compare how these attributes are related to the attitudes of candidates, to the relationship between these indicators and the voting behaviour of electors (from chapter 4). All variables are dummies in the model, except for age (in years).

Finally, we consider the relationship between the general personality traits captured in the Big Five (openness, conscientiousness, extraversion, agreeableness, and neuroticism) and support for online voting. Individual differences in personality are related to a variety of political outcomes and, as indicated earlier, we expect to find a positive relationship between support for online voting and openness and a negative relationship for neuroticism. The personality variables are based upon the Ten Item Personality Inventory (TIPI; Gosling et al. 2003).

The results of these analyses are found in table 5.1. The outcome variable in all models is the agree/disagree responses to the question about support for online voting. Given the ordinal nature of this variable, we employ ordered logistic regression models.[10] Though our survey response rate is more than respectable, our sample sizes are relatively modest. As such, we consider each type of variable separately (rather than together in a vastly over-specified model).[11]

Prior to discussing the individual models, it is interesting to note that candidates in a city that dropped online voting in 2018 (Guelph) have a particularly negative assessment of internet voting (see towards the bottom of the table). The variable is negative and significant in all models, and it is significantly different from both comparator groups at least at the 90 per cent level. Such a finding is particularly striking given the small sample size in this group (N = 27). There is no discernible difference between candidates from the other two types of cities (those that had online voting in both 2014 and those that adopted it new in 2018). The decision to eliminate online voting in Guelph appears to have been well-received by candidates.

Table 5.1 | The correlates of support for the use of online voting in municipal elections

	Political characteristics		Personal characteristics	Personality
Incumbent	0.14 (0.29)	0.39 (0.37)		
Ideology	-1.69 (0.64)***	-1.76 (0.65)***		
Councilor	-0.24 (0.45)	-0.23 (0.44)		
Regional council	-0.31 (0.88)	-0.26 (0.88)		
Trustee	0.05 (0.48)	0.16 (0.48)		
Age			-0.03 (0.01)**	
Woman			0.02 (0.27)	
University education			0.36 (0.27)	
Racialized			0.32 (0.58)	
Indigenous			0.59 (0.87)	
Immigrant			0.48 (0.47)	
High income			0.39 (0.27)	
Extraversion				-0.20 (0.52)
Agreeableness				0.57 (0.68)
Conscientiousness				0.72 (0.70)
Neuroticism				-1.36 (0.66)**
Openness				0.40 (0.72)
Had in 2018 only	-0.06 (0.25)	-0.32 (0.27)	-0.08 (0.28)	-0.05 (0.24)
2018 only X incumbent		1.30 (0.64)**		
Dropped for 2018	-0.88 (0.48)*	-1.22 (0.58)**	-1.28 (0.55)**	-0.95 (0.48)**
Dropped for 2018 X incumbent		1.17 (1.03)		
Cut 1	-30.6 (0.57)	-3.18 (0.57)	-3.40 (0.68_	-1.30 (0.89)
Cut 2	-2.60 (0.56)	-2.72 (0.56)	-3.03 (0.67)	-0.84 (0.89)
Cut 3	-1.37 (0.54)	-1.48 (0.54)	-1.60 (0.64)	0.38 (0.88)
Pseudo R2	0.0198	0.0273	0.0375	0.0263
N	303	303	254	315

Note: Entries report coefficients and standard errors (in parentheses).
*: p<0.10, **:p<0.05, ***: p<0.01

The "personal characteristics" models reveal perhaps the most interesting results in table 5.1. The first observation, which we see in both models, is that the position being sought by candidates is irrelevant to their opinions towards online voting. In contrast, we see statistically significant results in these models for our two variables of particular interest in this chapter: ideology and incumbency.

First, in both models (with and without the interactions) we see that ideology is negatively correlated with support for online voting, suggesting that right wing-candidates are less supportive of the use of such a system than are their left-wing counterparts. Such a finding makes sense in light of our finding in chapter 4, where we saw that left-wing voters are particularly likely to cast their ballots online. As far as ideology is concerned, therefore, voters and candidates appear to be in sync.

The results for incumbency are more difficult to make sense of. In the model without the interactions, the term is insignificant. That is, when incumbent candidates elected under a paper ballot system are pooled with those elected under an online system, the incumbency variable has no effect. However, when these groups are considered separately, we see that incumbency does indeed matter for candidates in cities that adopted online voting for the first time in 2018. The interaction term for such candidates is positive, suggesting that these individuals are more supportive of online voting than their challengers. The constituent term (which is indicative of the effect of incumbency in cities that used online voting in both elections) and the term interacted with the "dropped in 2018" variable are both insignificant (though the latter coefficient is large, the comparatively small size of this group is likely responsible for the large standard error). Only in cities that recently adopted online voting, however, does incumbency matter. In these cities, incumbency is associated with a relatively high level of support for the voting method.

Given that interaction terms can be quite difficult to interpret on their own, we have graphed the results of the second model. Figure 5.1 shows the predicted probability of falling into each category of the "support for online voting" outcome variable, depending upon incumbent status and whether the candidate's municipality employed online voting in both 2014 and 2018, in 2018 only, or in 2014 only. Results were determined using post-estimation, where the incumbency and "online voting in place" variables were manipulated, while other variables were kept unchanged.

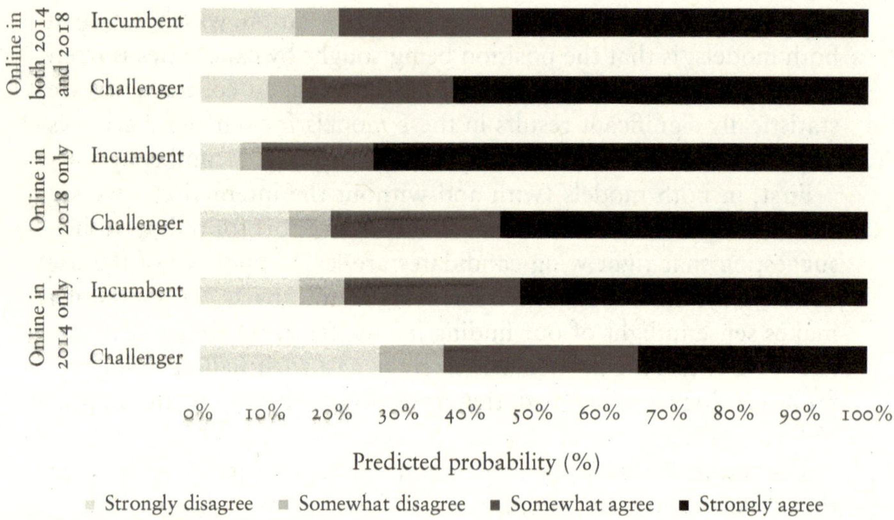

Figure 5.1 | Support for online voting by incumbency and 2014 online voting experience: Predicted probability

Figure 5.1 shows in a more intuitive manner the interaction results from table 5.1. The most striking finding from the figure is that incumbents in cities where online voting was not in place in 2014 are more supportive of the use of online voting than are challengers (see the second pair of bars). Recall that the results in table 5.1 suggest that the other within-city group comparisons are statistically insignificant. At first glance, the finding for the "2018 only" cities may seem counterintuitive. Why would someone elected just four years ago under a paper-voting system support the adoption of a new system? In our view, the answer to this lies in the fact that decisions to use online voting are made by incumbents on city council (councillors and mayors make up a substantial majority of the respondents in our sample). Current incumbents in cities that used online voting for the first time in 2018 are therefore the ones who, overall, supported the adoption of the new system.[12] Incumbent status has a clear effect upon support for internet voting, conditional upon the point in time at which online voting came into effect.

Returning to table 5.1, we see in the "personal characteristics" model that just one sociodemographic characteristic is related to support among candidates: age. Older candidates view online voting less favourably than their younger counterparts do, after controlling for a variety of other characteristics. Such a finding is perhaps intuitive if one accepts the conventional wisdom that older individuals have comparatively low rates of digital literacy. However, given that we saw in chapter 4 of this work that older voters are, in fact, more likely to vote online than are their younger counterparts, the finding is particularly striking. We also saw in that chapter, however, that most older candidates incorrectly believe that older electors are less likely than younger ones to vote online. This lack of understanding on the part of candidates might help to explain why, while older voters are seemingly fond of online voting, older candidates oppose it.

Finally, the "personality" model in the table reveals one trait to be significantly related to attitudes towards online voting. Consistent with our expectations, the trait of neuroticism is negatively related to support for online voting. Recall that those scoring higher in neuroticism tend to suffer from negative emotions such as fear, anxiety, and vulnerability. Given ongoing concerns about the security and safety of online voting, it is not surprising to find that these individuals view the voting method more skeptically. Until these issues are fully resolved, we expect individuals scoring higher on neuroticism to be relatively unsupportive of online voting. Our expectation regarding openness, by contrast, is not borne out by the data. While we expected these individuals (who are characterized as being imaginative, inquisitive, and open to new ideas and experiences) to be more supportive of online voting, this is not so. It may be the case that online voting is not as novel as it once was, and as a result, it does not capture the attention of highly open candidates. When combined with the results from the other models, we see that at least one variable from each model is related to support for online voting.

Who Do Candidates Think Benefits from Online Voting?

Overall, candidates for local office in Ontario are supportive of the use of online voting. We show above, however, that there are a variety of factors related to this support. Among these are two important candidate characteristics: incumbent status and ideology. In the

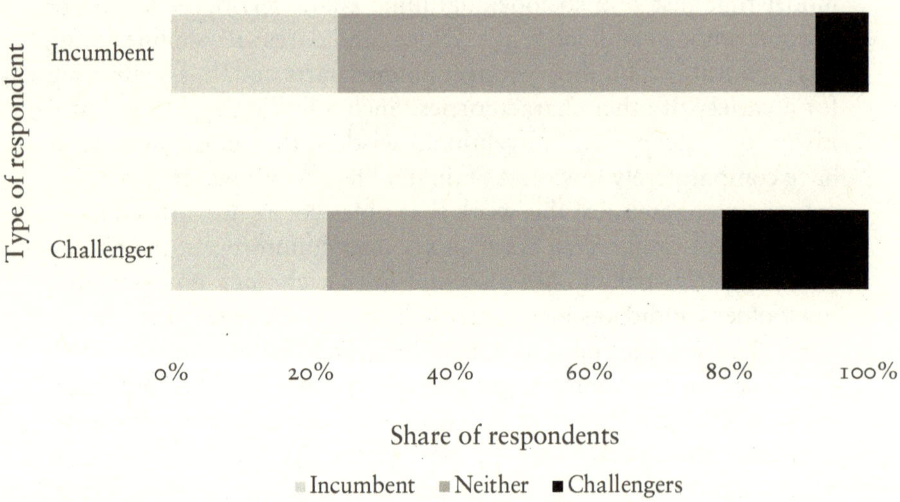

Figure 5.2 | Who benefits from online voting: Incumbent status

next stage of our analysis of the opinion of candidates we consider assessments of how the use of online voting might affect the electoral prospects of candidates, based upon these two factors. In the minds of candidates themselves, are there certain types of individuals who might benefit from online voting?

Respondents were asked whether they thought incumbents or challengers (or neither) would benefit from the use of online voting.[13] On the whole (N=305), incumbents are seen as having a slight advantage, with 22.6 per cent of respondents believing that incumbents are given an edge by online voting. Only 18.0 per cent selected challengers. Most respondents (59.3 per cent), however, did not believe that either group had an advantage. When we break down the sample based upon whether candidates are incumbents, however, we see important differences. Figure 5.2 shows the distribution of responses to the "who benefits" question, based upon incumbent status. [14]

Though most incumbents and challengers believed neither group was given an advantage by internet voting, challengers are nearly three times as likely to believe that they have an edge – 21.0 per cent

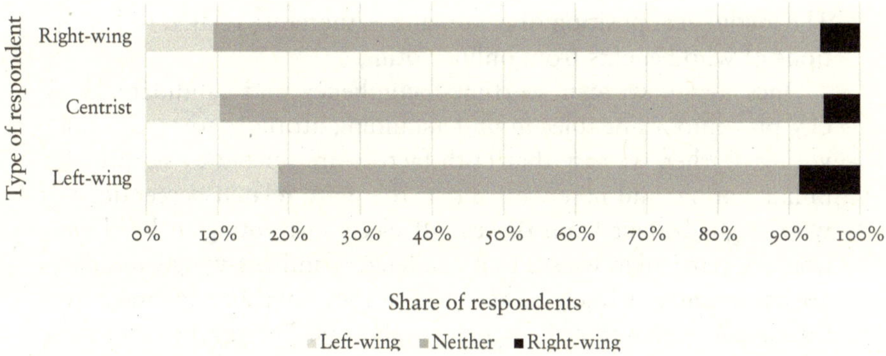

Figure 5.3 | Who benefits from online voting: Ideology

of challengers (N = 238) think that challengers benefit from online voting, as opposed to just 7.5 per cent of incumbents (N = 67). This gap is sizable and statistically significant at the 95 per cent confidence level. Thus, while more incumbents believe they have an advantage over challengers than vice-versa, challengers (as a whole) see benefits as roughly equally split between themselves and incumbents.

Next, survey respondents were asked if they believed left or right-wing candidates (or neither) benefit from use of online voting. Once again, we see that, on the whole, most candidates (82.5 per cent) believe that neither group has an advantage. However, among candidates who do think that one group benefits, more believe that left-wing candidates benefit (12.0 per cent) than do candidates on the right (5.5 per cent) (N = 274). Once again, however, we see that answers to this question are based upon candidate characteristics. Figure 5.3 shows the results of this survey question about the ideology of candidates, based on a standard 0–10 ideological self-placement question. We look at candidates that position themselves on the left (0–4), centre (5), and right (6–10).

While figure 5.3 shows no discernible difference between right-wing and centrist candidates, left-wing candidates do have distinct perceptions of what type of candidates benefit from online voting. They are more likely than their right-wing counterparts to believe candidates on the left benefit from online voting ($p=0.07$). They are also less likely to believe that neither type of candidate benefits (p<0.05 as compared to both right-wing and centrist candidates). The ideological position of candidates is therefore related to perceptions of who benefits from online voting.

Once again, we can see that incumbency and candidate ideology play important roles in understanding attitudes towards online voting. Earlier, we saw that both factors are related to support for online voting, and here we see that there are related perceptions of who might benefit from the use of electronic voting in local elections. In particular, we see that challengers and left-wing candidates are comparatively likely to believe that they have an advantage over their incumbent and right-wing competitors. The results from these two separate analyses make sense. Support for internet voting is relatively high among left-wing candidates, and this could be because these individuals are comparatively likely to think that they benefit from the use of such a system. The incumbent results are less straightforward, and do not as neatly suggest that support for online voting is related to opinions of who might benefit (recall that the model in table 5.1 without interaction reveals that, on its own, incumbent status is unrelated to support for internet voting). Regardless, the fact remains that there are clear differences in perception on the basis of both ideology and incumbency, with regard to evaluations of who benefits from online voting.

Did Candidates Campaign Differently Because of the Presence of Online Voting?

The final question we investigate is whether the use of online voting affected the way candidates campaigned. Those survey respondents who completed our post-election questionnaire were asked "Would you say that internet voting had an effect on the way you campaigned?" There are conceivably a variety of ways in which candidates may campaign differently in an online election (we return to this below), though we did not provide any details on what we meant by the question, leaving it up to respondents to interpret as they saw fit. A slight majority (51.1 per cent) responded "yes," while the remaining 48.9 per cent said "no" (N = 190).

As we have done above, in addition to focusing on aggregate results alone, we consider whether their differences in this regard are based upon either incumbent status or ideology. We have already shown that both factors are related to (a) support for internet voting and

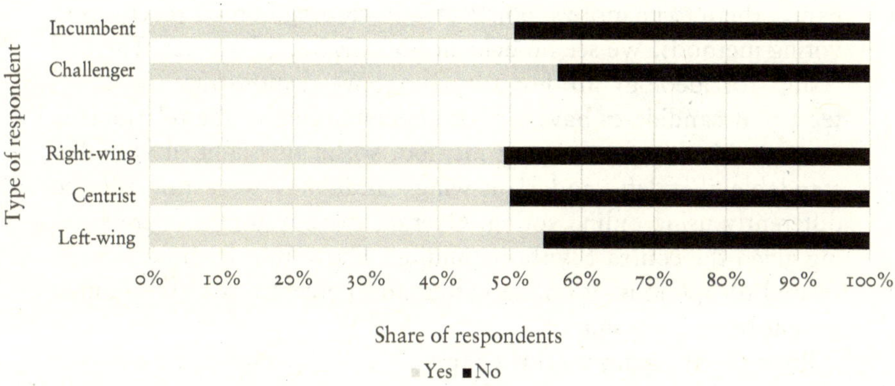

Figure 5.4 | Did online voting affect campaigning?

(b) opinions of who benefits from the use of online voting. There are good reasons to expect that both factors might matter here also. First, incumbents are likely to be more experienced campaigners than their competitors, and they may be expected to be relatively aware of what is required to campaign and thus may be well situated to respond to the use of different electoral systems. With respect to ideology, it was shown in chapter 4 that ideology has a strong relationship with whether electors cast their ballots online or in person, with left-wing voters considerably more likely to vote online. If savvy candidates are aware of this difference, they may choose to campaign using different methods (perhaps moving advertising online) to reach their target audience. To test these assertions, we present figure 5.4, which shows the breakdown of responses to the "campaigning" question, by incumbent status and candidate ideology.

Despite the fact that figure 5.4 hints at some differences on the basis of incumbency and ideology, none of the discrepancies in the figure are statistically significant. Incumbents and challengers are equally likely to report that their campaign strategies were affected by the presence of online voting. The same is true of candidates of different ideological stripes, with no differences between the groups on this measure.

These null findings are perhaps somewhat surprising for the incumbency variable. Sitting politicians, on balance, should have more experience campaigning than challengers, and one might expect them to be more sophisticated, including in their reactions to voting methods. We see no evidence of this here, however. The null results for ideology are less surprising. We demonstrated in chapter 4 that candidates have a poor understanding of the relationship between ideology and voting method, so, in this light, it is understandable that left- and right-wing candidates were not affected differently using online voting. Overall, these null results are striking given the contrast with the findings above that both factors are related to opinions of online voting and perceptions of who might benefit from the system.

Prior to wrapping up this chapter, we wish to delve a bit deeper into the way online voting affected the campaign strategies among those candidates who did react to the use of online voting. Though incumbency and ideology do not appear to matter in this respect, the fact remains that most candidates did shape their campaigning strategies with the voting method in mind.

After being asked if online voting affected their campaigning, respondents who answered "yes" were presented with an open-ended follow up question about how they had campaigned differently. Two distinct themes emerge from these data.[15] The first is that many candidates indicated that they increased their campaigning presence online, sometimes while also decreasing their "real world" campaigning. Some typical responses to this effect include:

"Relied on social media to a great extent"
"Got engaged in online conversations"
"Didn't bother with lawn signs, just shared online"
"I focused on online advertising to target online voters"
"I had to opt for FB/YouTube Ads in addition to my regular campaign"
"Used more social media and internet marketing methods to engage"
"I joined Facebook"

The implicit assumption among these respondents seems to have been that because voting was conducted online, voters would also collect their information online. Regardless of whether this assumption is correct or not, the fact that candidates are making this assumption is telling and suggests that the places where voters can find information during campaigns might depend, to some extent, upon the voting methods offered (and how candidates respond).

The second theme that emerges from the open-ended response is the provision of information to electors on how to vote online. Some typical responses to this effect include:

> "Informed voters that they could vote online – majority did not know"
> "Promoted online voting in all of my campaign efforts by providing the link to website"
> "Additional voting information was added in my campaign materials"
> "I encouraged people to vote online and provided information on how to do that"
> "I was able to inform the public that they cold contact the city for information on how to vote online"
> "During online voting periods, I posted frequently on social media about How to vote online. I also showed people a card and how to vote online with their VIN"
> "Ensured as many people as possible [are] aware of online voting, especially younger voters."

Even the simplest of online voting methods is quite different from traditional paper voting methods (to which electors are accustomed), so it is unsurprising that candidates devoted time and resources to attempting to educate potential voters on this. It is possible that candidates were concerned that their supporters might not be able to navigate the voting system. It is also plausible that some candidates expected electors to be thankful for such information, potentially leading to persuasion. Whether the goals of these efforts were to increase turnout, persuade potential voters, or perhaps some combination of both, "education" was a very common theme in the open-ended responses.

Although we find no evidence that campaign strategies were related to either incumbency or ideology, we do see that the presence of an online voting option affected the campaign strategies of many candidates. It affected both the mode of engaging with voters and the messages presented. Many candidates clearly responded in meaningful ways to the use of this non-traditional voting method.

CONCLUSION

This chapter helps us to understand the attitudes of local candidates in Ontario towards online voting. As a key player in the adoption of online voting, Ontario serves as an important case for study. While a great deal of research exists on how voters view and react to the new system, as is the case with the field of political behaviour more generally, comparatively less is known about the "supply side" of the electoral equation: candidates. However, given how integral candidates are to the political process, to begin to paint a complete picture of attitudes towards and behavioural response to online voting, it is vital to study both electors and candidates.

This chapter has revealed several noteworthy findings, both with respect to the aggregate sample and our key candidate characteristics of interest: ideology and incumbency. First, among the population as a whole, our survey data reveal that a majority of candidates are supportive of online voting. Because our sample is limited to cities that already employ online voting, such a finding is perhaps not surprising. However, the sky-high level of support (over 80 per cent) may be much more so. While we cannot speak here to levels of support for online voting in municipalities where online voting has never been used, the fact that such a potentially controversial voting method has achieved this substantial level of support among candidates with experience contesting an "online" election should be highly encouraging to proponents of such systems.

The second aggregate level finding is that most candidates see no advantages for candidates based upon either ideology or incumbent status. In both dimensions, substantial majorities of candidates believed the voting method did not provide an inherent benefit to any of these groups (though candidates were roughly three times as likely to think that incumbent/challenger status mattered than did ideology). The lack of a widespread belief that the voting method benefits any particular group no doubt helps to explain why support for online voting is so high among candidates. In fact, our data reveal that incumbents who thought online voting benefitted challengers, and vice versa, are considerably less likely to support online voting than those candidates who believed that they benefitted from the system ($p<0.01$).[16] Though we cannot conclusively state that such a pattern exists on the basis of perceptions of benefits on the basis of ideology (simply because so few of our respondents believed ideology to matter), there is an apparent link between perceptions of how one's chances of winning are affected by the voting method and support for online voting.

A third and final noteworthy finding based upon the sample as a whole is that a slight majority of candidates seem to have adapted their campaign strategies in response to the use of online voting. Our data suggest that roughly 51 per cent of candidates reacted, a figure which may seem low given the centrality of voting method to elections. However, a brief examination of the relationship between this "reaction" variable and success in the election suggests that victorious candidates were no more likely to alter their campaign strategies than were unsuccessful candidates.[17] This null finding seems to suggest that, at least at the aggregate, there is no clear evidence that candidates have found a way to adapt to the use of online voting to gain an electoral advantage. Among those candidates who did change their tactics in response to the use of online voting, the most common ways of doing so appear to be increasing online campaigning and attempting to educate electors regarding the process of online voting. Whether or not these activities are successful in attracting new voters needs to be considered, as the aforementioned null results seem to suggest that they may not be.

With respect to our key explanatory variables of interest, ideology and incumbency, each stage of our analysis provides insight into the importance of these two variables which, as argued above, play a central role in municipal politics in Ontario. Both factors are related to support for the use of online voting. Right wing candidates are relatively unsupportive of the method. Incumbency also matters but only in those cities that introduced online voting for the first time in 2018. Ideology and incumbency status are also both related to expectations of who might benefit from the use of online voting; challengers and left-wing candidates are comparatively likely to believe they have an advantage (the question of whether they actually do or not is another matter and one worthy of consideration in future research). Finally, candidates of all ideological and incumbent statuses are equally likely to alter the way in which they campaign in response to the use of online voting. On the whole, these factors which we know to be extremely important in local politics are also highly relevant to the study of the impact of online voting.

The study of municipal politics, as we allude to in our introductory chapter, has often been labelled the "black hole" of Canadian political science (Eidelman and Taylor 2016, 306) and the "poor cousins" in the study of Canadian political behaviour (Cutler and Matthews 2005, 359). While this, of course, is beginning to change, these labels still ring true when it comes to the study of local elites and municipal candidates. While our understanding of municipal electors has been advanced through numerous large-scale studies (McGregor et al. 2021; Lucas et al. 2021), very little is known about the individuals who run for local office. This chapter, therefore, makes an important advancement by turning our attention from voters to candidates. As the individuals who shape the substance and dynamics of local elections, candidates are a remarkably important piece of the puzzle. Moreover, as the set of individuals some of whom will ultimately serve in elected office and establish policy, it is crucial that we develop an understanding of their attitudes towards important public policy debates such as the adoption of internet voting.

6

What Do Administrators Think?

INTRODUCTION

The previous chapter made the case for studying municipal candidates as an important, though vastly understudied, group of political actors in Canada. If the literature on municipal candidates is limited, then the literature on local election administrators in Canada is virtually non-existent. Consistent with the argument presented in the fifth chapter, Krivonosova (2021, 2) argues that research on electoral technologies, specifically online voting, has tended to focus on voters rather than "election administration" and election administrators more specifically. Although there are, of course, some recent exceptions in the literature on Canada (Goodman and Spicer 2019), the views, attitudes, and preferences of local administrators remain largely unknown. This, of course, raises an important question: what do the individuals who administer local elections think about online voting and its adoption?

To call them "administrators," however, may be underestimating their role in local politics and governance. They do much more than simply administer; they are also important decision makers in many respects. While we dig into this later in the chapter, we asked administrators in cities that plan to make use of online voting the following question: "Who led the charge to adopt online voting in your municipality for 2022?" While we might think that elected politicians are responsible for such important decisions, this option garnered just 6.4 per cent of responses. The vast majority (83 per cent) reported that it was bureaucrats in the clerk's office who were primarily responsible for the adoption of online voting.[1] While these individuals may be overestimating their role to some extent, there is at least a clear perception of importance. What's more, this perception is consistent with recent accounts of the actual importance of these local actors (Goodman and Spicer 2019; Krivonosova 2021). Krivonosova (2021, 5), for example, argues that "it is crucial" to focus local election administrators precisely because these "street-level" bureaucrats tend to "have a high level of discretion in the delivery of elections." If administrators are, in fact, important local decision makers with considerable agency and autonomy, then it is crucial that we have an understanding of their attitudes and opinions.

Shifting our focus away from voters and candidates, this chapter considers several questions related to the motivations, opinions, and perceptions of municipal election administrators. The four questions we consider in this chapter are as follows: first, in cities that do use online voting, what are the motivations for doing so? Here local administrators can offer unique insight into the debates and rationale surrounding a municipality's adoption and usage of online voting. This is important as it is administrators, not necessarily politicians as noted above, who have spearheaded the move to online voting. Understanding their views, therefore, is an essential piece of the puzzle when seeking to understand variation in the adoption of online voting. Second, how do the attitudes of administrators compare to those of electors and candidates? While administrators may be leading the charge, voter and candidate attitudes are undoubtedly relevant, informing, framing, and ultimately shaping public debates on these matters. As such, we are interested in better understanding whether administrators have attitudes that are distinctive from the other actors we have examined in previous chapters. Third, and relatedly, what do administrators think that electors want? If public opinion is to inform decisions, then perceptions of these opinions matter. Do administrators in towns that employ online voting have different perceptions than those in places that do not and how does this match up with electors? Fourth, and finally, how did administrators perceive the effects of two recent and important exogenous shocks: COVID-19 and the technical incident that occurred in the 2018 Ontario municipal elections? Exogenous shocks have the potential to affect the machinery of elections, including the adoption and use of online voting. Interestingly, COVID and the technical incident may have pulled in different directions – COVID should presumably make the adoption of online voting more likely and the technical incident less likely. We consider this very possibility.

To explore these questions and to better understand a crucial, though understudied, set of local decision makers, we draw upon an original survey of municipal election administrators that was conducted in the spring of 2022. The final dataset includes responses from 281 administrators from across the province of Ontario. Taken together, the results of this chapter help us to develop a better understanding of the decision-making processes that inform election administration and the considerations taken when engaging in election reforms, including those necessary to respond to exogenous shocks. In other words, we provide insight into why (and when) electoral administrators might support or oppose online voting in their municipalities. Results reveal several important, perhaps even counterintuitive, findings. On the question of motivations, for example, we find that a desire for higher turnout is not explicitly the most important factor. Here we find that several other factors (i.e., accessibility) – factors that are undoubtedly linked to turnout – are viewed as more important. The chapter highlights that local administrators are an important piece of the puzzle and should not be overlooked.

BACKGROUND

Local Election Administration

As mentioned at the outset of the book, the province of Ontario provides remarkable leeway to municipalities in determining vote method. Other aspects of elections, such as the timing of the election and rules regarding candidate financing, are strictly regulated by the province through the Municipal Elections Act. Procedures for running elections locally are all contained in the act, meaning that there is a great deal of standardization across the province. For instance, the act sets out who can and cannot be a candidate and who can and cannot vote in the municipal election. It specifies who can raise funds for a campaign and permits only certain sources of donations. The act also provides key dates for reporting and mandates penalties for both voters and candidates that fail to abide by its rules. One of the more permissive aspects of the act, however, is that which allows municipalities to determine the vote method for their community. It further allows for the use of alternative voting methods, opening the door for internet voting locally across Ontario.

The Municipal Elections Act also places responsibility for administering the election onto the clerk (section 11[2]). A municipal clerk is a legislative requirement for each municipality in Ontario through the Municipal Act. As one of the few members of the staff that municipalities are legally required to have, the clerk has broad responsibilities for providing legislative and corporate support to council, managing council's agenda, and acting as a key interface between council and the public (Sancton 2011). Elections, as mentioned above, also fall into this broad job requirement. Depending on the size of the community, the election logistics may fall on an election administrator or a deputy clerk, but legislatively the clerk is ultimately responsible for the election (Garnett and Keir 2022).

For municipal clerks, the election process begins quite early. Clerks are responsible for hiring staff to ensure they have enough support throughout the election period. They certify the voters list, prepare candidate nominations, ensure there are enough ballots, distribute voter information to the public, secure the sites that would be used for advanced voting or polling stations on election day, and generally engage the public, encouraging them to become candidates and vote. After the election period, they will review candidate finances, refer any matters to the assembled compliance audit committee (which they are also responsible for forming by a provincially imposed deadline prior to the election) and begin the onboarding of newly elected councillors.

Upon conclusion of the election, clerks will often prepare a report, making recommendations for council on how the process could be improved. Council is generally quite deferential to the clerk and mindful of their position as a neutral administrator of the election. Incumbent councillors understand that if they are seen to be interfering with the administration of the election, the integrity of the vote may well be called into question. While politicians are involved in setting the broad parameters in which the election will be contested, they are not involved with the implementation, making studies focused on election administrators important sites for better understanding democratic function (Krivonosova 2022).

While council ultimately makes the decision on vote choice, they do consider the perspective of clerks and election administrators while making those decisions (Goodman and Spicer 2019). For those reasons, it is important to understand the factors that may influence clerks and election administrators to make such decisions and recommendations to council. While past literature has not shown that the overall administrative burden of facilitating an election is greatly lifted while adopting internet voting (Yard 2010), research has shown the possibility that internet voting may reduce errors in the counting process that could arise due to human error (Krivonosova 2022) – a potentially valuable improvement given the responsibility clerks carry for electoral integrity in Ontario. With that said, internet voting has also been shown to introduce a new swath of private actors to the administrative mix, which can create another level of complexity for clerks but may alleviate them of certain administrative functions throughout the election period (James 2019). Many are also hopeful that the integration of technology into the electoral process will boost convenience and, with it, potentially turnout as well (Goodman and Pyman 2016; Carter and Campbell 2012). As a result, internet voting may have both negative and positive consequences for the role clerks play during an election. Some of which may potentially persuade them to promote the adoption of internet voting in their communities. However, very little of this work focuses on Canadian municipalities.

Exogenous Shocks: Recent Shocks in Ontario

Reforms to electoral systems, as well as major changes to the machinery of elections, are relatively rare occurrences (Norris 1995; Norris 1997). Indeed, the rules governing elections tend to be remarkably stable. Nonetheless, reform does happen. Why? A large body of research suggests that exogenous shocks are often responsible for creating the conditions that allow major institutional and organizational change (Harmel and Janda 1994; Cross and Blais 2012). Importantly, many suggest that this applies to electoral reform as well (Renwick 2010). Whether responding to economic crises (Alhquist et al. 2020), war (Walter 2018), natural disasters (Stein 2015), or public health emergencies (Umberg et al. 2020), there have been many instances where election officials around the world have altered the machinery of their elections in times of uncertainty.

Ontario has experienced two such shocks in recent years. The first was a technical incident that occurred during the 2018 municipal elections. Just hours before the polls were set to close on voting day, websites in forty-three municipalities that were being supported by internet voting vendor Dominion Voting Systems slowed or stopped, preventing many voters from casting their ballots online (Hayes et al. 2022). Thirty-five of these communities declared a state of emergency under the Municipal Elections Act to allow voting to continue the following day. The remaining eight continued voting by one to two hours on election day (Cardillo et al. 2019). As Hayes et al. (2022) note, the incident and accompanying emergency response "sparked discussion about whether online voting uptake in Ontario municipalities would consequently be curbed or halted."

The second exogenous shock occurred two years later when COVID-19 was declared a global health pandemic. As Blais et al. (2021, 1) write, "The terms 'lockdown' and 'social distancing' became part of the global vocabulary as governments closed schools, parks, and businesses, limited international travel, and mandated that individuals keep their distance from one another (working from home, restricting unnecessary travel, staying six feet of physical distance in public spaces, etc.)." In response to these new public health measures, eighty countries around the world postponed a variety of elections, and many more modified their delivery or undertook voting reforms to continue to offer regular elections that were accessible to voters (IDEA 2021). Not surprisingly, many during this time suggested that online voting may be a useful response to allow elections to continue while still promoting public health compliance.

These recent shocks experienced by Ontario raise the final question tackled by this chapter: how did local administrators perceive the impact of the 2018 technical incident and the COVID-19 pandemic as it relates to the adoption and usage of online voting? And importantly, did these two shocks pull decision makers in different directions? Here we consider whether the 2018 incident dissuaded adoption and whether the onset of the pandemic encouraged it.

DATA AND ANALYSIS

The results presented in this chapter are drawn primarily from a survey of election administrators, fielded in the spring of 2022 (roughly six months prior to the 2022 municipal elections).[2] The contact list was procured from the Association of Municipal Managers, Clerks and Treasurers of Ontario, a professional association for municipal administrators across the province who maintain the most comprehensive contact list of municipal elected officials and staff in Ontario. Elected officials were removed from the list, as were any staff without a direct role in election administration. The resulting list included only those with a direct role in election administration. The job title of these individuals may vary. Clerk is the standard for much of the province, but in some municipalities, variations, including clerk-treasurer, clerk-administrator, or clerk-counsel were included given their responsibilities would include election administration. A total of 281 administrators completed at least part of the survey.

The survey includes a variety of questions about the motivations, opinions, and perceptions of election administrators. This includes questions on their views on the use of online voting, the perceptions of the views of electors, reasons for supporting online voting, and their views on the effects of important external events that may impact the use of online voting – note that appendix 6.I contains information on the survey questions analyzed in this chapter. We also have information on the personal characteristics of respondents and these show that the dataset includes respondents with variation on many dimensions. A majority of respondents (63.3 per cent) are from cities that are employing online voting in 2022 (N=275). Most participants (72.2 per cent) are from municipalities that they would describe as "rural," 10.6 per cent report being from "suburban" municipalities, and the remaining 17.3 per cent are from "urban" municipalities (N=237). A total of 74.8 per cent of respondents reported being female, 17.7 per cent were male, and the remaining 7.6 per cent preferred not to report this information (N=238). The average age was 46.5 years old (standard deviation: 10.7 years) (N=216). Finally, respondents were largely quite experienced in their roles, with fewer than a quarter (24.1 per cent) having worked in electoral administration for less than five years and 48.3 per cent having served in such a role for more than ten years (N=232).

We answer this chapter's research questions in four stages. First, we consider the question of why some administrators support online voting. As we note below, there is substantial support for the use of online voting among our sample. A majority (82.9 per cent) of respondents believe that online voting should be employed in local elections, while only 12.3 per cent do not (5 per cent were unsure) (N=240). Most of the administrators in our sample are from municipalities with online voting (as is the case in a majority of Ontario municipalities in 2022). Among respondents in places where internet voting is in use, we consider the importance of four common justifications for its employment: accessibility, convenience, public health and safety, and to improve voter turnout.

Next, we consider the opinions of administrators in response to two questions central to the debate over the use of online voting: Should online voting be used in local elections, and should local governments take action to increase turnout? We also consider the similarity of the views of administrators as compared to those of electors and candidates (using results from our 2018 elector and candidate surveys). Do the preferences of these powerful bureaucrats reflect those of their citizenry? Here we differentiate between administrators from municipalities that use online voting and those that do not.

Third, we continue to strive to understand the motivation for implementing online voting. Here, we consider perceptions of attitudinal change between 2018 and 2022, a period during which two noteworthy events occurred which have the potential to affect attitudes towards online voting: a major technical glitch in the 2018 elections and the COVID-19 pandemic. Separate from, and perhaps more important than, the question of whether these events actually influenced public attitudes, is the question of how administrators interpreted such shifts. The question considered here is whether administrators perceive a shift in public opinion between 2018 and 2022 and if respondents in municipalities with online voting differ from those without.

Finally, we consider how local electoral administrators perceived the effects of two significant events that occurred between the 2018 and 2022 elections. The first is the COVID-19 pandemic. Many democratic countries around the world have adapted their elections in response to this major health crisis. In some instances, elections were postponed, but in most cases, non-traditional voting methods have been either introduced or their use expanded. Though voting by mail is the most common of these voting methods employed in response to the pandemic, online voting was considered seriously in many places. At the local level in Ontario, where online voting is already very common, we should expect support for online voting to increase because of the pandemic.

The second event considered is a technical incident that occurred on election day when the websites of Dominion Voting Systems' online voting system slowed due to an unapproved restriction in bandwidth by their colocation provider (Cardillo et al. 2019; Essex and Goodman 2022). This restriction in bandwidth went undetected until election day when voting traffic reached its peak. As noted above, the result was that the websites of forty-three municipalities either did not work or operated so slowly that casting a ballot was either very difficult or not possible. Though technical incidents had previously arisen in Ontario local elections, none had this magnitude, which made national news.

Together, these analyses provide detailed insights into the views of electoral administrators towards online voting. They tell us the importance of various considerations for the adoption of online voting, the position of electoral administrators towards online voting, how administrators view the opinions of the residents they serve, and how major incidents were perceived by administrators. The answers to this chapter's research questions go a great distance towards helping to understand why online voting is utilized in as many Ontario municipalities as it is.

RESULTS

Why Do Administrators Support Online Voting?

As already noted, most municipalities in Ontario are employing online voting in 2022. The spread of this voting method has been steady and significant since it was first introduced in 2003. This chapter's first analysis is focused on understanding the perceived importance of various factors for the adoption of online voting. That is, as far as administrators are concerned, why is online voting adopted?

As noted in our introductory chapter, there are various reasons that municipalities might choose to adopt online voting. Among these arguments is to make voting more accessible or to provide options for people for whom voting in person may be difficult. Another argument is that online voting is more convenient or easier. Citizens live busy lives and online voting might simply be easier and less time consuming than voting in person. Considering the COVID-19 pandemic, another argument for online voting is that it is safer. A trip to the voting booth involves going to a public space, where the health statuses of those around the voter are unknown. A fourth and extremely common argument in favour of online voting

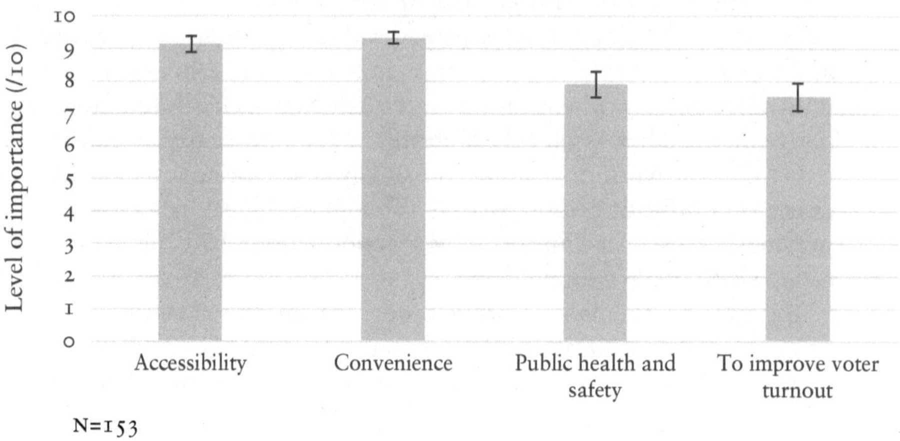

Figure 6.1 | Perceived importance of reasons for employing online voting

is that it could potentially boost turnout. The argument here is that improvements to accessibility, convenience, and even the protection of public health might increase the likelihood of participation.

To test the perceived importance of each of these factors, administrators in those municipalities where online voting has been implemented were asked how important (on a scale from 0 to 10) each factor was in the decision of their municipality to adopt remote voting.[3] Figure 6.1 shows the average score for each category (represented by the height of the vertical bars). Whiskers show 95 per cent confidence intervals.

Figure 6.1 shows that all factors were viewed by administrators as important (all scored higher than 7.5 out of 10) but that some are clearly more important than others. Accessibility and convenience were seen as more central to the decision to using online voting that were either public health and safety or voter turnout. This is perhaps surprising given that much of the public and media discussion around online voting is focused on these last two factors (see, for example, Chandler 2022). In the face of dual crises of health and declining voter turnout, accessibility and convenience are stronger drivers of the choice to using online voting among electoral administrators.

How Do Administrators Compare to Electors and Candidates?

Now that we are beginning to get a sense of the views of administrators, it seems logical to compare their views to those of other important electoral stakeholders, namely candidates and electors themselves. If administrators are "driving the bus," so to speak, it seems important that their views are compatible with these other actors. To consider whether this is the case, we compare results from our administrator survey to those from the elector and candidate surveys (introduced and described in earlier chapters of this book). More specifically, we compare these three groups (administrators, electors, and candidates) on two dimensions (or two questions that were common to all three surveys). First, we consider opinions of whether online voting should be used in municipal elections. Second, we compare attitudes on whether local governments have a responsibility to take action to increase voter turnout. This has long been the primary stated motivation for introducing online voting among the system's proponents (though we have shown above that this is not the most important consideration for administrators). Tables 6.1 and 6.2 show the distribution of answers to agree/disagree questions when presented with statements about whether online voting should be used and if municipalities have a responsibility to take action to increase turnout.

Some important caveats must be kept in mind when interpreting the data from these tables. First, the administrator data was collected four years later than the elector and candidate data. During this time, online voting has been adopted by many more municipalities. If public opinion has shifted in concert with this growth, then one may expect support for online voting among electors and candidates to be somewhat greater in 2022 than it was in 2018. Though we cannot test this contention, readers should keep this difference in the timing of data collection in mind when interpreting results. Second, the elector and candidate data are only from cities where online voting was in place prior to 2022.[4] However, we have administrator data from cities that use and do not use online voting. To account for this difference and make our comparison more valid, we differentiate between administrators from places that used online voting in 2018 and those which did not.[5]

The first finding of note in table 6.1 is that, unsurprisingly, administrators in municipalities where online voting was in place in 2018

Table 6.1 | Internet voting should be available in municipal elections

	Administrators		Electors	Candidates
	Cities without online voting	Cities with online voting		
Strongly agree	45.6%	83.2%	59.3%	59.2%
Somewhat agree	34.2%	12.4%	26.8%	13.3%
Somewhat disagree	11.4%	1.8%	7.0%	3.5%
Strongly disagree	8.8%	2.7%	6.8%	4.9%
N	114	113	3851	347

are significantly more likely to support the system's use than are their colleagues elsewhere. A mere 4.5 per cent of respondents in the former type of cities and towns are disagree with the system's use and a staggering 83.2 per cent strongly agree with it (this is the highest percentage in any category in the table). Still, we see that a sizable majority of administrators (nearly 80 per cent) in places without online voting support its adoption at the municipal level.

Electors and candidates in our samples are also highly supportive of online voting – almost 60 per cent of both groups agree strongly with the system's use. However, these groups are considerably less positive about online voting than are administrators in those towns where the system was in place in 2018 ($p<0.01$ for both comparisons).[6] Though most of the variation here is between the "agree" and "strongly agree" categories, there is a clear gap between administrators and the other stake holding groups. Administrators in municipalities that employ online voting are much more enthusiastic about the system's use.

Together, these results help to explain the consistent growth of online voting throughout the province. Administrators, electors, and candidates in all three of our surveys strongly support the use of

Table 6.2 | Government should take action to maximize voter turnout in municipal elections

	Administrators		Electors	Candidates
	Cities without online voting	Cities with online voting		
Strongly agree	56.3%	65.8%	52.0%	78.4%
Somewhat agree	32.8%	26.1%	37.7%	13.3%
Somewhat disagree	8.4%	3.6%	7.8%	3.5%
Strongly disagree	2.5%	4.5%	2.5%	4.9%
N	119	111	3815	347

online voting. In fact, this pattern raises the question of why internet voting is not more widespread than is currently the case. We expect that inertia plays a prominent role in the maintenance of the paper-based status quo in so many places, but further research would be helpful to determine why so many municipalities in the province still have not embraced the use of online voting.

Table 6.2 addresses a related question, speaking to the motivation for supporting online voting (or not). The table shows the share of respondents who agree or disagree with the view that governments should strive to maximize turnout in local elections. In our sample, attitudes towards the use of online voting and opinions of whether government should strive to maximize turnout have a strong positive correlation for all groups – administrators, electors, and candidates ($p<0.001$ in all groups). Though there are certainly other factors that influence opinions of the use of online voting, this is certainly an important factor in this consideration. There is a strong societal norm suggesting that voting is important (Blais et al. 2019), and the question posed to administrators here is whether their organizations have a role to play in seeking to maximize turnout in local democracies.

While it appears that we see a difference between administrators in cities with and without online voting, these distributions are not statistically distinguishable from one another (the sample sizes of these groups potentially play a role in this null finding). In both groups, roughly 90 per cent of respondents agree that governments have a role to play in shaping turnout. Administrators are also no different from electors. However, all other comparisons in the table are significant at least at the 95 per cent level. Candidates are the most likely to support a role for government in maximizing turnout – they differ from all other groups. The contrast with electors is particularly striking. While this group is generally supportive of government intervention, they are relatively unlikely to agree strongly with such a position. Whereas administrators are on the extremes (high and low) with respect to support for online voting, their views of administrators are between those of electors and candidates on the question of whether the government should strive to maximize turnout.

While, as noted above, the relationship between these two attitudes is related, this distinction in the position of administrators relative to the other groups under study is important. It suggests that administrators are not simply supportive of online voting because of an expectation that it will increase turnout. Such a finding is compatible with our earlier finding, that turnout is not as important in decisions to adopt online voting as are other factors, such as convenience and accessibility.

What Do Administrators Think Electors Want?

Having shown that the views of administrators are different from electors (the group which, some might argue, administrators are working for), we turn to examine how administrators perceive the views of the public. Normatively speaking, it is desirable that even unelected officials in a democracy act in such a way that fits with the wishes of the citizenry. If administrators are at all swayed by public opinion, their perceptions of the public's views are worthy of our consideration.

In this third section of our analysis, we consider how administrators perceive the public's views towards the use of online voting and how these opinions might have changed between 2018 and 2022. As noted above, much occurred between the two events, including the technical disaster in dozens of municipalities that led to the

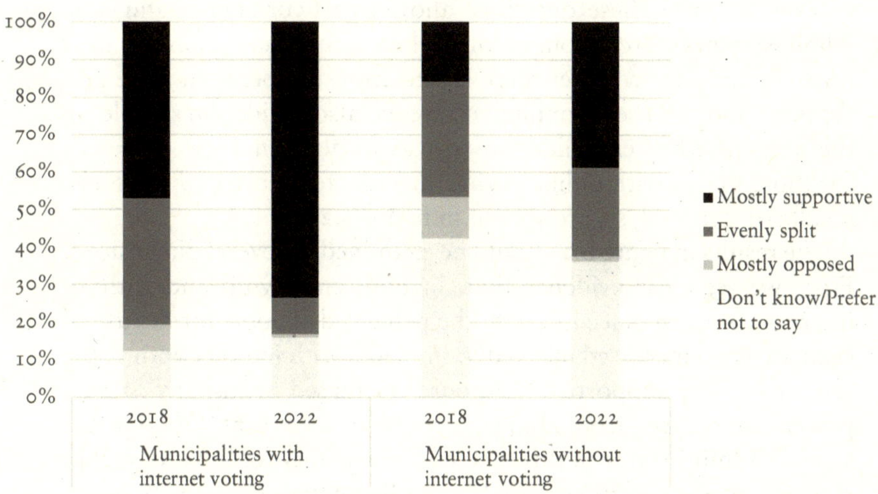

Figure 6.2 | Perceptions of public support for internet voting

extension of voting hours in 2018 and the COVID-19 pandemic, which has been a significant consideration for election administrators of all levels, for years now (we consider in more detail below how the effects of the two events were perceived by administrators). On top of these events, other factors might influence perceptions of public support for online voting. In particular, the consistent growth of online voting among Ontario's cities (as demonstrated in our introductory chapter) might lead to a normalization of the practice, creating a sense of inevitable expansion of online voting over time. It is also possible that citizens are continuing to become more comfortable with using the internet for things they might not have in the past; the pandemic increased rates of internet use for things like schooling and ordering groceries, among other things. Regardless of the exact sources of public opinion, and changes in public opinion, the fact remains that public perceptions can be, at least theoretically, important to the decisions of administrators.

Respondents to the administrator survey were asked how supportive they believe electors in their municipality were of online voting in 2018 and in 2022 (either mostly supportive, mostly opposed, or evenly split). These questions allow us to consider if and how administrators' perceptions of the public's views have changed over time. To consider whether there is a relationship between these perceptions and the use of online voting, we also divide the sample on the basis of whether online voting was in place in 2018 (N = 113 for those places with online voting and 127 for those without). The results of this analysis are shown in figure 6.2.

The results in figure 6.2 should be examined in several dimensions. First, we see clear evidence that, in both cities with and without internet voting in place in 2018, the perceived support for the use of such a system increased markedly. In places with internet voting, the rate of "mostly supportive" responses increased by just shy of 26.5 percentage points – from 46.9 per cent to 73.4 per cent. Of note, just a single administrator in this type of municipality took the view that residents were "mostly opposed" to online voting in 2022. We see a similar trend in locations without online voting, though the magnitude of the difference is slightly smaller. The "mostly support" group grew by 22.8 points, jumping from 15.8 per cent to 38.6 per cent. Administrators in both types of cities therefore took the view that their electorate has become more supportive of online voting in the past four years (note that both differences are significant at $p<0.05$).

The second striking result from the figure is that perceptions of support for online voting differ greatly between types of municipalities. At both points in time, administrators perceived greater support in places where online voting was in use in 2018 ($p<0.01$ in both comparisons). We hesitate to make strong causal claims about this gap (perceived support could translate to use of the system, or vice-versa). The finding is nevertheless striking and suggests that, for the most part, administrators view the voting method in place in their municipalities as being largely in line with public support.

A final finding worthy of note from figure 6.2 is that the rates of "don't know" responses are considerably higher in municipalities without internet voting. Roughly four in ten respondents chose this in both 2018 and 2022 in such cities, while less than one in five administrators did so in places with online voting. Such a result could suggest that administrators in municipalities without internet voting have thought less, talked less with their colleagues, and perhaps consulted with the public less about the electorate's views of online voting. For them, consideration of internet voting is a relatively unimportant aspect of their job.

The question of the accuracy of administrator perceptions aside, there are multiple important findings in this analysis. Electors are perceived as becoming more supportive of online voting over time, and those individuals with online voting in place are viewed as particularly supportive. We turn in the fourth and final stage of this chapter's analysis to consider the perceived effects of some important events that might help to account for these gaps.

How Do Administrators View the Effects of Exogenous Shocks?

To conclude our analysis of the attitudes and evaluations of electoral administrators, we consider their perceptions of the effects of two major events of clear and significant relevance to the administration of (online) elections. The first is a technical incident experienced by municipalities which employed Dominion Voting Systems as their vendor in the 2018 elections. A significant decrease in bandwidth allowed to websites running those elections meant that, for many electors, voting was difficult or impossible, and balloting periods had to be extended. This technical problem made national news and sparked discussion about the future of internet voting in Ontario municipalities (Britneff 2018). An incident of this nature should be expected to decrease support for the use of online voting, both among electors and administrators. The second event which we consider is COVID-19, the global public health emergency which affected elections around the world. Dozens of countries around the world postponed their elections and many others considered changes to voting methods. As voting remotely is clearly safer than voting in person, we expect that there was pressure upon administrators in Ontario municipalities to expand remote voting. The two events – the technical incident and COVID-19 – therefore pull in opposite directions.

In this section of our results, we consider the perceptions of administrators about the effects of these two events on the likelihood that their municipality would employ online voting in 2022. We consider the direction of perceived effects, as well as the magnitude. This analysis allows us to compare the perceived impacts of these two potentially significant factors upon the adoption of online voting in Ontario municipalities. First, survey respondents were asked separately questions about if they believed the two events

Table 6.3 | Perceived direction of impact of shocks upon likelihood of use of online voting

	Dominion incident	COVID-19
Less likely	19.2%	0.0%
No effect	80.8%	52.7%
More likely	0.0%	47.3%
N	240	241

made online voting in their municipalities more likely, less likely, or if they had no effect. Table 6.3 shows the frequency distributions for these questions.

Table 6.3 contains two notable findings: First, it confirms that the perceived impacts of the two shocks are indeed pulling in different directions. About one-fifth of respondents believed that the technical incident decreased the likelihood that online voting would be adopted (not a single respondent thought it made it more likely). In contrast, nearly half of respondents thought that COVID-19 made the use of online voting more likely (here, not a single respondent replied that COVID made online voting less likely). There are clear directional effects here. The second finding of note from the table is that administrators were much more likely to believe that COVID-19 influenced online voting decisions than the technical incident. More than 80 per cent reported that the technical incident had no effect, while fewer than half took this opinion of the pandemic.

Considering respondents individually, we see that respondents were much more likely to believe that COVID-19 had an effect but the 2018 technical incident did not, rather than the other way around. A total of 38.5 per cent of respondents thought that the COVID-19 pandemic was the only factor that affected the adoption of online voting, while just 9.7 per cent thought only the 2018 technical incident mattered (8.4 per cent said that both mattered, and 43.4 per cent said that neither did). This supports the conclusion that COVID-19 was widely considered to be the more influential of the two events.

Table 6.4 | Perceived magnitude of impact of shocks on decision to use online voting in 2022

	Dominion incident	COVID-19
None	71.7%	53.1%
A little	7.1%	9.5%
Somewhat	12.1%	23.7%
A lot	9.2%	13.7%
N	240	241

Note: Numbers do not all add to 100, due to rounding.

A subsequent analysis shows that respondents from municipalities that were affected by the 2018 technical incident did not perceive it to have a different impact on the likelihood of using online voting than those in municipalities that were not affected. Forty administrators from twenty-nine municipalities affected by the technical incident responded to the survey, and the remaining respondents were from unaffected municipalities. We see no statistically significant differences between respondents from the two groups. Though the 2018 technical incident only affected a small share of Ontario's municipalities, its effects were just as likely to be felt in affected and unaffected municipalities.

Now that we understand the perceived directional perceptions, we can build upon these findings by examining the results of a second set of survey questions that asked respondents how much of an impact the two shocks had on the administration of elections (response options were "a lot," "somewhat," "a little," and "not at all"). Table 6.4 contains the frequency distributions for these two variables.

Table 6.4 provides more evidence that the COVID-19 pandemic is perceived to have a greater impact than the technical incident upon the use of online voting among Ontario municipalities in our sample. Respondents are considerably more likely to say that the technical incident had no effects, and they were more likely to report that COVID had either "a lot" or "somewhat" of an effect. A chi-square test reveals that the differences between these distributions is significant at $p<0.01$.

Overall, then, we see differences in the perceived effects of these events both in terms of direction and magnitude. Unsurprisingly, survey respondents saw COVID as making the use of online voting more likely and the technical incident less so. More surprising, perhaps, is the fact that the magnitude of the perceived effect was greater for COVID than for the technical incident. Administrators were considerably more likely to take the view that COVID had any effect at all, and when they did view either event as having an impact, the perceived extent of this impact was greater for COVID.

On the one hand, it is not at all shocking that COVID is viewed by administrators as being the more important of the two "shocks" considered here. On the other hand, it is perhaps surprising that the technical incident did not have more of an impact than it did. Dozens of municipalities were affected by this serious event, and the high-profile nature of the disruption was such that one might reasonably expect municipalities to seriously reconsider the use of online voting. It appears, however, that the trend towards increasing use of online voting in Ontario municipalities is simply too strong for technical issues to overcome. It is impossible to say how many communities would have decided to employ internet voting in 2022 had the technical issue not occurred, but dozens of municipalities adopted such a system between 2018 and 2022. Technical considerations were clearly not enough to dissuade them from adopting this new and, considering the technical issues experience in 2018, potentially controversial method of voting.

CONCLUSION

Despite their title, local administrators do more than simply administer. In many respects they are important decision makers in the arena of municipal governance. In Ontario, clerks are responsible for ensuring local elections are conducted fairly and do not contravene provincial election legislation. They also make the necessary preparations for election logistics, verify the voters list, and certify the results. While council makes the final determination of voting system choice, clerks can be highly influential in recommending alternative voting methods to council and determining the capacity of the municipal administration to administer either an electronic or traditional paper election. A central aim of this chapter, therefore, has been to better understand what motivates administrators to implement (or not) online voting technologies in their municipalities, as well as to better understand their perceptions of online voting more generally.

Drawing on original survey data, this chapter provides several important insights into this remarkably understudied set of local political actors. First, when considering general motivations, administrators placed considerably less emphasis on increasing turnout than conventional wisdom might suggest. Here administrators placed greater weight on outcomes like convenience and accessibility, which are distinct but closely related to turnout. It is surprising (especially given popular narratives) that turnout is not top of mind for admins when thinking about the "why" of online voting.

Second, we find that administrators are more supportive of the adoption of online voting for municipal elections than are local candidates seeking election. This likely speaks to their very different roles. As the previous chapter makes clear, some types of candidates may have good reason to be skeptical of the adoption of online voting precisely because some candidates may benefit from the adoption of internet voting more than others. At the same time, as the individuals responsible for overseeing local elections, administrators appear more persuaded by arguments to modernize the machinery of elections, despite some complications that online voting introduces into the clerk's office. Third, and perhaps relatedly, administrators view public support for online voting as expanding over time. Their perception of widespread public support for online voting may also inform their own opinions regarding the matter and help explain why clerks are so favourable. Finally, the data suggest that administrators viewed the impact of the two exogenous shocks examined in this chapter very differently. In their view, the pandemic contributed to the adoption of online voting in recent years. Conversely, while the 2018 technical incident has had some effect in the opposite direction, this effect is considerably less than that of COVID.

Interestingly, we do uncover some meaningful differences when comparing cities with and without online voting. At least two are worth highlighting here in the conclusion. First, while administrators are generally supportive of online voting in the aggregate, a 15 percentage point gap separates administrators in municipalities with and without online voting. Not surprisingly, it is administrators in cities with online voting that are the more supportive of the two. With that said, those in cities without internet voting are still strongly supportive of adopting online voting for municipal elections (80 per cent agreeing strongly or somewhat). Second, administrators in cities without online voting are more unsure of public opinion on the matter. This uncertainty with regard to public support may speak to their hesitancy to move forward with online voting.

Overall, this chapter reveals the importance of including municipal administrators in the analysis. These individuals offer valuable insight and differ from other actors (specifically electors and candidates) in several important ways. Given the centrality of these actors to decision making about the administration of elections, these results go a long way towards improving our understanding of why internet voting has spread, and continues to spread, so widely across Ontario.

7

Conclusion

INTRODUCTION

Elections are the defining feature of any democracy, but there is enormous variation in how democratic elections are administered across the globe.[1] Some of the most notable differences are voter eligibility, the scheduling of elections and electoral cycles, electoral and party systems, voting windows, and other rules about election administration. Only in the past two decades have technological advances led to the addition of a high-profile and often controversial voting reform: online voting.

Public opinion, measured either at election time or otherwise, is a cornerstone of decision making in a democracy (Burstein 2003). Just as the opinions of the governed decide who governs, those opinions also affect the actions that governors take, including in decision-making processes related to administrative protocols for elections. Prior to this book, however, relatively little has been written about Canadian electors' views on the use of online voting in binding elections, despite such systems being deployed in several provinces and territories, and in hundreds of municipalities across Canada, most notably in Ontario. In fact, most writing on this topic has focused superficially on how the widespread use of the internet, coupled with electors' increasing familiarity and comfort with it, has or has not convinced politicians and elections administrators of the value of adopting remote online voting technologies (Kamenova and Goodman 2015).

But electors' opinions do not solely shape policy. Politicians and election administrators themselves have direct decision-making power over municipal voting methods and their administration and may have views that differ from those of their constituents, as we have demonstrated earlier in this book. Similarly, administrators have their own motivations when making decisions about voting methods, and these may not match those of the public or elected officials. In fact, one could argue that these individuals are relatively well insulated from public opinion in their role as unelected officials.

For these reasons, amongst others, the administration of elections is unlike any other policy area. The legitimacy of a democracy hinges upon electoral integrity, the trustworthiness of elections, and the credibility of election outcomes (Mauk 2020). All other policies hinge upon those outcomes and, as recent experience from the United States shows, if even part of an electorate loses faith in the legitimacy of an election, then all policies implemented by election winners can be seen as illegitimate. It is therefore vital that administrators prioritize public trust in elections when crafting, adopting, or amending election policies.

Understanding the attitudes of all three of these groups – electors, politicians, and administrators – including in how they view and understand online voting adoption and deployment, has been a central goal of this book. In this final chapter, we conclude by accomplishing three final tasks: first, we recount the findings from our data-driven chapters (3–6) and consider what they teach us about attitudes towards online voting in Ontario. When doing so, we incorporate insights from a focus group and series of interviews with election administrators conducted between April and August 2022. Together, the data sources (from electors, candidates, and administrators) paint a rich picture of the online voting landscape in Ontario, allowing for a thorough depiction of the current and future states of online voting in this setting.

Second, we return to some of the topics introduced in the early chapters of this volume (chapters 1 and 2) to contemplate how our findings speak to larger themes relevant to online voting discourse. Do our results further our understanding of the effects of decentralized decision making in local elections? Do our findings provide lessons for policy makers regarding policy learning or experimentation? Are there lessons for legislators regarding the regulation of online voting going forward? Lastly, in the case of online voting, is technology a solution for the electoral-related problems plaguing our democracy?

Finally, we discuss opportunities for future research on internet voting in Ontario municipal elections. Though this volume makes some notable advances to our understanding of the phenomenon of online voting in this context, much remains to be learned. This is particularly important since Ontario will likely remain a world leader in the use of, and experimentation with, online voting for some time. In addition to more research on the attitudes of electors, candidates, and election administrators, we discuss possibilities for studies into how different variations in remote online voting (related to factors such as voting period, complementary voting options, and authentication and verification methods) might be appropriate for municipalities of different types and the potential long-term impacts of the COVID-19 pandemic upon research in this field. We also include a discussion of perhaps the toughest question facing proponents of online voting: how can a public be convinced that online elections are secure? This discussion highlights, once again, the importance of public opinion to the study of online voting in Canada and elsewhere. We conclude with a call for Canadians – researchers, electors, and elites alike – to consider not just empirical questions but also normative ones about the future of online voting in this country.

WHAT THE DATA SAY

The data chapters in this volume speak to many questions about the attitudes and behaviour of electors and elites towards online voting in Ontario local elections. Individually, the chapters provide important insights about each of our groups of interest, including how these different actors compare to one another. Combined, the results of our analyses point to some more general findings about the current state of attitudes towards, and engagement with, internet voting in Ontario. Here, we provide a brief reminder of the findings of our chapters and discuss how they speak to larger lessons about online voting adoption and deployment.

Central to the third chapter is a vitally important question: what happens when changes are made to voting methods? Whereas existing work has focused overwhelmingly upon whether the introduction of online voting affects turnout rates or other aspects of participation, the goal of this chapter was different. Here the aim was to identify the effects of adopting or abandoning online voting upon less studied public attitudes. Using a survey experiment, survey data from electors revealed that the introduction of online voting increases satisfaction with democracy. Such a finding is somewhat heartening given that faith in democracy has declined across the West for many years (Rainie and Perrin 2019; OECD 2022), suggesting that institutional change can serve as a bulwark against such trends. The chapter also investigated opinions of the use of online voting at other levels of government in Canada (provincial and federal) and whether experiences with online voting at the local level affect support for the diffusion of such systems to higher-order elections. According to our data, the introduction of online voting at the local level had no discernible effect upon levels of support for online voting either provincially or federally. However, the elimination of an online voting option locally has the effect of damping enthusiasm for online voting either provincially or federally. In short, institutional changes matter for public opinion, and making changes to voting methods have effects upon things other than turnout rates.

The behaviour of electors continued to serve as the focal point of chapter 4. In literature on political behaviour, the term "vote choice" tends to be synonymous with decisions about which candidate to support (Anderson and Stephenson 2011). But, electors make other vote choices at each election, including the basic question of whether or not to vote at all. As we know, in many municipalities in Ontario, individuals who vote can also choose whether to cast an online or in person ballot (and in some instances, whether to vote via mail-in ballot or by telephone). In chapter 4, we learned that, when given a choice of voting method, older voters, those with high incomes, homeowners, white voters, and those on the ideological left are relatively more likely to vote online, as opposed to in-person. This combination is perhaps surprising, given that each of the sociodemographic indicators listed tends to be associated with the ideological right. These findings perhaps speak to the unique nature of local elections and upon contests in the context of Ontario in particular, as they differ in some ways from the results of similar analyses conducted elsewhere. The chapter also showed that neither electors nor candidates have a particularly good understanding of these patterns and that neither group significantly outperforms the other in this respect. If assessments of such voting patterns do somehow affect debates over the adoption of online voting, the fact that these perceptions are not particularly in-touch with reality is striking.

Chapter 5 shifts the focus to candidates for local office. Drawing upon survey questions about the views and behaviours of these elites, we were able to provide a profile of the type of candidate that supports online voting, who candidates perceive as benefitting from the use of online voting, and if and how candidates react to the use of internet voting. On the first matter, the survey data show that candidates on the "left," who are older and are low in "neuroticism" (those who are less prone to negative emotions such as fear, anxiety, and vulnerability) are particularly supportive of the introduction and use of online voting. We also saw that incumbent status mattered but only in certain contexts. Incumbents were more supportive of online voting in municipalities that had recently adopted online voting – such a finding makes sense, as it is those incumbents who, as a group, voted to support the introduction of this new method. The chapter also finds that candidates vary in their view of the type of candidate that benefits from the employment of internet voting. While most are of the opinion that online voting advantages neither challenger nor incumbent, nor candidates of the right or left, a sizable majority believed that the success of candidates, based upon both dimensions, is affected by the presence of online voting. Specifically, candidates were more likely to believe incumbents and candidates of the left benefit. Finally, chapter 5 also considers whether and how the presence of internet voting affected the manner in which candidates campaign. Somewhat surprisingly, a small majority of candidates reported that they campaign the same under an online system as they would under a traditional paper system. Among those who did campaign differently, the most common reactions were to campaign more heavily online and to attempt to provide information to potential voters on how to cast electronic ballots. We saw significant variation, therefore, in levels of candidate support for, perceptions of the effects of, and reactions to the use of online voting among municipal candidates.

Chapter 6 focused on the views of electoral administrators who, by their own assessment, are highly influential in decisions on the type of voting options provided in their municipalities. During our focus group and interviews of administrators in the spring and summer of 2022, many expressed that they "play a central role in deciding elections methods" by drafting elections reports, including those about election technologies and making recommendations about vote processes, "although, elected council[s] have ultimate say in the voting methods deployed."

Our survey of administrators was likewise conducted in 2022, nearly four years after data collection from electors and candidates. This difference allowed us to assess how administrators viewed elections processes considering the exogenous shocks they faced between 2018 and 2022: notably, a technical incident that affected internet voting in forty-three municipalities and the onset and persistence of the COVID-19 pandemic (Hayes et al. 2022). As such, the chapter began with a consideration of the motivations for adopting online voting and found that concerns over accessibility and convenience were more important drivers than either health concerns or the goal of improving voter turnout (though these factors are no doubt related to one another). Similarly, in the focus group and interviews we conducted, administrators explained that while COVID-19 influenced changes in voting modes in some instances, in others it did not play a role at all given that decisions had either been made prior to the commencement of the pandemic or because the municipality had already made a more fulsome online transition.

One administrator's comment in an interview captures this perspective by noting that "COVID would be an excuse [to adopt online voting], but, it's also about the convenience for the elector. We also don't have to hire as much polling staff." Others, however, pointed to their municipal government and services already being offered largely online: "we made no changes to the process itself [as a result of COVID-19] except by bringing in a corporate resource policy. We were already doing e-meetings and livestreaming them on YouTube before COVID hit. We have 10k followers on Facebook." There were, however, some administrators that noted that the pandemic played a role in their municipality's decision making. As one administrator commented, "COVID played a very large part in our decision-making between lockdowns. Things are good now, but you can't know what the future will hold. This is our first time using tech and it was our big deciding factor." These focus group and interview responses indicate that, while COVID-19 was not a huge changemaker with respect to the growth of online elections, in some cases it was cited as the deciding factor to take the online voting leap.

Chapter 6 then turned to consider how the views of administrators compare to those of electors and candidates. The data showed that administrators in cities with online voting in place are more supportive of online voting than either of our other groups of focus. Results also indicated that administrators believed that the public in their respective municipalities were in favour of the use of online voting. This was not the case among administrators in municipalities without online voting, where perceived support for the system was considerably lower. Finally, the chapter examined the perceived effects of COVID-19 and the 2018 technical incident and concluded that the former had more of an impact upon their decisions on whether to adopt online voting in 2022. As administrators play such a central role in decision making, this chapter provided invaluable insight into the growth of online voting in Ontario.

While these chapter-specific findings are by themselves noteworthy, when considered holistically, they also speak to at least three general lessons about online voting. These lessons correspond with the three questions outlined in our introduction, which we mention are recurring themes in the book: How consistent are orientations within groups, across groups, and across time? What accounts for variation in attitudes and behaviour? Does internet voting affect attitudes and behaviour?

The first lesson learned by combining results from multiple chapters is that attitudes about internet voting vary in important ways, both within groups (i.e., electors) but also between different types of actors and across time. Chapter 4 illustrates that there are several individual-level factors related to the use of online voting amongst electors. Some types of voters are much more likely to embrace the voting method than others. Acceptance of the voting method, however, is far from universal, even in locations where it is widely embraced. In chapter 5, we identified several characteristics of candidates associated with support for or opposition to online voting. Among administrators, we saw large differences in support for online voting based on whether the voting mode was in place. This is not surprising, but it is noteworthy, given the strong relationship between these bureaucrats and the "facts on the ground" in their municipalities. It provides further evidence that administrators are influential in making decisions on voting methods.

We also saw variations in the attitudes of the different groups studied here. Administrators in cities with online voting in place are more supportive of its use than both electors and candidates in those same settings (candidates are slightly more supportive than electors). In this instance, the fact that the opinions of unelected elites differ from candidates, who are engaged directly in the democratic process, is particularly notable. In our focus group and interviews, many administrators whose municipalities had used online voting in at least one prior election cycle noted their enthusiasm about the method, despite hiccups with online voting services in 2018. In fact, contrary to what many administrators perceived as "dissatisfaction with online voting from some electors who experienced voting issues in 2018," the method "is the way of the future" and is "here to stay." This incongruence is potentially a red flag of note for opponents of online voting.

Finally, if the assessments of election administrators are to be believed, Ontarians are becoming increasingly accepting of internet voting over time. Administrators in cities both with and without online voting took the view that their residents became considerably more supportive of the voting method between 2018 and 2022. Given the significant uptick in the adoption of online voting among Ontario municipalities over that period, we see no reason to doubt that support is indeed increasing over time.

The second lesson learned builds upon the idea that attitudes towards online voting are context specific. That is, these attitudes are dependent upon the environment and change in that environment. Chapter 3 shows that changes to voting methods affect elector support for these methods. Here, we see that institutional change can precede support for (or opposition to) such change. In chapter 6, we find that support for online voting among administrators is significantly higher in places where internet voting is in place. The chapter also shows that support for online voting was affected by both the COVID-19 pandemic and the 2018 technical incident. Though most of our data (the elector and candidate surveys) are limited to municipalities that employ online voting, it is undeniable that support for the voting mode varies greatly across the province.

Finally, our data show that making changes to voting methods has important effects, other than those upon turnout. This is highlighted most clearly in chapter 3, which showed that changes to voting methods can affect satisfaction with democracy and support for online voting. We hope that this chapter encourages other researchers to broaden their examination of the effects of online voting past the focus of voter participation. In chapter 5, we also saw that the presence of online voting affects the manner in which many candidates campaign. Campaign tactics have shifted to include greater online campaigning, either via website or social media. Perhaps more striking is that many candidates have begun to play an informational role, aiding electors with respect to the technical minutiae of voting. Given the many variations of online voting used in Ontario, with respect to factors such as authentication requirements, verification processes (if any), and voting windows, it is logical that voters might need additional information and reminders regarding the specifics of the voting process since these intricacies may change between elections (even in municipalities that have been long-term adopters and users of online voting systems). Election management bodies would be wise to take note of this finding and recognize that candidates can play an important role in educating their electorates.

Finally, chapter 5 also shows that the use of online voting has perceived effects – many candidates were of the view that incumbents and candidates of the ideological left benefit from the use of internet voting. In this instance, reality is perhaps less important than perception, as candidates have a significant role to play in determining voting methods (if elected) and of legitimizing election outcomes. As we mentioned above, when electoral integrity is called into question, significant social problems can arise. In this context, if some candidates see the system used to vote as disadvantageous to them, it can breed resentment and, in extreme instances, an unwillingness to accept election results. Once again, election administrators would be wise to recognize this possibility.

LESSONS LEARNED

In addition to empirical findings, our results highlight several broader lessons related to some of the ideas introduced in the early chapters in this book. Our data speak to the wider effects of electoral experimentation, the importance of online voting regulation, and debates about internet voting as a solution to electoral problems. Ontario provides important insights on each of these topics.

The decentralized nature of election administration coupled with the absence of online voting regulation has helped to facilitate widespread experimentation with voting methods in Ontario. Municipalities in the province differ in whether they offer online voting, the specific features of deployment of online voting including when they offer it, and what other complementary methods are available, if any. Such freedom to experiment has caused several municipalities, like Guelph, to implement online voting and then later remove it as an option. Our results, however, reveal that such decisions do not have strictly local effects. The multi-level nature of Canadian politics, wherein municipal elections have less perceived significance, allows for policy attitudes and preferences to spill over into other jurisdictions. Indeed, we provide compelling evidence that removing online voting in municipal elections has downstream consequences for how people view the technology's suitability at other levels. Removing online voting locally decreases support for its adoption provincially and federally. Despite being referred to as the "poor cousin" of provincial and federal politics (Cutler and Matthews 2005) and a "black hole" (Eidelman and Taylor 2010), municipalities' political and administrative decision making has effects far beyond the local arena. During interviews, however, some administrators noted their skepticism about the influence that municipally adopted online voting technology may have on provincial, let alone federal, voting methods: "given the diversity of [Ontario's] electorate, I'm unsure whether online voting will be deployed throughout all municipalities, let alone provincially. But, I do think that if online voting is adopted provincially, most municipalities will hop on the bandwagon." This view also illustrates the reciprocal relationship between levels of government.

Second, our interviews with administrators point to changing attitudes about the importance of regulation to the adoption of online voting. While a lack of standards allows municipalities to experiment with different variations of online voting approaches, likely contributing to its adoption in earlier phases of diffusion, municipalities that have yet to adopt internet voting may wait to do so until such time as standards are in place. Some administrators explicitly noted that "standards setting is integral to council's willingness to adopt online voting ... without it, it's unlikely that our municipality's elected officials would feel comfortable voting to adopt it in the next election cycle." This sentiment is illustrative of why our interviews gave us good reason to believe that many municipalities in the "late majority" and "laggard" categories are cautiously waiting for the online voting standards process to advance before moving forward with adoption. Likewise, on the topic of oversight from higher level authorities, some interview and survey comments emphasized the importance of updating the legislation governing municipal elections to provide greater clarity around how to manage the implementation of both alternative and unsupervised voting methods like online voting, now and into the future. During our focus group and interviews, administrators were keen to point to a future in five to ten years where aspects of the voting process continue to become increasingly electronic, meaning that both regulatory and legislative frameworks will need to evolve over time in effort to keep up with technology and its related social change. As one administrator commented, "there will be a lot of online stuff. The days of going door to door knocking are slowly deteriorating. I think we're going to run out of people [i.e. poll workers and other election workers] too."

Although municipalities have now seen nearly two decades of binding online elections conducted online across hundreds of cities, regulations and further legislative clarity alike may be needed for some reluctant municipalities to adopt remote online voting in their own elections. This is likely made more salient due to (a) the 2018 technical incident and possibility for future issues (Hayes et al. 2022) and (b) debates about electoral integrity and alternative voting methods in the aftermath of the 2020 US presidential election (Biggers et al. 2022).

There is, of course, another perspective worth noting which was captured by an administrator of a municipality who had at one point used the voting reform and then changed course: "I think standards would help, but I hesitate to say it would be the silver bullet." While the final completion of standards will no doubt help to bring some consistency to municipal online voting approaches, it is important to remember that they will be voluntary and therefore municipalities can decide whether to pay attention to and seek counsel from them when developing their online voting plans and requests for proposals by vendors. For many small municipalities that currently do not have the resources to conduct research on online voting, reading through and understanding the components of these standards without an IT team and potentially limited technical capacity could be an issue. It is possible that the emergence of standards will create two-tiers with respect to online voting administration: those that are part of the standards club and those that continue to operate as they have been, extending the "patchwork" of online voting development across of the smaller communities and more rural areas of the province (Goodman and Pammett 2014).

Finally, the findings presented throughout the previous chapters speak to debates surrounding "tech-solutionism." Recall from the first chapter that this theory suggests that technology can be a solution to address social and political problems, including widespread and growing concerns about the democratic deficit (e.g., declining turnout, growing apathy, eroding trust, etc.). Although our results do not speak to this question directly (since we did not ask respondents about their views regarding technology's ability to solve political problems), our work nevertheless provides some relevant insights.

First, online voting is expected to address low turnout – and nowhere is this more applicable than in municipal elections, where turnout is routinely less than 50 per cent (Andrews and Pruysers 2022). The existing evidence regarding online voting and turnout, however, is mixed. Some, such as Goodman and Stokes (2020), who look at the Ontario case specifically, have identified modest effects for online voting and turnout. Other assessments, by contrast, which look at other countries such as Switzerland, are less convinced: Petitpas et al. (2021, 1), for example, have written that online voting "does not seem to have to have measurable effects on turnout." Our data provide some support to this later contention as online voters in our study resemble traditional paper voters in many ways. Chapter 4 revealed that, unlike voters aged thirty-five and older, younger voters are not more likely to vote online. Such findings raise questions about the ability of online voting to mobilize new cohorts of voters into the electoral process. On the other hand, our data also reveal some benefits. Specifically, the adoption of online voting appears to result in increases in positive democratic attitudes, including satisfaction with democracy. In this regard, electors do not need to cast a ballot online to receive the benefit; the mere availability of online voting in their municipality increases their satisfaction. It is likely fair to conclude that online voting has some potential benefits to offer, but it is not a silver bullet to address the democratic malaise felt by many democracies worldwide. This conclusion has been stated again and again in online voting research in Ontario (Goodman et al. 2010; Goodman and Gabel 2020). In fact, even in jurisdictions where support for online voting is high, a significant portion of actors in each of the cohorts we examined – voters, candidates, and administrators – remain skeptical of both online voting and its democratic impacts. Such skepticism is consistent with the fact that nearly half of municipalities in the province, representing a sizable majority of Ontarians, have opted against online voting.

To recap, this book has pointed to important lessons about three major topics: first, our results are an important reminder that municipal politics matters. Attitudes and preferences that are formed with respect to local politics can spill over and inform attitudes about other jurisdictions. Second, there may be a potentially unique relationship between overly permissive legislation and the absence of regulation, and adoption. While a lack of municipal oversight via the absence of legislative and regulatory details contributed to easy, early adoption as municipalities had tremendous freedom to experiment, "laggards" may be waiting for standards or further legislative direction before they adopt the voting technology. Finally, our results suggest that claims of tech-solutionism are overstated. While online voting undoubtedly offers some important benefits, it is not a singular solution to the democratic malaise that has characterized contemporary democratic politics.

LESSONS STILL TO BE LEARNED

In addition to teaching us a great deal about how Ontarians (in the role of electors, candidates, or administrators) view and behave towards online voting, this book demonstrates just how fertile the topic of online voting is for social researchers. Though we have answered many novel questions here, our work points to several new ones for researchers to consider going forward, to understand the causes, consequences, and correlates of online voting use in Ontario. These questions should be viewed considering the steep growth in online voting in the province, as outlined in chapter 2. Readers will recall that, according to Rogers' (2003) theory of the diffusion of technology across society over time, Ontario is now entering the "late majority" phase of the adoption of online voting. Whether growth continues or stagnates remains to be seen, but the future of online voting, both in Ontario and elsewhere, may depend upon the answers to important social science research questions. In other words, research on online voting is of practical, rather than just academic, interest. Decision makers in municipalities in Ontario and other provinces, at the provincial and federal levels, and outside of Canada, can learn a great deal from the experience of Ontario's towns and cities.

We therefore use the closing pages of this book to propose several research questions that can inform future debates on this topic. Important questions remain about online voting's impact on electors, candidates, and administrators, about the features of online voting systems that might be best suited to different types of municipalities, the long-term effects of the COVID-19 pandemic on the administration of local elections, and how security concerns might be successfully addressed. Though some of these matters have been investigated to some extent in other settings, they need to be fully examined in Canada, as the answers may be context dependent.

Though our research has added substantially to our collective understanding of the orientations of electors and elites in Ontario, given the relative paucity of research on this subject, our work represents but a sizable scratch on the surface of this field of study. Many important questions remain to be asked and answered regarding how relevant political actors view and react to internet voting.

Electors are the backbone and most studied group of any democracy, and there remains a great deal to be learned about how Canadians view and react to internet voting. We have shown here that support for the use of online voting is quite high among our sample, but research should delve into greater detail on the precise reasons for support or opposition to online voting. For instance, we know that security concerns are an important consideration for electors, but what exactly is it that some electors are most worried about, and can these concerns be addressed by service providers? A related and particularly promising topic of study of this group is persuasion. It is unclear how firmly anchored attitudes towards online voting are. Can attitudes be changed and, if so, how? What types of messages or interventions might be effective in this respect, and who is more or less likely to change views? A third set of questions about electors is if and how attitudes towards online voting are shaped by one's personal experience but also the experience of other Canadians. How and why does experience with online voting at one level of government affect attitudes towards the potential use of the voting mode at other levels? Does knowledge of the experience of others affect such views? In a federation like Canada, where election campaigns at every level of government include discussions (at least by the media) of the appropriateness of online voting, there is great value in determining how receptive Canadians are to electoral modernization and experimentation or many forms. Discussions about the adoption of online voting are not going away, and decision makers need to be as informed as possible regarding the wishes of those who they serve.

Candidates are another central part of our democracy, and this group is no less worthy of future study than electors. Indeed, there is reason to believe that this group is of particular relevance to the topic of online voting. As we saw in chapter 5, candidates have an important role to play in educating the public about how to navigate the online voting process. Many reported having done so as part of their campaign. A number of outstanding questions remain about candidates, including more detail on why it is that candidates support or oppose the use of online voting, whether the use of online voting attracts or repels certain types of candidates, and if any types of candidates do actually benefit or suffer from the use of internet voting (recall that we focused only on perceptions of benefit in chapter 5). Candidates also have the potential to influence the views of electors regarding online voting and, if successful in their election campaigns, to participate directly in discussions about the voting methods used in their municipalities. To understand the future growth (or lack thereof) in online voting in Ontario, therefore, this group must be of central concern.

Another major contribution here has been the focus on electoral administrators, who, given their importance to relevant decision-making processes, have been vastly understudied in existing research. Still, significant questions remain about this group. First, a more detailed analysis of the relationships between administrators would help to understand the patterns of diffusion of online voting. What networks, formal or otherwise, exist and what types of information are shared via these networks? Furthermore, how has the involvement of online voting vendors affected online voting approaches and uptake? Second, the motivations of these individuals need to be better understood. What are their priorities when making decisions on voting methods, and how do these motivations vary across cities? Third, we see great value in an examination of the compatibility of the views of administrators with those of electors. These individuals are insulated from the democratic pressures in a way that elected officials are not. This provides them with the freedom that can sometimes be necessary to make difficult decisions, but the argument could easily be made that administrators should be cognizant of the wishes of the citizenry they represent. We have found administrators to be particularly amenable to aiding our work on Ontario, and we expect them to be invaluable and important partners on future research of this type.

Finally, it is important to consider this constellation of actors – electors, candidates, and administrators – holistically. This book provides some insight into how the views of members of these groups compare to one another, but much more can be done on this front. How do the groups view the advantages and challenges brought about by online voting? Do different priorities drive their opinions? Importantly, what happens when the views of the groups are different: whose views win out, and whose views should win out? A thorough evaluation and comparison of the orientations of these groups, both in Ontario and in other contexts, can go a long way towards explaining rates and patterns of growth of online voting.

Perhaps the most important puzzle involving data from these three groups is the question of how much each actor matters for decisions regarding the adoption of online voting. Here, researchers have an ideal opportunity to study institutional change as it happens. Online voting is growing not just in Ontario, but consideration of the voting reform is happening in other places. As part of a university research project where Elections Quebec and the City of Longueuil served as partners, a citizens' assembly considered four voting reforms in the summer of 2023, including online voting. There has also been discussion of possible use in municipalities in British Columbia and Alberta (Kamenova and Goodman 2015). Online voting also continues to be adopted at a rapid rate by municipalities in Nova Scotia. Researchers therefore have the chance to study electors, candidates, and administrators in settings where debates over online voting are ongoing but also where this reform has a realistic chance of being adopted. Such research can help us understand with more clarity why online voting is growing the way that it is and the specific factors that play a role in its adoption or in decisions not to proceed.

In addition to research into electors, candidates, and administrators, a second set of new research questions revolves around the specific features of remote voting and precisely what methods are best (or worst) for municipalities of different types. With the experience of hundreds of municipalities and several election cycles spanning nearly two decades, decision makers now have a great deal of data available to them about how different variations in approaches function. Municipalities have provided ample data in terms of variation in the length of fielding dates of online voting, the types of authentication processes used, options for verification, and the other voting modes used to complement the online ballots (either in-person, telephone, or mail). Coupled with the large number of cases represented by Ontario's numerous municipalities, this variation presents an ideal situation for social researchers to study key questions. The opportunity exists for a thorough examination of how each of these factors, as well as other types of variation, are related to the success (however defined) of the adoption of online voting. For example, though research findings are mixed with respect to the effects of online voting on turnout, it is possible that different combinations of these factors produce different outcomes than others, in different settings. Notably, one article finds that 35 per cent fewer voters vote online when a two-step authentication approach is required (Goodman and Stokes 2020); such impacts could be felt from other aspects of variation in adoption and application. Furthermore, it could be the case that different deployment approaches are better suited to municipalities of various types, based upon factors such as size, density, or sociodemographic composition. Ontario's municipalities provide the sample size necessary to delve into the effects observed in each of these types of systems.

Perhaps principal among the dimensions worthy of study of variation is city size. For proponents of online voting in Ontario, it is no doubt frustrating that large cities have been more reluctant to adopt the voting mode; Markham and Vaughan are the only cities of the largest ten in the province to have adopted online voting. What is it about large municipalities that makes them less willing to run online elections? Conversely, is there something about small municipalities that drives them to online voting? Cities of different sizes face different challenges and constraints, and which of these are responsible for the vastly different decisions made based on city size? Might different types of online voting systems appeal to municipalities of different sizes and why? Based on informal conversations with officials in large cities such as Toronto and Ottawa a key consideration is security.

The City of Toronto had authorized an online advance poll voting pilot for persons with disabilities for the 2014 municipal election but cancelled the project due to hesitations regarding technology and security after consulting with professors in software engineering and information systems (City of Toronto 2014). In their report, the professors noted, "From a security design perspective, internet voting is a particularly challenging problem and carries the greatest number of risks of any ballot casting method." Election administrators have continued to recommend that the City of Toronto not proceed with online voting for municipal elections due to perceived security risks (City of Toronto 2016; City of Toronto 2020). In the 2022 municipal elections Toronto opted for voting by mail as an alternative convenience voting mode.

While not planning an official project, the City of Ottawa continues to share similar concerns to Toronto. In addition to possible security risks, the city also identified platform stability and availability as risks to conducting an election supported by online voting. In recent reports, city staff further outlined additional concerns related to internet voting, including the lack of standards, absence of a physical paper trail, poor quality of the voters list, presumed cost, and the disenfranchisement of certain electors, and possibilities for the exacerbation of the digital divide (City of Ottawa 2022; City of Ottawa 2023). Finally, elections in larger cities can carry a greater degree of importance in the eyes of voters. This, coupled with the unique political sensitivities faced by some big cities, creates a different profile of risk exposure, which has prevented some larger municipalities from pulling the trigger and adding online voting to their elections.

These experiences aside, there is a great deal of room for research into the exact conditions under which online voting has proven successful, and size is just one variable that should be considered. Until more large cities have positive experiences with online voting, however, it will be difficult to determine if current uses of online voting will be informative for debates of implementation either provincially or federally. However, in our focus group and interviews, administrators emphasized the efficiencies brought about by online elections and their surprise that higher levels of government had not bought into electronic elections to the same extent. As one administrator expressed, "I can't believe that the federal and provincial governments still do polls. It probably has to do with a lack of internet in remote communities. It's an easier way to do it, it works fine, you get your results within 30 minutes of the election. It's a lot cheaper to do it electronically."

A third set of questions that must be answered revolve around how COVID-19 has affected the rate and type of online voting adoption. Given the timing of our data collection, we are only partially able to consider this topic, from the perspective of election administrators. However, COVID has become the "elephant in the room" in many research fields; the effects of the pandemic must be addressed to properly understand a variety of social phenomena. This is particularly true as far as research on online voting is concerned. The use of remote voting (most notably, via mail) has increased drastically globally since the onset of the pandemic, and this trend has seen discussions of internet voting become more common than ever before. Governments of all types will have to demonstrate to their electorates that they value the wellbeing of their citizens. From this point forward, discussions of remote voting are not just about the health of a democracy but also of citizens themselves.

Research should identify the types of individuals who are most likely to abstain from in-person elections due to COVID or other health concerns and the extent to which online voting mitigates these effects. Are health concerns significant enough to overcome concerns about the security of online voting? Will the effects of COVID upon support for online voting last or will it be fleeting? There is good reason to expect that COVID will be a central consideration in both academic research and practical debates on internet voting for the foreseeable future.

While pandemic-related concerns seemingly increase the likelihood of adopting online voting, security and technical concerns are a major countervailing force, with the potential to dampen support for system use. In a context where the accuracy of election results is frequently being called into question (most famously by prominent Republicans in the United States), proponents of online voting have a particularly high bar to meet to convince others of the credibility of online election results. People need to be convinced that elections are safe and that votes are counted properly. A shortage of confidence in voting systems can have a variety of effects, including but not limited to effects upon turnout (among the electorate as a whole or among specific segments of the population) and attitudes towards the legitimacy of election outcomes and the right of winners to govern.

The development of new methods of securing electronic elections from external threats is an obvious priority for computer science researchers and vendors, but social researchers should investigate whether and how various types of technical advances influence the opinions of electors and elites. Do newer security methods, such as those that use "blockchain" technology or verifiable types of voting, provide greater peace of mind than more generic methods? How aware are electors of the security measures in place? Would any security measures be sufficient to provide enough confidence for, for example, decision makers and electors in large cities to embrace online voting? What types of public information campaigns can be employed to increase support for such systems? System security and public opinions towards security, should become a major preoccupation of social researchers. As part of this, an important area of research is going to be understanding what specific policies can best protect electoral integrity without stifling the innovation of online voting and other voting technologies. Such contributions will have an important impact on scholarly reviews but more importantly for practitioners.

Finally, though this book has largely avoided normative questions, this is perhaps the most important type of question for Canadians to consider, as far as internet voting is concerned. Online voting has benefits and costs, both real and perceived. In our view, the Canadian electorate has yet to sufficiently debate these issues, but social researchers can play a vitally important role by creating knowledge that can inform these important discussions. One of the benefits of the spread of online voting in Ontario elections is that it is forcing online voting into the public discourse and providing evidence of experience (both good and bad) with internet voting in the Canadian context. It is up to Canadians – electors and elites alike – to make informed decisions about how best to run elections of the future and to what extent this future will be a digital one.

Epilogue

Ontario's most recent municipal elections were held on 24 October 2022. It is, therefore, worthwhile to share some brief notes on the impacts of the 2022 election on online voting adoption and deployment in Ontario. As noted in the second chapter, the 2022 municipal elections were Ontario's most digitized to date, with 231 of the 414 local governments that run elections providing voters with the option to cast their ballots online. With this, Ontario positioned itself as the largest case study for internet voting usage in the world, necessarily raising a host of considerations about technical safety, voter trust, and changing attitudes about electoral reform amongst voters and elections administrators alike (Hayes et al. 2022).

Despite majority uptake of online voting systems in 2022, Ontario's municipal election saw a record low average turnout for the province at 36.3 per cent (Association of Municipalities of Ontario 2022).[1] Likewise, fewer candidates ran for office (6,306 in 2002 as opposed to 6,658 in 2018) (Association of Municipalities of Ontario 2022), suggesting a less competitive landscape in nearly every region across the province. Far more candidates were acclaimed than in 2018 as well (Association of Municipalities of Ontario 2022).

These figures led many to call for reform in the wake of the growing election malaise to increase voter engagement, with blame being spread widely among electors, candidates, and municipalities (Kiwanuka, 2022). Looming over this election was the presence of COVID-19. While most public health measures and restrictions in Ontario were removed by the time municipal elections took place in Ontario, it is conceivable that some voters declined to enter a polling station out of fear of contracting COVID-19. Vote methods, however, escaped much of this blame, demonstrating that few viewed the presence of internet voting as a culprit of relatively low voter engagement (or, conversely, as the savior to the problem).

The 2022 municipal elections faced a series of administrative controversies, albeit only one (that we are aware of) related to the use of internet voting.[2] In contrast to the 2018 municipal election, wherein forty-three municipalities were affected by a technical incident causing voting outages and delays in vote casting and counting (Hayes et al. 2022), the 2022 elections were run largely without a similar incident. In fact, as of this writing, we are aware of only seventeen[3] municipalities having had faced some type of technical or administrative disruption. Most of these municipalities (Barrie, Brantford, New Tecumseh, Prince Edward County, Sault Ste Marie, Toronto, Wasaga Beach, Scugog, and Oro-Medonte) experienced some delay in counting and announcing results on election night. Greater Sudbury experienced a delay in processing ballots in some on-site locations using tabulators, while Peterborough's election website temporarily crashed on election day, causing some confusion finding polling locations until it was restored. Thunder Bay and Vaughan experienced delays in opening a few voting stations on election day, leading to slight extensions in the voting period at those locations.

Three municipalities – Cambridge, Dryden, and Hamilton – declared emergencies under s.53 of the Municipal Election Act.[4] None of these declarations, however, resulted from internet voting issues. Electors in Cambridge were provided with ballots that did not have two school board trustee candidates listed, while ballots in Dryden allowed electors to vote in more than one school board race. Meanwhile, some voters in Hamilton experienced an hour delay in poll openings on election day. The clerk, in this instance, used her ability to extend voting hours. Only Collingwood experienced technical challenges related to online voting when voters were faced with a thirty-minute delay in accessing the online voting system. To remedy this incident, voting was extended until 9:00 pm to allow anyone affected to comfortably cast their ballot.

Given the relatively smooth deployment of internet voting in 2022 and the record low level of turnout we can likely expect increased calls for the use of online voting in the 2026 municipal elections. Data from our focus group and interviews likewise suggest a consensus among elections administrators that, despite potentially not having perfect conditions to expand use of internet voting, that municipal elections in Ontario have a digital future that will eventually integrate into a "digital way of living."

While a digital elections future for local governments in Ontario is expected, the transition is likely to continue to occur incrementally. Our focus group participants and interviewees also expressed the view that change would be incremental in the coming years and decades. Concerns were raised about the elimination of paper ballots but also about electoral integrity and security. Indeed, one official commented, "I don't expect us, even in 2026, to adopt Internet voting and replace the paper ballots outright. It takes time. My colleagues in Markham still offer paper ballots and they started Internet voting back in 2003." Other officials, by comparison, focused on vendors, noting that improvements to current options are required before broader uptake occurs, particularly among the largest municipalities. This perspective was captured by one clerk who remarked, "I don't think we're going to see a trend of the larger jurisdictions going exclusively online until they're able to assure themselves that the vendors are providing a product which will meet their standards." The lessons here are that municipal elections in Ontario will likely continue to become increasingly digital in terms of expansion in uptake and scope of online voting but this will likely not happen quickly. There are important obstacles to be overcome before the system is implemented more fully across the province, including concerns about electoral integrity and security and garnering public support for the voting mode. Social scientists will have an important part to play in this process of growth, as they help us to understand how electors and elites view online voting.

Appendices

APPENDIX 1.1: LIST OF MUNICIPALITIES THAT ADOPTED ONLINE VOTING IN 2018 AND 2022

2018 (177)

Addington Highlands, Adelaide-Metcalfe, Ajax, Alfred and Plantagenet, Alnwick/Haldimand, Amaranth, Arnprior, Ashfield-Colborne-Wawanosh, Asphodel-Norwood, Augusta, Aurora, Aylmer, Belleville, Blue Mountains, Bluewater, Bracebridge, Bradford West Gwillimbury, Brantford, Brockton, Brockville, Burlington, Cambridge, Carleton Place, Carling, Carlow/Mayo, Casselman, Cavan-Monaghan, Central Frontenac, Central Huron, Centre Hastings, Centre Wellington, Champlain, Chatham-Kent, Clarence-Rockland, Clearview, Cobourg, Collingwood, Deep River, Douro-Dummer, Dryden, East Zorra-Tavistock, Edwardsburgh/Cardinal, Elizabethtown-Kitley, Fort Frances, Frontenac Islands, Gananoque, Georgian Bay, Georgian Bluffs, Goderich, Grand Valley, Gravenhurst, Greater Madawaska, Greater Napanee, Greater Sudbury, Greenstone, Grey Highlands, Grimsby, Hamilton, Hanover, Hastings Highlands, Havelock-Belmont-Methuen, Hawkesbury, Howick, Huntsville, Huron East, Huron-Kinloss, Innisfil, Kawartha Lakes, Kenora, Killarney, Kincardine, Kingston, Lake of Bays, Lambton Shores, Lanark Highlands, Lasalle, Laurentian Valley, Leamington, Leeds and the Thousand Islands, Limerick, Lincoln, Loyalist, Lucan Biddulph, Markham, Marmora and Lake, McDougall, McKellar, McNab-Braeside, Meaford, Melancthon, Merrickville-Wolford, Middlesex Centre, Minden Hills, Mississippi Mills, Mono, Montague, Morris-Turnberry, Mulmur, Muskoka Lakes, Newmarket,

North Dumfries, North Dundas, North Glengarry, North Grenville, North Huron, North Kawartha, North Middlesex, North Stormont, Northern Bruce Peninsula, Oil Springs, Oro-Medonte, Otonabee-South Monaghan, Owen Sound, Parry Sound, Pembroke, Penetanguishene, Perth East, Perth Town, Petawawa, Peterborough, Petrolia, Pickering, Plympton-Wyoming, Point Edward, Port Hope, Prescott, Prince Edward County, Quinte West, Ramara, Red Lake, Renfrew, Rideau Lakes, Russell, Sarnia, Saugeen Shores, Seguin, Selwyn, Shelburne, Shuniah, Sioux Lookout, Smiths Falls, South Bruce, South Dundas, South Frontenac, South Glengarry, South Huron, South Stormont, South-West Oxford, Southgate, Southwest Middlesex, Springwater, St Thomas, Stone Mills, Stratford, Strathroy-Caradoc, Tay Valley, Tecumseh, Thames Centre, The Archipelago, The Nation, Thunder Bay, Tillsonburg, Timmins, Trent Hills, Trent Lakes, Tudor and Cashel, Tweed, Warwick, Wasaga Beach, Wawa, Wellesley, West Elgin, West Grey, West Perth, Whitestone, Whitewater Region, Woolwich.

Note that, for 2022, the list contains notes (in brackets). Notes describe changes made since 2018, and indicate those elections that were acclaimed.

2022 (231)

Addington Highlands, Adelaide-Metcalfe, Adjala-Tosorontio (Adopted), Ajax, Alfred and Plantagenet, Algonquin Highlands (Adopted), Alnwick/Haldimand, Amaranth, Arnprior, Arran-Elderslie (Adopted), Ashfield-Colborne-Wawanosh, Asphodel-Norwood, Atikokan (Adopted), Augusta, Aurora, Aylmer, Baldwin (Adopted), Bancroft (Adopted), Barrie (Adopted), Belleville, Black River-Matheson (Adopted), Blind River (Acclaimed), Blue Mountains, Bluewater, Bracebridge, Bradford West Gwillimbury, Brant (Adopted), Brantford, Brighton (Adopted), Brockton, Brockville, Burlington, Calvin (Adopted), Cambridge, Carleton Place, Carling, Carlow/Mayo, Casselman, Cavan-Monaghan, Central Frontenac, Central Huron, Centre Hastings, Centre Wellington, Champlain, Chapleau (Acclaimed), Chatham-Kent, Clarence-Rockland, Clarington (Adopted), Clearview, Cobourg, Cochrane (Adopted), Collingwood, Cramahe (Adopted), Deep River, Douro-Dummer, Drummond/North Elmsley (Acclaimed), Dryden, Dysart et al (Adopted), Ear Falls (Adopted), East Garafraxa (Acclaimed), East Gwillimbury (Adopted), East Hawkesbury (Adopted), East Zorra-Tavistock, Edwardsburgh/Cardinal, Elizabethtown-Kitley, Espanola (Adopted), Fort Frances, French River (Adopted), Front of Yonge (Acclaimed), Frontenac Islands, Gananoque, Georgian Bay, Georgian Bluffs, Georgina (Adopted), Goderich, Grand Valley, Gravenhurst, Greater Madawaska, Greater Napanee, Greater Sudbury, Greenstone, Grey Highlands, Grimsby, Haldimand (Adopted), Halton Hills (Adopted), Hamilton Township (Adopted), Hanover (Adopted), Hastings Highlands, Havelock-Belmont-Methuen, Hawkesbury (Dropped), Highlands East (Adopted), Hornepayne (Acclaimed), Howick (Acclaimed), Huntsville, Huron East, Huron Shores (Adopted), Huron-Kinloss, Ignace (Adopted), Innisfil, Kawartha Lakes, Kenora, Killarney, Kincardine, Kingston, Lake of Bays, Lambton Shores, Lanark Highlands, LaSalle, Laurentian Valley, Leamington (Dropped), Leeds and the Thousand Islands, Limerick, Lincoln, Loyalist, Lucan Biddulph, Madoc (Adopted), Magnetawan (Adopted), Malahide (Adopted), Manitouwadge (Adopted), Mapleton (Adopted), Marathon (Adopted), Markham, Marmora and Lake, McDougall, McKellar, McNab-Braeside, Meaford (Dropped), Melancthon, Merrickville-Wolford, Middlesex Centre, Midland (Adopted), Minden Hills, Mississippi Mills, Mono, Montague, Morris-Turnberry, Mulmur, Muskoka Lakes, New Tecumseth (Adopted), Newmarket, North Bay (Adopted), North Dumfries, North Dundas, North Frontenac (Adopted), North Glengarry, North Grenville, North Huron, North Kawartha, North Middlesex, North Shore (Adopted), North Stormont, Northern Bruce Peninsula, Oil Springs (Dropped), Oliver Paipoonge (Adopted), Oro-Medonte (Dropped), Otonabee-South Monaghan, Owen Sound, Parry Sound, Pembroke, Penetanguishene, Perth, Perth East, Petawawa, Peterborough, Petrolia, Pickering, Plympton-Wyoming, Point Edward, Port Hope, Prescott, Prince Edward County, Quinte West, Ramara, Red Lake, Renfrew, Richmond Hill (Adopted), Rideau Lakes, Russell, Sables-Spanish Rivers (Adopted), Sarnia, Saugeen Shores, Scugog (Adopted), Seguin, Selwyn, Severn (Adopted), Shelburne, Shuniah, Sioux Lookout, Smiths Falls, South Bruce, South Bruce Peninsula (Adopted), South Dundas, South Frontenac, South Glengarry, South Huron, South Stormont, South-West Oxford, Southgate, Southwest Middlesex, Springwater, St Thomas, Stirling-Rawdon (Adopted), Stone Mills, Stratford, Strathroy-Caradoc, Tay (Acclaimed), Tay Valley, Tecumseh, Temiskaming Shores (Adopted), Thames Centre, The Archipelago (Acclaimed), The

Nation, Thorold (Adopted), Thunder Bay, Tillsonburg, Timmins, Trent Hills, Trent Lakes, Tudor and Cashel, Tweed, Tyendinaga (Adopted), Vaughan (Adopted), Warwick, Wasaga Beach, Wawa, Wellesley, West Elgin, West Grey, West Lincoln (Adopted), West Perth, Whitestone, Whitewater, Wilmot (Adopted), Wollaston (Adopted), Woolwich, Zorra (Adopted)

APPENDIX 3.1: SURVEY QUESTIONS

Experimental outcome variables
Treatment 1: City group specific preambles.

Group 1: In 2018, internet voting was added as a voting option for municipal elections in [city name]. Residents could vote either ONLINE or IN PERSON (using traditional paper ballots), for local elections.

Group 2: Internet voting has been an option for municipal election in [city name] since [2014/2010]. In 2018, residents could vote either ONLINE or IN PERSON (using traditional ballots), for local elections.

Group 3: In 2018, municipal elections in [city name] were run completely online. That is, residents COULD vote ONLINE, but they COULD NOT vote IN PERSON (using traditional paper ballots) for local elections.

Group 4: In 2018, municipal elections in Guelph were run using IN PERSON voting (using traditional paper ballots). In the 2014 local elections, residents were able to vote either ONLINE or IN PERSON, but the online option was not offered in 2018.
Treatment 2: No preamble (control).

For each statement below, please indicate if you strongly agree, somewhat agree, somewhat disagree, or strongly disagree.

Table A3.I.1 | Experimental outcome questions

	Strongly agree	Somewhat agree	Somewhat disagree	Strongly disagree	Don't know
I am satisfied with the quality of democracy in [city name].	❑	❑	❑	❑	❑
Internet voting should be available in MUNICIPAL elections	❑	❑	❑	❑	❑
Internet voting should be available in PROVINCIAL elections	❑	❑	❑	❑	❑
Internet voting should be available in FEDERAL elections	❑	❑	❑	❑	❑

Variable for interaction results discussed in conclusion
Voting method: In the recent Municipal Election did you vote ...

❑ In person by paper
❑ Online
❑ By telephone
❑ By mail
❑ Don't know/Don't remember

Variables for Appendices 3-II and 3-III
Age: In what year were you born?
Please enter your year of birth in the box below.

❑ Prefer not to say

Gender: Are you:

- ❑ Male
- ❑ Female
- ❑ Other/gender non-binary
- ❑ Prefer not to say

Race: Do you identify as:

- ❑ White
- ❑ Indigenous (e.g. First Nations, Inuit, Métis)
- ❑ Visible minority (e.g. South Asian, Chinese, Black, Filipino, Arab,
- ❑ Southeast Asian, West Asian, Korean, Japanese, etc.)
- ❑ Other (please specify) (Open ended box)
- ❑ Prefer not to answer

Immigrant status: Were you born in Canada?

- ❑ Yes
- ❑ No
- ❑ Prefer not to say/Don't know

University education: What is the highest level of education that you have completed?

- ❑ No schooling
- ❑ Some elementary school
- ❑ Completed elementary school
- ❑ Some secondary/high school
- ❑ Completed secondary/high school
- ❑ Some technical, community college
- ❑ Completed technical, community college
- ❑ Some university
- ❑ Bachelor's degree
- ❑ Master's degree
- ❑ Professional degree or doctorate
- ❑ Prefer not to say/Don't know

(Dis)ability: Are you a person with a disability?

- ❑ Yes
- ❑ No
- ❑ Don't know/prefer not to answer

Income: The confidentiality of your responses to this survey is guaranteed, and knowing the approximate income of respondents helps researchers to identify important patterns and trends.

Which of the following best indicates your annual household income before taxes?

- ❑ Less than $25,000
- ❑ $25,000–$49,999
- ❑ $50,000–$74,999
- ❑ $75,000–$99,999
- ❑ $100,000–$124,999
- ❑ $125,000–$149,999
- ❑ $150,000–$174,999
- ❑ $175,000–$199,999
- ❑ $200,000 or more
- ❑ Prefer not to say/Don't know

Home owner: Do you or someone else in your household own your home?

- ❑ Yes
- ❑ No
- ❑ Don't know/prefer not to answer

Voter turnout: In each election we find that a lot of people were not able to vote because they were not registered, they were sick, or they did not have time. Others do not want to vote.

Did you vote in the recent MUNICIPAL election in [CITY NAME]? Please select the statement that best describes you.

- ❑ I did not vote in the election
- ❑ I thought about voting but didn't
- ❑ I usually vote but didn't in that election
- ❑ I am sure I voted in the election
- ❑ Don't remember/Don't know

Table A3.II.1 | Balance Tests – Logistic regression models

	Group 1	Group 2	Group 3	Group 4
Age	0.00 (0.00)	0.00 (0.00)	0.01 (0.01)	0.01 (0.01)*
Female	-0.03 (0.10)	0.14 (0.14)	0.01 (0.16)	-0.02 (0.19)
Racialized	-0.13 (0.17)	-0.01 (0.24)	0.15 (0.24)	-0.57 (0.33)
Immigrant	-0.29 (0.16)	-0.35 (0.20)	-0.07 (0.23)	-0.13 (0.29)
University education	0.02 (0.11)	-0.03 (0.15)	-0.11 (0.17)	0.03 (0.20)
High income	0.01 (0.11)	-0.18 (0.16)	-0.26 (0.18)	0.02 (0.21)
Home owner	-0.07 (0.14)	-0.04 (0.18)	0.21 (0.22)	0.15 (0.24)
Disabled	0.24 (0.15)	0.04 (0.21)	0.10 (0.23)	-0.11 (0.28)
Voter	0.05 (0.12)	0.15 (0.16)	-0.07 (0.19)	0.20 (0.20)
Bradford West Gwillimbury	Base/omitted			
Kawartha Lakes	-0.14 (0.26)			
Pickering	0.25 (0.25)			
Sarnia	0.05 (0.25)			
St Thomas	-0.04 (0.28)			
Thunder Bay	0.21 (0.24)			
Brantford		Base/omitted		
Cambridge		0.40 (0.28)		
Chatham-Kent		0.28 (0.30)		
Kingston		-0.16 (0.28)		
Timmins		0.23 (0.38)		
Quinte West		0.15 (0.40)		
Belleville		0.40 (0.36)		
Burlington		0.44 (0.26)		
Markham		0.37 (0.28)		
Ajax			Base/omitted	
Sudbury			-0.20 (0.21)	
Newmarket			-0.23 (0.25)	
Innisfil			0.06 (0.31)	
Guelph				Base/omitted
Constant	-0.20 (0.30)	-0.19 (0.36)	-0.31 (0.40)	-0.81 (0.37)*
N	1,607	890	679	493
Pseudo R2	0.0073	0.0126	0.0100	0.0243

Note: Entries report coefficients and standard errors (in parentheses)

*:p<0.05, **:p<0.01

APPENDIX 3.II: BALANCE TESTS

Table A3.II.1 shows the results of four logistic regression models – one for each city group. The outcome variable in each model is the experimental treatment (0/1). Explanatory variables include a series of sociodemographic variables, voter turnout (versus abstainer), and fixed effects for city. Age is coded in years, and all other variables are dummies (divided at the median when not already binary). Significant results indicate a lack of balance between experimental groups.

The above table reveals that group 4 is unbalanced in one dimension – age. To confirm the findings from the body of the chapter, a subsequent analysis must be performed in order to account for this lack of balance in this one group. As such, we present here a series of ordered logistic regression models (one for each of the outcome variables considered in figures 3-1 to 3-4. The explanatory variables include the experimental treatment and the age variable. Results reveal that the substantive conclusions from the uncontrolled analyses is unchanged. The experimental treatment is statistically insignificant in the "satisfaction" model and significant and in the negative direction in the models where the outcome variables indicate support for the use of online voting. These results confirm that the lack of balance on age is not problematic in this instance.

Table A3.II.2 | Experimental analysis with control for Age – Ordered logistic regression

	Satisfaction with local democracy	Support for online voting		
		Local	Provincial	Federal
Experimental treatment	-0.17 (0.16)	-0.46 (0.16)**	-0.34 (0.16)*	-0.34 (0.15)*
Age	0.00 (0.00)	-0.02 (0.00)**	-0.01 (0.00)*	-0.01 (0.00)
Cut 1	-3.15 (0.32)	-3.12 (0.28)	-2.23 (0.26)	-1.90 (0.26)
Cut 2	-1.48 (0.26)	-2.25 (0.27)	-1.36 (0.25)	-1.21 (0.25)
Cut 3	0.90 (0.25)	-0.95 (0.25)	-0.19 (0.24)	-0.01 (0.24)
N	566	566	566	566
Pseudo R2	0.0011	0.0196	0.0062	0.0045

Note: Entries report coefficients and standard errors (in parentheses)
*:p<0.05, **:p<0.01

APPENDIX 3.III: CORRELATES OF OUTCOME VARIABLES

The following table shows the results of ordered logistic regression models, for each of the four outcome variables of interest in this chapter. Explanatory variables include a series of sociodemographic variables, voter turnout (versus abstainer), and fixed effects for city. Age is coded in years, and all other variables are dummies (divided at the median when not already binary). Note that the baseline category for city is Bradford West Gwillimbury.

Table A3.III.1 | Correlates of outcome variables

	Satisfaction with local democracy	Support for online voting		
		Local	Provincial	Federal
Age	0.01 (0.00)**	0.00 (0.00)	0.00 (0.00)	0.01 (0.00)*
Female	-0.21 (0.07)**	0.18 (0.07)**	0.15 (0.07)*	0.13 (0.07)*
Racialized	0.02 (0.11)	-0.21 (0.11)	-0.19 (0.11)	-0.14 (0.11)
Immigrant	0.06 (0.10)	0.11 (0.10)	0.07 (0.10)	0.04 (0.10)
University education	0.17 (0.07)*	0.09 (0.07)	0.05 (0.07)	0.09 (0.07)
High income	0.06 (0.07)	0.31 (0.07)**	0.26 (0.07)**	0.29 (0.07)**
Home owner	0.12 (0.08)	0.12 (0.09)	0.08 (0.09)	0.07 (0.08)
Disabled	-0.23 (0.09)*	-0.15 (0.10)	-0.13 (0.09)	-0.07 (0.10)
Voter	0.46 (0.07)**	-0.01 (0.08)	-0.05 (0.08)	-0.03 (0.08)
Bradford West Gwillimbury		Baseline		
Kawartha Lakes	-1.67 (0.25)**	0.03 (0.25)	0.04 (0.24)	-0.02 (0.24)
Pickering	-1.12 (0.25)**	0.15 (0.24)	0.13 (0.23)	0.11 (0.24)
Sarnia	-1.51 (0.25)**	-0.06 (0.24)	-0.11 (0.23)	-0.12 (0.23)
St Thomas	-0.80 (0.27)**	0.23 (0.26)	0.30 (0.26)	0.25 (0.26)
Thunder Bay	-1.60 (0.24)**	0.48 (0.24)*	0.40 (0.23)	0.40 (0.23)
Brantford	-1.17 (0.29)**	0.02 (0.29)	0.08 (0.29)	-0.05 (0.29)
Cambridge	-1.13 (0.29)**	-0.10 (0.29)	-0.14 (0.28)	-0.24 (0.28)
Chatham-Kent	-1.13 (0.31)**	0.40 (0.31)	0.26 (0.30)	0.17 (0.30)

Table A3.III.1 | Correlates of outcome variables ... *continued*

	Satisfaction with local democracy	Support for online voting		
		Local	Provincial	Federal
Kingston	-0.95 (0.29)**	0.49 (0.30)	0.10 (0.28)	-0.05 (0.28)
Timmins	-1.09 (0.37)**	0.23 (0.38)	0.43 (0.39)	0.38 (0.39)
Quinte West	-0.35 (0.40)	0.33 (0.40)	-0.16 (0.39)	-0.15 (0.39)
Belleville	-0.76 (0.35)*	0.86 (0.40)*	0.62 (0.37)	0.35 (0.36)
Burlington	-0.69 (0.27)*	0.36 (0.27)	0.38 (0.27)	0.29 (0.27)
Markham	-1.02 (0.26)**	0.50 (0.26)	0.63 (0.25)*	0.51 (0.26)*
Ajax	-0.61 (0.27)*	0.28 (0.27)	0.11 (0.26)	0.08 (0.26)
Sudbury	-2.02 (0.24)**	0.07 (0.24)	0.02 (0.23)	-0.01 (0.24)
Newmarket	-0.73 (0.28)**	-0.25 (0.27)	-0.40 (0.26)	-0.37 (0.27)
Innisfil	-0.90 (0.33)**	-0.04 (0.33)	0.01 (0.32)	-0.11 (0.32)
Guelph	-1.04 (0.24)**	-0.46 (0.23)*	-0.54 (0.22)*	-0.59 (0.22)**
Cut 1	-3.34 (0.26)	-2.12 (0.25)	-1.84 (0.24)	-1.63 (0.24)
Cut 2	-2.00 (0.25)	-1.26 (0.25)	-1.02 (0.24)	-0.89 (0.24)
Cut 3	0.44 (0.25)	0.14 (0.25)	0.26 (0.24)	0.34 (0.24)
N	3, 669	3, 669	3, 669	3, 669
Pseudo R2	0.0374	0.0184	0.0174	0.0168

Note: Entries report coefficients and standard errors (in parentheses)
*:p<0.05, **:p<0.01

APPENDIX 4.1: SURVEY QUESTIONS

Elector Survey

<u>Voting method</u>
In the recent Municipal Election did you vote:

- ❑ In person by paper
- ❑ Online
- ❑ By telephone
- ❑ By mail
- ❑ Don't know/Don't remember

Digital literacy
How would you describe your ability to use the internet? Is it …

❑ Poor
❑ Fair
❑ Good
❑ Very good
❑ Don't know

Explanatory factors
Are you:

❑ Male
❑ Female
❑ Other/gender non-binary
❑ Prefer not to say

Were you born in Canada?

❑ Yes
❑ No
❑ Prefer not to say/Don't know

In what year were you born?
Please enter your year of birth in the box below.

❑ Prefer not to say (999)

Do you identify as:

❑ White
❑ Indigenous (e.g. First Nations, Inuit, Métis)
❑ Visible minority (e.g. South Asian, Chinese, Black, Filipino, Arab,
❑ Southeast Asian, West Asian, Korean, Japanese, etc.)
❑ Other (please specify) (Open ended box)
❑ Prefer not to answer

What is the highest level of education that you have completed?

❑ No schooling

- ❑ Some elementary school
- ❑ Completed elementary school
- ❑ Some secondary/high school
- ❑ Completed secondary/high school
- ❑ Some technical, community college
- ❑ Completed technical, community college
- ❑ Some university
- ❑ Bachelor's degree
- ❑ Master's degree
- ❑ Professional degree or doctorate
- ❑ Prefer not to say/Don't know

In politics people sometimes talk of left and right. Where would you place yourself on a scale from 0 to 10, where 0 means left and 10 means right?

- ❑ 0 (left)
- ❑ 1
- ❑ 2
- ❑ 3
- ❑ 4
- ❑ 5 (centre)
- ❑ 6
- ❑ 7
- ❑ 8
- ❑ 9
- ❑ 10 (right)
- ❑ Don't know/prefer not to say

<u>Perceptions of group voting method</u>

In many cities, residents are able to vote either online or in person. Of the following paired groups of individuals, which residents are MORE LIKELY to vote ONLINE? You have the option of choosing that you believe that paired groups would be EQUALLY likely to vote online. Considering the following pairs of individuals, which group would you expect to be MORE LIKELY to vote ONLINE?

Men	Women	The same
❑	❑	❑
Canadian born residents	Foreign born residents	The same
❑	❑	❑
People under 35	People over 35	The same
❑	❑	❑
Those with LOWER than average income	Those with HIGHER than average income	The same
❑	❑	❑
Visible minority residents	White residents	The same
❑	❑	❑
People with a university education	People without a university education	The same
❑	❑	❑
Homeowners	Renters	The same
❑	❑	❑
"Left-Wingers"	"Right-wingers"	The same
❑	❑	❑

Candidate Survey

Perceptions of who benefits from online voting

Which candidates benefit most from internet voting?

❑ Left-wing candidates
❑ Right-wing candidates
❑ Neither has an advantage
❑ Don't know/prefer not to say

Perceptions of group voting method:
Same as with elector survey

Incumbent
Are you the incumbent for this position?

❑ Yes
❑ No
❑ Don't know/prefer not to say

APPENDIX 4.II: FULL MODEL RESULTS FOR FIGURE 4.1

The following models show the results of logistic regression models where voting by internet (as opposed to by paper) serves as the outcome variable. Entries report marginal effects. The effects from the eight models are reported in figure 4.1, while the final model includes all variables simultaneously.

Table A4.II.1 | Full model results for figure 4.1

Female	0.02 (0.02)								0.05 (0.03)*
Under 35		-0.21 (0.03)***							-0.20 (0.04)***
University education			0.00 (0.02)						-0.01 (0.03)
High income				0.05 (0.02)**					0.02 (0.03)
Homeowner					0.16 (0.03)***				0.16 (0.04)***
Immigrant						-0.04 (0.03)			-0.04 (0.04)
Racialized							-0.20 (0.04)***		-0.11 (0.06)*
Left-of-centre								0.09 (0.03)***	0.11 (0.03)***
Prob. > chi2	0.335	0.000	0.827	0.028	0.000	0.169	0.000	0.001	0.000
Number of observations	2,239	2,175	2,247	1,973	2,235	2,246	2,135	1,262	1,063
Number of groups	15	15	15	15	15	15	15	15	15

Note: Entries report coefficients and standard errors (in parentheses)
*:p<0.05, **:p<0.01

APPENDIX 5.1: SURVEY QUESTIONS

To what extent to you agree with the following statement: Internet voting should be available in municipal elections.

- ❑ Strongly agree
- ❑ Somewhat agree
- ❑ Somewhat disagree
- ❑ Strongly disagree
- ❑ Don't know/prefer not to say

Political characteristics

Are you the incumbent?

- ❑ Yes
- ❑ No
- ❑ Don't know/prefer not to say

In politics people sometimes talk of left and right. Where would you place yourself on a scale from 0 to 10, where 0 means left and 10 means right?

- ❑ 0 (left)
- ❑ 1
- ❑ 2
- ❑ 3
- ❑ 4
- ❑ 5 (centre)
- ❑ 6
- ❑ 7
- ❑ 8
- ❑ 9
- ❑ 10 (right)

For which position are you contesting election?

- ❑ School board
- ❑ City council/councillor
- ❑ Regional chair or councillor
- ❑ Other

Sociodemographic characteristics
Age: In what year were you born?
Please enter your year of birth in the box below.

- ❑ Prefer not to say

Gender: Are you:

- ❑ Male
- ❑ Female
- ❑ Other/gender non-binary
- ❑ Prefer not to say

Race: Do you identify as:

- ❑ White
- ❑ Indigenous (e.g. First Nations, Inuit, Métis)
- ❑ Visible minority (e.g. South Asian, Chinese, Black, Filipino, Arab, Southeast Asian, West Asian, Korean, Japanese, etc.)
- ❑ Other (please specify) (Open ended box)
- ❑ Prefer not to answer

Immigrant status: Were you born in Canada?

- ❑ Yes
- ❑ No
- ❑ Prefer not to say/Don't know

University education: What is the highest level of education that you have completed?

- ❑ No schooling
- ❑ Some elementary school
- ❑ Completed elementary school
- ❑ Some secondary/high school
- ❑ Completed secondary/high school
- ❑ Some technical, community college
- ❑ Completed technical, community college
- ❑ Some university
- ❑ Bachelor's degree

- ❑ Master's degree
- ❑ Professional degree or doctorate
- ❑ Prefer not to say/Don't know

Personality

Here are a number of personality traits that may or may not apply to you. Please indicate the extent to which you agree or disagree that these traits apply to you. You should rate the extent to which the pair of traits applies, even if one characteristic applies more strongly than the other.

	Disagree strongly	Disagree moderately	Disagree a little	Neither agree nor disagree	Agree a little	Agree moderately	Agree strongly
Extraverted, enthusiastic	❑	❑	❑	❑	❑	❑	❑
Critical, quarrelsome	❑	❑	❑	❑	❑	❑	❑
Dependable, self-disciplined	❑	❑	❑	❑	❑	❑	❑
Anxious, easily upset	❑	❑	❑	❑	❑	❑	❑
Open to new experiences, complex	❑	❑	❑	❑	❑	❑	❑
Reserved, quiet	❑	❑	❑	❑	❑	❑	❑
Sympathetic, warm	❑	❑	❑	❑	❑	❑	❑
Disorganized, careless	❑	❑	❑	❑	❑	❑	❑
Calm, emotionally stable	❑	❑	❑	❑	❑	❑	❑
Conventional, uncreative	❑	❑	❑	❑	❑	❑	❑

❑ Prefer not to answer

APPENDIX 5.II: FULL TABLE RESULTS

Table A5.II.1 | Who benefits from online voting – Incumbent status

		Type of candidate	
		Challenger	Incumbent
Who benefits?	Incumbent	22.3%	23.9%
	Neither	56.7%	68.7%
	Challengers	21.0%	7.5%
	N	238	67

Table A5.II.2 | Who benefits from online voting – Ideology

		Type of candidate		
		Left-wing	Centrist	Right-wing
Who benefits?	Left-wing	18.6%	10.3%	9.2%
	Neither	72.9%	84.6%	82.5%
	Right-wing	8.6%	5.1%	5.5%
	N	70	117	87

Table A5.II.3 | Did online voting affect campaigning?

	Type of candidate				
	Challenger	Incumbent	Left-wing	Centrist	Right-wing
Yes	56.7%	50.6%	54.7%	50.0%	49.2%
No	43.3%	49.4%	45.3%	50.0%	50.9%
N	254	81	53	78	59

APPENDIX 6.1: SURVEY QUESTIONS

Who led online voting decision?

Who led the charge to adopt online voting in your municipality for 2022?

- ❑ Politicians (e.g. council, mayor/reeve)
- ❑ Clerk's office
- ❑ Senior executives/CAO
- ❑ Other (please specify)
- ❑ Don't know/prefer not to say

Importance of factors in adopting online voting

Please rate the importance of the following reasons for your municipality's decision on whether to adopt online voting. Responses options range from 0 (not at all important) to 10 (extremely important).

- ❑ Accessibility
- ❑ Convenience
- ❑ Public health and safety
- ❑ To improve voter turnout

Attitudes towards online voting

To what extent to you agree with the following statement: Internet voting should be available in municipal elections.
[Asked of administrators, electors, and candidates]

- ❑ Strongly agree
- ❑ Somewhat agree
- ❑ Somewhat disagree
- ❑ Strongly disagree
- ❑ Don't know/prefer not to say

Attitudes towards government intervention on turnout

To what extent to you agree with the following statement: Government should take action to maximize voter turnout in municipal elections. [Asked of administrators, electors, and candidates]

- ❑ Strongly agree
- ❑ Somewhat agree

- ❑ Somewhat disagree
- ❑ Strongly disagree
- ❑ Don't know/prefer not to say

Estimated support for online voting

A lot has changed since the 2018 Ontario Municipal elections. In your view, how supportive were Ontarians of the use of online voting in 2018?

- ❑ Mostly supportive
- ❑ Evenly split
- ❑ Mostly opposed
- ❑ Don't know/prefer not to say

In your view, how supportive of the use of online voting are Ontarians now (in 2022)?

- ❑ Mostly supportive
- ❑ Evenly split
- ❑ Mostly opposed
- ❑ Don't know/prefer not to say

Estimated effects of shocks

In your view, did the COVID-19 pandemic make the use of online voting more or less likely in your municipality?

- ❑ More likely
- ❑ Less likely
- ❑ Did not have an effect
- ❑ Don't know/prefer not to say

In your view, did the 2018 Dominion technical incident make the use of online voting more or less likely in your municipality?

- ❑ More likely
- ❑ Less likely
- ❑ Did not have an effect
- ❑ Don't know/prefer not to say

Notes

CHAPTER ONE

1 This is not to say municipal candidates have been fully ignored. Research has considered the personality profile of candidates (Scott and Mederios 2021), opportunity structures for diverse candidates (Spicer et al. 2017), as well as the competitive dynamics of candidate campaigns (Breux et al. 2019; Lucas et al. 2021).

2 While there is some debate regarding the definition of online voting and which elements of a vote need to take place "online," the definition we present here is consistent with the Council of Europe's CM/Rec(2017)5 on e-voting wherein votes are received and counted online. This document is regarded as the "international legal standard in the field" (Rodríguez-Pérez 2022).

3 Note, however, that the use of online voting in other contexts can be found even earlier (see, for example, the 2000 Arizona Democratic primary; see Solop 2001).

4 In Switzerland, for example, prior to the halting of the online voting program, the voting mode was only offered to a certain percentage of the voting population based on the level of security the system tested for (Puiggali et al. 2017). Even now, as online voting has resumed, it is only useable in certain areas (Federal Chancellery 2023).

5 A notable exception is the federal Conservative party.

6 These numbers are based on information obtained from online voting vendors and municipalities leading up to and following the 2022 municipal elections.

7 Two maps are included to highlight the northern and southern portions of the province.

8 Two of the five were smaller municipalities with electorates with fewer than 25,000 persons, while the other three had electorates between 75,000 and 100,000.
9 A small number of municipalities used online voting in 2018 but not in 2022, and we were unable to recruit any participants from these locations.

CHAPTER TWO

1 The Act is silent in expressing a preference on voting method, as long as a first-past-the-post system is used. The provincial government revoked a section of the Act that allowed municipalities to use ranked ballots on 20 November 2020.
2 This is not only a security issue, as the number of steps it takes for voters to access and cast their ballots affects their voter participation (Goodman and Stokes 2020) and their satisfaction (Goodman and Harvey 2022) which can impact their use of the technology and attitudes towards it.
3 Data from the 2019 Canadian Election Study, a survey of electors during the 2019 federal election, reveal similar patterns of support: a majority of respondents said that they would make use of online voting if it were available (Stephenson et al. 2020).
4 There was not demand for increased security until the 2018 technical incident where voters were prevented from casting ballots on election day as the system of one vendor slowed so that the platform was not useable (Cardillo et al., 2019).
5 These include Dominion Voting Systems, Intelivote, Neuvote, Scytl, Simply Voting, Smartmatic, and Voatz. Neuvote and Smartmatic provided services in partnership.
6 Some computer scientists argue that blockchain is not a solution to online voting and in fact causes more problems than it solves (Park et al., 2021).
7 Percentages are based upon a denominator of 414. Though there are 444 municipalities in Ontario, only 414 hold elections.
8 Data on voting method are unavailable from four of these forty-four cities, so this average is based upon the forty cities which we have information on.
9 Innovation is "an idea, practice, or object perceived as new by an individual" (Rogers and Shoemaker 1971) and the "process by which new products and techniques are introduced into the economic system" (Nelson 1968).
10 When adoption is not 100 per cent, the five categories are not completely exhaustive, as there is another category not shown: non-adopters.

11 These include Champlain, Clarence-Rockland, East Hawkesbury, Hawkesbury, North Dundas, North Glengarry, North Stormont, South Dundas, South Glengarry, South Stormont, and The Nation (Goodman et al. 2010).

12 For example, to cover the costs to develop broadband technologies and adopt online voting in 2003, the city obtained funding through the Applied Research in Interactive Media Program, a program sponsored by CANARIE and the Department of Canadian Heritage (Kapica 2003; Goodman et al. 2010). It also partnered with Delvinia, to assess the effectiveness of online voting and support voter education. Delvinia carried out surveys with online and paper voters to evaluate different user experiences and created a digital Interactive Guide to facilitate voter outreach (Delvinia 2003). In addition to these partnerships, the City of Markham partnered with a York University professor to perform a risk assessment of all voting modes, including traditional paper and online ballots (Goodman et al. 2010).

13 The Township of North Glengarry is an example of this. The Township used online voting in 2003, dropped the voting mode in the 2006 and 2010 elections, and then adopted it once again in 2014.

14 Markham offered online voting during the advanced voting period only, did not introduce telephone voting simultaneously, and used a two-step process to authenticate voters. By contrast, most of the other municipalities offered online voting for the full election period, including election day, they also adopted telephone voting, and they used a one-step authentication process.

15 While a numerical majority did not technically adopt online voting during this period, the distribution and classification put forward by Rogers (2003) represents a series of ideal types that cannot match empirical reality perfectly.

16 This problem will likely diminish as infrastructure across the province continues to improve.

CHAPTER THREE

1 The Spicer Commission was formally known as the "Citizens' Forum on Canada's Future."

2 The democratic deficit, however, encompasses more than just voter attitudes. Savoie (2019), for instance, writes about the "disintegration" of Canadian political institutions. Likewise, Axworthy (2004), writes that "Canada's democratic deficit goes much beyond the role of Parliament.

Literally every institution in our system of democratic governance – the electoral system, parties, Parliament, federalism, and the public service – as they operate presently, contribute to the democratic deficit." We focus on a particular aspect of this phenomenon: attitudes towards democracy, in general.

3 Kousser and Mullin (2007, 428), for example, conclude that "voting by mail does not deliver on the promise of greater participation in general elections."

4 Diffusion among users has been slow, moving beyond young tech-savvy users only after three or so election cycles (Vassil et al. 2016).

5 While a majority (57 per cent) of voters supported electoral reform in BC's 2005 referendum, the vote failed to meet the 60 per cent super-majority threshold.

6 The exception would be the claim by the Liberal Party, during the 2015 election campaign, that they would adopt a new electoral system. The party changed positions, however, once winning power under first-past-the-post.

7 In 2016, the (Liberal) provincial government amended the Municipal Elections Act to allow municipalities to adopt (a specific form of) ranked ballots for their elections. London was the only municipality to adopt such a system by 2018. Other cities (Cambridge and Kingston) held referenda on the adoption of the system in conjunction with the 2018 election, and planned to adopt it in time for the 2022 elections. However, in 2020, the (Conservative) provincial government amended the Municipal Elections Act once again, revoking the power granted to municipalities to employ a ranked ballot system. During the 2022 provincial election campaign, Liberal Leader Steven Del Duca pledged to adopt a ranked ballot electoral system in provincial elections, if his party were elected (Jones 2016).

8 Respondents opted into the survey after being explicitly told of its focus on local politics.

9 An alternative approach might be to conduct a long-term panel study of respondents, with data collected over the course of multiple years, including before and after changes to voting methods have been made.

10 Balance tests confirm that, with one exception, the groups are balanced on a variety of dimensions. One group (four) is slightly unbalanced on age, but a controlled analysis reveals that this has no substantive effect upon the analysis below. See Appendix 3.II for more details.

11 There are some differences in levels of satisfaction between the city groups (overall satisfaction levels are higher in groups two and four than in groups one and three). We do not suggest, however, that these are due to

differences in voting method options. We expect that satisfaction levels and voting options may, in fact, affect one another. Our interest is in disentangling this relationship by focusing on voting method as the causal factor, hence our experiment.

12 Ideally, we would like to compare our results to levels of satisfaction outside of our case cities. The only way to do so, however, is to draw upon data from a different dataset (perhaps data from the Consortium on Electoral Democracy or the Making Electoral Democracy Project). Doing so, would not provide a valid comparison, however, given differences in recruitment methods. We have therefore decided to refrain from making such comparisons here.

13 For group four/Guelph, voting method from 2014 was used.

14 These models reveal that online voters are particularly supportive of the use of online voting but that they are not more or less satisfied with democracy than their counterparts.

CHAPTER FOUR

1 There are exceptions to the elite-driven nature of electoral reform. Notably, a movement towards "citizens' assemblies" and similar public consultations have been used in electoral reform in Canada and elsewhere (Fournier et al. 2011; LeDuc 2011; Rose 2007), albeit the recommendations of these deliberative forums are still under the purview of elites. Likewise, cultural explanations such as citizen dissatisfaction with regimes can also explain how the subject of reform makes it on the policy agenda (Norris 2011).

2 Alterations to election laws and voting processes such as extending the advance voting period, increasing poll hours during voting time, adopting or dropping voting modes can affect how electors choose to vote and whether they show up to do so (Burden et al. 2013; Berinsky et al. 2001; Berger et al. 2008).

3 The cities are Bradford West Gwillimbury, Brantford, Belleville, Burlington, Cambridge, Chatham-Kent, Kawartha Lakes, Kingston, Markham, Pickering, Sarnia, St Thomas, Thunder Bay, Timmins, and Quinte West.

4 See appendix 4.I for a complete list of survey questions used here.

5 This is the most common method, in Canada, for categorizing respondents on the basis of education. Though there is evidence that there is value, in some instances, of using a categorization scheme with additional detail (i.e. more categories) (see McGregor & Pruysers 2022), the analysis below

requires binary variables. Hence the degree versus no-degree distinction is used here.

6 One aspect the survey did not ask about was Indigenous ancestry. Indigenous peoples make up roughly 2 per cent of respondents in the sample.

7 For this last comparison, we omit those respondents who locate themselves at the midpoint of the ideological scale, as they cannot accurately be classified as either left- or right-of-centre voters.

8 The candidate survey was programmed and fielded by the researchers, using the Qualtrics platform.

9 Note that we indicate the reported rate of online voting and not the actual rate in the electorate.

10 See appendix 4.II for full model results. The appendix also contains the result of a multivariate analysis, containing all of the variables in figure 4.1 simultaneously. The results of this model are largely, though not entirely, consistent with the bivariate findings. Our primary interest is in describing simple bivariate relationships, without adding the conceptual complexity of controls and confounding variables, so we focus on each variable individually in figure 4.1.

11 We use a cutoff point of thirty-five here, as we employ binary variables in this analysis. A more detailed investigation of the age variable suggests, however, that the relationship between age and online voting use is not monotonic. The rate of online voting among voters under thirty-five in our sample is 46.8 per cent (N=267). These values increase for voters between thirty-five and forty-nine (61.7 per cent, N=371) and between fifty and sixty-four (67.4 per cent). However, we see a slight decrease in the rate of online voting among seniors – 62.9 per cent (N=730). Use of internet voting therefore increases with age until voters reach retirement age, then it decreases.

12 For reasons noted above, we focus on voters who do not place themselves at the ideological centre. Though they are excluded in the figure, we did conduct a separate analysis that suggests that they participate online in levels somewhere between those of left- and right-wing voters. Using the same approach used to generate the results in figure 4.1, centrist voters are roughly 4.6 points less likely to vote online than are left-wingers (p=0.096), and 4.7 points more likely to vote online than right-wingers (p=0.074). The relationship between ideology and voting online is therefore monotonic.

13 Both candidates and electors were given a "don't know" option. These cases are not considered in the results here, but there are no differences between the two types of respondents and don't know responses.

14 Rates of correctly understanding voting patterns are likely lower than indicated here, given that there were almost certainly respondents who simply guessed when giving answers.

CHAPTER FIVE

1 hile Elections Canada has asked *federal* candidates about their support for online voting in recent years, their reports devote little time to this question and provide only basic bivariate relationships.
2 As they conclude (2021, 217): "socio-demographic factors appear to be relatively unimportant for mayoral vote choice ... By contrast, ideological indicators are much more consistently significant."
3 Recall that the 2019 federal election occurred *before* the COVID-19 pandemic.
4 Consistent with our expectations, an Elections Canada (Phoenix Strategic Perspectives 2011) survey of federal candidates in 2011 found that "support for internet voting increased as respondents' number of candidacies decreased." A 20-percentage-point gap separated the most and least experienced candidates.
5 Note, however, that the empirical evidence suggests that internet voting is not especially beneficial for candidates from underrepresented backgrounds (Wigginton and Stockemer 2021).
6 For a somewhat more critical take on the causal relationship between personality and political behaviour see Bakker et al. (2021).
7 The "Report of the Standing Committee on Electoral Reform," for instance, recommended that the federal government not implement online voting. Justifying this recommendation, the committee focused on security concerns: "the secrecy and integrity of an online ballot cannot be guaranteed to a sufficient degree to warrant widespread implementation in federal elections" (2016, 115). Similarly, a majority (67 per cent) of federal candidates in 2019 reported that online voting was "risky" while less than a quarter (22 per cent) viewed online voting as "safe" (Ekos 2020).
8 While it is possible that our survey captured some staffers responding on behalf of the candidate, this is less likely municipally than it is at other levels in Canada as municipal candidates tend to have fewer resources (especially organizational in nature given the lack of organized parties).
9 Fortunately, the response from candidates in Guelph was reasonably good – twenty-seven candidates from the city completed our survey.
10 For two reasons, we do not run multi-level models. First, given our limited sample size, and the fact that candidates come from twenty cities, multi-

level models inflate standard errors in such a way as to make it nearly impossible to find significant results. Second, the introduction of the cross-level interaction term in a multi-level model for the "political characteristics" results in the model not converging. While we do not believe that the single-level models we employ here introduce bias into our exploratory analysis, we nevertheless see value in conducting future studies of this nature with a larger sample to test our findings in a more extensive manner.

11 Also due to our modest sample size, we discuss statistical significance all the way to the 90 per cent level.

12 While in theory this explanation is testable, given our sample size limitations, we are unfortunately unable to do so here. That is, there are too few respondents within these cities to compare incumbent city councilors and mayors to regional and school board trustees in this respect.

13 We provided no additional clarification regarding what the word "benefit" meant, so incumbents were free to interpret this statement as they saw fit.

14 The results of figures 5.2–5.4 are found in tabular format in appendix 5.II.

15 Due to sample size limitations, we cannot compare incumbent and ideological groups based on the type of open-ended responses they provided. We expect that it is conceivable however that, among those candidates in the population who did campaign differently because of online voting, incumbents and challengers might have reacted differently, as might have candidates of different ideologies. This remains an open question.

16 Among respondents who believed that their incumbent/challenger status benefitted them in an online voting system, support for online voting (strongly agree and agree) was 83.4 per cent. Among those who saw themselves as disadvantaged, the comparable figure is only 63.2 per cent

17 The cross-tabulation of these two variables returns a chi-square p-value of 0.79, suggesting that the two factors are not related to one another (N = 190).

CHAPTER SIX

1 Note that Section 11(2) of the Municipal Elections Act places the responsibility for conducting the election upon the clerk. The clerk is one of two statutory roles required for each Ontario municipality. The clerk manages services, policy processes, elections, and matters of legislative compliance in their respective municipality.

2 Field dates were 21 April to 26 May 2022.

3 This question was only asked to administrators from municipalities using online voting. Respondents were also given the option to name, in open-ended format, some other factor that might have influenced their decision. Fewer than a third of respondents did so. Among these responses, the most common answer was around the theme of convenience and cost for administrators. The average score for these responses was lower than any included in figure 6.1, at 6.96/10.
4 This includes cities that had it in place in 2018 and Guelph, that had used it in 2014.
5 We also ran the analysis using 2022, rather than 2018 use. Results change little, and the substantive conclusions of the analysis are unchanged.
6 All of our surveys were of an opt-in nature, so there is some self-selection among potential respondents. Given that all surveys were conducted online, our intuition is that levels of support for online voting are higher among respondents than among the entire population. However, as noted in the introductory chapter of this book, the response rate was considerably lower for the elector survey than the candidate and administrator surveys. We expect that this overestimation of support for online voting is particularly pronounced among this group. If correct, however, this would only serve to increase the gap in the attitudes of electors and administrators.

CHAPTER SEVEN

1 Even so-called "minimalist" definitions of democracy highlight the foundational role of elections (see Schumpeter 1942).

EPILOGUE

1 Overall turnout across the province (rather than municipal averages), based upon data available from the AMO, is an estimated 31.0 per cent.
2 This incident occurred in Collingwood, Ontario.
3 These municipalities include Barrie, Brantford, Cambridge, Collingwood, Dryden, Greater Sudbury, Hamilton, New Tecumseh, Peterborough, Prince Edward County, Sault Ste Marie, Thunder Bay, Toronto, Vaughan, Scugog, Oro-Medonte, and Wasaga Beach.
4 Under s.53 of the Municipal Elections Act, a "clerk may declare an emergency if he or she is of the opinion that circumstances have arisen that are likely to prevent the election being conducted in accordance with this Act." When an emergency has been declared, a clerk may make

arrangements that he or she sees fit under the circumstances, so long as they are consistent with the principles of the act. These arrangements, if "made in good faith" are not "reviewed or set aside on account of unreasonableness or supposed unreasonableness." Emergencies continue until a clerk declares that the circumstances are thus that the emergency ceases to pose issues for the carrying out of the election.

References

Alcantara, C., and J. Roy. 2014. "Reforming Election Dates in Canada: Towards an Explanatory Framework." Canadian Public Administration. 57 (2): 256–74.

Alhquist, J., M. Copelovitch, and S. Walter. 2020. "The Political Consequences of External Economic Shocks: Evidence from Poland." *American Journal of Political Science* 64 (4): 904–20.

Alvarez, R.M., M. Duchin, G. Macht, and C. Stewart III. 2021. "Election Science: A Proposed NSF Convergence Accelerator." MIT Election Lab. https://electionlab.mit.edu/sites/default/files/2021-07/Election-Science-Proposed-NSF-Convergence-Accelerator.pdf.

Alvarez, R.M., and T.E. Hall. 2004. *Point, Click, and Vote: The Future of Internet Voting*. Washington, DC: Brookings Institution Press.

— 2010. *Electronic Elections: The Perils and Promises of Digital Democracy*. Princeton, NJ: Princeton University Press.

Alvarez R.M., T.E. Hall, and A.H. Trechsel. 2009. "Internet Voting in Comparative Perspective: The case of Estonia." *PS: Political Science and Politics* 42 (3): 497–505.

Alvarez, R.M., G. Katz, and J. Pomares. 2011. "The Impact of New Technologies on Voter Confidence in Latin America: Evidence from E-voting Experiments in Argentina and Colombia." *Journal of Information Technology & Politics* 8 (2): 199–217.

Alvarez, R.M., I. Levin, and Y. Li. 2018. "Fraud, Convenience, and E-voting: How Voting Experience Shapes Opinions about Voting Technology." *Journal of Information Technology & Politics* 15 (2): 94–105.

Alvarez, R.M., I. Levin, J. Pomares, and M. Leiras. 2013. "Voting Made Safe and Easy: The Impact of E-voting on Citizen Perceptions." *Political Science Research and Methods* 1 (1): 117–37.

Anderson C., A. Blais, S. Bowler, T. Donovan, and O. Listhuag. 2005. *Losers' Consent: Elections and Democratic Legitimacy*. Oxford: Oxford University Press.

Anderson, C., M. McGregor, and S. Pruysers. 2020. "Incumbency and Competitiveness in City Council Elections: How Accurate Are Voter Perceptions?" *Canadian Journal of Political Science* 53 (4): 853–71.

Anderson, C., and L. Stephenson, eds. 2011. *Voting Behaviour in Canada*. Vancouver: UBC Press.

Andrews, B., and S. Pruysers. 2022. "Does Democracy Die in Darkness? An Examination of the Relationship Between Local Newspaper Health and Turnout in Municipal Politics." *Canadian Journal of Political Science* 55 (4): 958–71.

Association of Municipalities Ontario. 2018. *2018 Municipal Elections Fast Facts*. https://elections.amo.on.ca/web/en/stats.

— 2022. *2022 Municipal Election – Context*. Toronto: Association of Municipalities of Ontario. https://www.amo.on.ca/municipal-election-statistics.

— 2022. *AMO submission on Bill 23, Better Municipal Governance Act, 2022 Introduced – Expanding "strong mayor" tools*. https://www.amo.on.ca/advocacy/health-human-services/amo-submission-bill-23-better-municipal-governance-act-2022.

Axworthy, T. 2004. "Addressing the Accountability Deficit: Why Paul Martin's Minority Government Must Pay More Attention to the Three A's." *Institute for Research on Public Policy, Working Paper Series*, 1 December. https://policyoptions.irpp.org/fr/magazines/sovereignty-in-turmoil/addressing-the-accountability-deficit-why-the-martin-minority-government-must-pay-more-attention-to-the-three-as/.

Babyan, V., I. Marques II, M. Mironyuk, and A. Turobov. 2021. "Public Trust in Internet Voting Systems: Evidence from Russian Public Opinion." *Basic Research Program Working Papers*. https://wp.hse.ru/data/2021/12/22/1776945193/83PS2021.pdf.

Bakker, B., Y. Lelkes, and A. Malka. 2021. "Reconsidering the Link between Self-Reported Personality Traits and Political Preferences." *American Political Science Review* 115 (4): 1482–98.

Barbaranelli, C., G.V. Caprara., M. Vecchione, and C.R. Fraley. 2007. "Voters' Personality Traits in Presidential Elections." *Personality and Individual Differences* 42 (7): 1199–208.

Béland, D., S. Dinan, P. Rocco, and A. Waddan. 2022. "COVID-19, Poverty Reduction, and Partisanship in Canada and the United States." *Policy and Society* 41 (2): 291–305.

Bélanger, F., and L. Carter. 2010. "The Impacts of the Digital Divide on Citizens' Intentions to Use Internet Voting." *International Journal on Advances in Internet Technology* 3 (3 & 4): 203–11.

Benaloh, J., R. Rivest, P.Y.A Ryan, P. Stark, V. Teague, and P. Vora. 2014. "End-to-end Verifiability." Available at: https://escholarship.org/content/qt7c9994dg/qt7c9994dg_noSplash_97d64dc5a809c55270107925of47b4cb.pdf.

Berger, J., M. Meredith, and S.C Wheeler. 2008. "Contextual Priming: Where People Vote Affects How They Vote." *Proceedings of the National Academy of Sciences* 105 (26): 8846–9.

Berry, F.S., and W.D. Berry. 2018. "Innovation and Diffusion Models in Policy Research." In *Theories of the Policy Process*, edited by Christopher M. Weible and Paul A. Sabathier, 253–97. London: Westview Press.

Biggers, D.R., E.M Elder, S.J. Hill, T. Kousser, G. Lenz, and M. Lockhart. 2022. "Can Addressing Integrity Concerns About Mail Balloting Increase Turnout? Results from a Large-Scale Field Experiment in the 2020 Presidential Election." *Journal of Experimental Political Science* 10 (13): 413–25.

Blais, A. 2006. "What Affects Voter Turnout?" *Annual Review of Political Science* 9: 1111–25.

Blais, A., and K. Carty. 1990. "Does Proportional Representation Foster Voter Turnout?" *European Journal of Political Research* 18 (2): 167–81.

Blais, J., P.G. Chen, and S. Pruysers. 2021. "Who Complies and Who Defies? Personality and Public Health Compliance." *Frontiers in Political Science*. https://doi.org/10.3389/fpos.2021.660911.

Blais, A., and J.F. Daoust. 2020. *Motivation of Vote: Explaining Electoral Participation*. Vancouver: UBC Press.

Blais, A., J.F. Daoust, R. Dassoneville, R., and G. Péloquin-Skulski. 2019. "What is the cost of voting?" *Electoral Studies*, 59: 145–57.

Blais, A., and A. Dobrzynska. 1998. "Turnout in Electoral Democracies" *European Journal of Political Research* 33 (2): 239–61.

Blais, A., A. Dobrzynska, and P. Loewen. 2007. *Incidences Potentielles de la Prolongation du Vote Part Anticipation sur la Participation Electorale*. Ottawa: Elections Canada.

Blais, A., and C. Galais. 2016. "Measuring the Civic Duty to Vote: A Proposal." *Electoral Studies* 41: 60–9.

Blais, A., C. Galais, and D. Mayer. 2019. "Is It a Duty to Vote and to be Informed?" *Political Studies Review* 17 (4), 328–39.

Blais, A., and F. Gelineau. 2007. "Winning, Losing and Satisfaction with Democracy. *Political Studies* 55 (2): 425–41.

Blais, A., E. Gidengil, N. Nevitte, and R. Nadeau. 2004. "Where Does Turnout Decline Come From?" *European Journal of Political Research* 43 (2): 221–36.

Blais, A., A. Morin-Chassé, and S.P. Singh. 2017. "Election Outcomes, Legislative Representation, and Satisfaction with Democracy." *Party Politics* 23 (2): 85–95.

Blais, J., L. Mungall, and S. Pruysers, (2022). "Personality, Political Ideology, and Partisanship in Canada." *Canadian Journal of Behavioural Science*. Advance online publication. https://doi.org/10.1037/cbs0000355.

Blais, J., S. Pruysers, and P. Chen. 2019. "Why Do They Run? The Psychological Underpinnings of Political Ambition." *Canadian Journal of Political Science* 52 (4): 761–79.

Blais, A., and D. Rubenson. 2013. "The Source of Turnout Decline: New Values or New Contexts?" *Comparative Political Studies* 46 (1): 95–117.

Blais, A., and S.L. St-Vincent. 2011. "Personality Traits, Political Attitudes, and the Propensity to Vote." *European Journal of Political Research* 50 (3): 395–417.

Blais, André, and M. Turgeon. 2004. "How Good Are Voters at Sorting Out the Weakest Candidate in Their Constituency?" *Electoral Studies* 23 (3): 455–61.

Bochsler, D. 2010. "Can Internet Voting Increase Political Participation? Remote Electronic Voting and Turnout in the Estonian 2007 Parliamentary Elections." Prepared for presentation at the conference Internet and Voting, Fiesole, 3–4 June.

Boix, C. 1999. "Setting the Rules of the Game: The Choice of Electoral Systems in Advanced Democracies." *American Political Science Review* 93 (3): 609–24.

Bol, Damien. 2016. "Electoral Reform, Values, and Party Self-Interest." *Party Politics* 22 (1): 93–104.

Bol, D., J.B. Pilet, and P. Riera. 2015. "The International Diffusion of Electoral Systems." *European Journal of Political Research* 54:384–410.

Boyd, B. 2021. "Introduction: Theorizing about Provinces as Provincial Laboratories for Policy Diffusion and Transfer." In *Provincial Policy*

Laboratories Policy Diffusion and Transfer in Canada's Federal System, edited by B. Boyd and A. Olive. Toronto: University of Toronto Press.

Brand, J.A. 1969. "Councillors, Activists, and Electors: Democratic Relationships in Scottish Cities." In *Comparative Legislative Behavior: Frontiers of Research*, edited by S.C. Patterson and J.C. Wahlke. De Moines: University of Iowa Press.

Breux, S., J. Couture, and R. Koop. 2017. "Turnout in Local Elections: Evidence from Canadian Cities, 2004–2014." *Canadian Journal of Political Science* 50 (3): 699–722.

Bridgmon, P., and M. Milewicz. 2004. *E-politics: Technology in American Government*. New York: Kendall Hunt Publishing Company.

Britneff, B. 2018. "Online Voting in 51 Ontario Municipalities Marred by Election-Day 'System Load Issue." Global News. https://globalnews.ca/news/4585577/ontario-voting-issues/.

Broockman, D., and C. Skovron. 2013. "What Politicians Believe about Their Constituents: Asymmetric Misperceptions and Prospects for Constituency Control." https://www.vanderbilt.edu/csdi/miller-stokes/08_MillerStokes_BroockmanSkovron.pdf.

— 2018. "Bias in Perceptions of Public Opinion among Political Elites." *The American Political Science Review* 112 (3): 542–63.

Broussard, M. 2018. *Artificial Unintelligence: How Computers Misunderstand the World*. Massachusetts: MIT Press.

Brossard, M., and M. James. 1997. "Changing Attitudes in America." In *Why People Don't Trust Government*, edited by J.S. Nye, P.D. Zelikow, and D.C. King. Cambridge, MA: Harvard University Press.

Brown, Lawrence A. 1981. *Innovation Diffusion: A New Perspective*. New York: Methuen.

Budd, B., C. Gabel, and N. Goodman. 2019. "Online Voting in a First Nation in Canada: Implications for Participation and Governance." In *Electronic Voting. E-Vote-ID 2019. Lecture Notes in Computer Science*, edited by R. Krimmer et al., 50–66. Cham: Springer International Publishing.

Budd, B., N. Goodman, and R.M. McGregor. 2021. *Electronic Voting Alternatives to Support the Canadian Constituency*. Report prepared for the Nunatsiavut Assembly.

Burstein, P. 2003. "The Impact of Public Opinion on Public Policy: A Review and an Agenda." *Political Research Quarterly* 56 (1): 29–40.

Cardillo, A., N. Akinyokun, and A. Essex. 2019. "Online Voting in Ontario Municipal Elections: A Conflict of Legal Principles and Technology? In *Electronic Voting. E-Vote-ID 2019. Lecture Notes in*

Computer Science, edited by R. Krimmer et al., 67–82. Cham: Springer International Publishing.

Carter, L., and F. Bélanger. 2005. "The Utilization of E-government Services: Citizen Trust, Innovation and Acceptance Factors." *Information Systems Journal* 15 (1): 5–25.

Carter, L., and R. Campbell. 2012. "Internet Voting Usefulness: An Empirical Analysis of Trust, Convenience and Accessibility." *Journal of Organizational and End User Computing* 24 (3): 1–17.

Carty, K. 2010. "Canadian Democracy: An Assessment and an Agenda." In *Auditing Canadian Democracy*, edited by William Cross. Vancouver: UBC Press.

CBC News. 2017. "Incumbents Have the Advantage in Municipal Politics, but Not Always." https://www.cbc.ca/news/canada/calgary/ward-8-voters-incumbent-1.4311322.

— 2017. "Sudbury Moves to Digital-only Voting System for 2018 City Election." Retrieved from https://www.cbc.ca/news/canada/sudbury/sudbury-city-election-digital-only-1.4140064.

Chandler, J. 2022. "Vote Anywhere. At Any Time: What Happens When Elections Move Online." TVO. https://www.tvo.org/article/vote-anywhere-at-any-time-what-happens-when-elections-move-online.

Chanley, V., R. Rudolph, and W. Rahn. 2000 "The Origins and Consequences of Public Trust in Government: A Time Series Analysis." *The Public Opinion Quarterly* 64 (3): 239–56.

Chen, E., H. Chang, A. Rao, K. Lerman, G. Cowan, and E. Ferrara. 2021. "COVID-19 Misinformation and the 2020 US Presidential Election." *The Harvard Kennedy School Misinformation Review*, 1(7): DOI: 10.37016/mr-2020-57.

Chen, P., S. Pruysers, and J. Blais. 2021. "The Dark Side of Politics: Participation and the Dark Triad." *Political Studies* 69 (3): 577–601.

CIO Strategy Council. 2021. "CIO Strategy Council Developing National Standards for Online Electoral Voting Technologies." Press release, 21 January 2021.

Citizens' Forum on Canada's Future. 1991. *Report to the people and Government of Canada*. Ottawa: Supply and Services Canada.

Citrin, J., H. McClosky, J.M. Shanks, and P.M. Sniderman. 1975. "Personal and Political Sources of Political Alienation." *British Journal of Political Science* 5 (1): 1–31.

City of Guelph. 2013. "Staff Report: 2014 Municipal Election: Methods of Voting." https://guelph.ca/wp-content/uploads/StaffReport_Guelph MethodsOfVoting.pdf.

City of Ottawa. 2022. "2022 Report on the Elections Office." https://pub-ottawa.escribemeetings.com/filestream.ashx?DocumentId=123582.

— 2023. "Finance and Economic Development Committee Report 35." 23 March 2023. https://pub-ottawa.escribemeetings.com/filestream.ashx?documentid=87905.

City of Toronto. 2014. "Staff Report: Contract Award – RFP No. 3405-13-3197 – 2014 Municipal Election – Internet Voting Service for Persons with Disabilities." https://www.toronto.ca/legdocs/mmis/2014/cc/bgrd/backgroundfile-66912.pdf.

— 2016. "Report for Action: Changes to the Municipal Elections Act and related matters impacting the 2018 Election." https://www.toronto.ca/legdocs/mmis/2014/cc/bgrd/backgroundfile-66912.pdf.

— 2020. "Report for Action: The Impact of COVID-19 on 2022 Election Preparation Activities." https://www.toronto.ca/legdocs/mmis/2020/ex/bgrd/backgroundfile-156443.pdf.

Clark, J., A. Essex, and C. Adams. 2007 "Secure and observable auditing of electronic voting systems using stock indices." Conference paper for the 2007 Canadian Conference on Electrical and Computer Engineering. Vancouver: IEEE.

Clarke, H., and M. Stewart. 1998. "The Decline of Parties in the Minds of Citizens." *Annual Review of Political Science* 1 (1): 357–78.

Colomer, J, ed. 2004. *The Handbook of Electoral System Choice*. New York: Palgrave.

Courtney, J. 2010. "Elections." In *Auditing Canadian Democracy*, edited by William Cross, 118–43. Vancouver: UBC Press.

Council of Europe. 2017. "Recommendation Recc(2017)5 of the Committee of Ministers to Member States on Standards for E-Voting."

Couture, J., S. Breux, and N. Goodman. 2017. "La Vote par Internet Augmente-t-il la Participation Electorale?" In *Cyberspace et science politique*, edited by H. Loiseau and E. Waldispuehl, 123–48.

Cross, W. 2008. "Democratic Norms and Party Candidate Selection: Taking Contextual Factors into Account." *Party Politics* 14 (5): 596–619.

Cross, W., and A. Blais. 2012. "Who Selects the Party Leader?" *Party Politics* 18 (2): 127–50.

Cross, W., and S. Pruysers. 2019. "Sore Losers? The Costs of Intra-party Democracy." *Party Politics* 25 (4): 483–94.

Cross, W., S. Pruysers, and R. Currie-Wood. 2022. *The Political Party in Canada*. Vancouver: UBC Press.

Culnane, C., M. Eldridge, A. Essex, and V, Teague. 2017. "Trust Implications of DDoS Protection in Online Elections." In *Electronic Voting. E-Vote-ID 2017. Lecture Notes in Computer Science,* edited by R. Krimmer et al., 127–45. Cham: Springer International Publishing.

Cutler, F. 2008. "One Voter, Two First-Order Elections?" *Electoral Studies* 27 (3): 492–504.

Cutler, F., and J.S. Matthews. 2005. "The Challenge of Municipal Voting: Vancouver 2002." *Canadian Journal of Political Science* 38 (2): 359–82.

Dalton, R.J., and M.P. Wattenberg. 2000. *Parties without Partisans: Political Change in Advanced Industrial Democracies.* Oxford: Oxford University Press.

Dandoy, R., and T. Kernalegenn. 2021. "Internet Voting from Abroad: Exploring Turnout in the 2014 French Consular Elections." *French Politics* 19 (4): 421–39.

Daoust, J.F., and R. Nadeau. 2021. "Context Matters: Economics, Politics and Satisfaction with Democracy." *Electoral Studies* 74: 102–33.

Daoust, J.F., H.M. Ridge, and P. Mongrain. 2023. "Electoral Outcomes and Satisfaction with Democracy: A Comparison of Regional and National Elections." *Electoral Studies* 84: 102–42.

Delli Carpini, M.X., and S. Keeter. 1996. *What Americans Know about Politics and Why it Matters.* New Haven, CT: Yale University Press.

Delvinia. 2003. "Internet Voting and Canadian Democracy in Practice: The Delvinia Report on Internet Voting in the 2003 Town of Markham Municipal Election." Elections Canada. https://verifiedvoting.org/wp-content/uploads/2020/07/Canada-2004-Delvinia_Voting_Report_04.pdf.

DeWinter, L. 2005. "Empowering Voters or Party Elites?" In *The Politics of Electoral Systems*, edited by M. Gallagher and P. Mitchell, 417–32. New York: Oxford University Press.

Dodek, A. 2010. "The Past, Present and Future of Fixed Election Dates in Canada." *Journal of Parliamentary and Political Law* 4: 215–38.

Downs, A. 1957. *An Economic Theory of Democracy.* New York: Harper.

Duenas-Cid, D., I. Krivonosova, R. Serrano, M. Freire, and R. Krimmer. 2021. "Tripped at the Finishing Line: The Åland Islands Internet Voting Project." In *Electronic Voting. E-Vote-ID 2020. Lecture Notes in Computer Science*, edited by R. Krimmer et al., 36–49. Cham: Springer International Publishing.

Dumitrica, D. 2014. "Politics as 'Customer Relations': Social Media and Political Authenticity in the 2010 Municipal Elections in Calgary, Canada, Javnost" *The Public* 21 (1): 53–69.

Dynes, A.M., H.J.G. Hassell, and M.R. Miles. 2019. "The Personality of the Politically Ambitious." *Political Behavior* 41: 309–36.

Easton, D. 1965. *A Systems Analysis of Political Life*. New York: Wiley.

Ehin, P., M. Solvak, J. Willemson, and P. Vinkel. 2022. "Internet Voting in Estonia 2005–2019: Evidence from Eleven Elections." *Government Information Quarterly* 39 (4): 1–14.

Eidelman, G., and Z. Taylor. 2010. "Canadian Urban Politics: Another "Black Hole"? *Journal of Urban Affairs* 32 (3): 305–20.

Ekengren, A.M., and H. Oscarsson. 2011. "Party Elites' Perceptions of Voters and Public Opinion." *Scandinavian Political Studies* 34 (2): 101–22.

EKOS. 2016. "The Case for Internet Voting." https://www.ekospolitics.com/index.php/2016/10/the-case-for-internet-voting/.

— 2016. "Survey of Candidates Following the 42nd General Election." Report prepared for Elections Canada. https://www.elections.ca/res/rec/eval/pes2015/can/can_surv_e.pdf.

— 2020. "Survey of Candidates Following the 43rd General Election." Report prepared for Elections Canada. https://www.elections.ca/res/rec/eval/pes2019/can/can_surv_e.pdf.

Elections BC. 2014. *Independent Panel on Internet Voting: Recommendations Report to the Legislative Assembly of British Columbia*. Victoria: Legislative Assembly of British Columbia.

Elections Canada. 2022. *Voter Turnout at Federal Elections and Referendums*. Ottawa: Elections Canada.

Elections Ontario. 2013. *Alternative Voting Technologies Report: Chief Electoral Officer's Submission to the Legislative Assembly*. Toronto: Elections Ontario.

Elections Nova Scotia. 2022. "Request for Proposals for a Nova Scotia Internet Voting System." Elections Nova Scotia. https://elections novascotia.ca/node/822.

Elections Quebec 2022. "Internet voting: call for expressions of interest." Quebec City: Quebec, 15 November.

Enders, A.M., J.E. Uscinski, C.A. Klofstad, K. Premaratne, M.I. Seelig, S. Wuchty, M.N. Murthi, and J.R. Funchion. 2021. "The 2020 Presidential Election and Beliefs about Fraud: Continuity or Change?." *Electoral Studies* 72 (August 2021): 1–9.

Essex, A. 2016 "Internet Voting in Canada: A Cyber Security Perspective." Brief submitted to the House of Commons Special Committee on Electoral Reform (Canada). Ottawa: House of Commons.

Essex, A., and N. Goodman. 2020. "Protecting Electoral Integrity in the Digital Age: Developing E-voting Regulations in Canada." *Election Law Journal: Rules, Politics, and Policy* 19 (2): 162–79.

Essex, A., and N. Goodman. 2022. "A Cyber-Threat Analysis of Online Voting in Canada." In *Cyber-Threats to Canadian Democracy*, edited by Holly Garnett and Michael Pal, 87–115. Montreal and Kingston: McGill-Queen's University Press.

Feist, J, and G. Feist. 2009. *Theories of Personality*. 7th ed. New York: McGraw- Hill.

Fisher, J., and M.M. Savani 2022. "Who's in Charge? The Impact of Delivery and Perception of Risk on the Willingness to Voting Online." *The British Journal of Politics and International Relations*. Online First. https://doi.org/10.1177/13691481221120143.

Fivaz, J., and G. Nadig. 2010 "Impact of Voting Advice Applications (VAAS) on Voter Turnout and Their Potential Use for Civic Education." *Policy & Internet* 2 (4): 167–200.

Flickinger, R., and D. Studlar. 1992. "The Disappearing Voters? Exploring Declining Turnout in Western European Elections." *West European Politics* 15 (2): 1–16.

Fournier, P., H. Van der Kolk, R.K. Carty, A. Blais, and J. Rose. 2011. *When Citizens Decide: Lessons from Citizen Assemblies on Electoral Reform*. Oxford: Oxford University Press.

Foucault, M., and É. Montpetit. 2013. "Diffusion of Policy Attention in Canada: Evidence from Speeches from the Throne, 1960–2008." In *Agenda Setting, Policies, and Political Systems. A Comparative Approach*, edited by C. Green-Pedersen and S. Walgrave. Chicago: University of Chicago Press.

Franklin M. 2004. *Voter Turnout and the Dynamics of Electoral Competition in Established Democracies Since 1945*. Cambridge, UK: Cambridge University Press.

Federal Chancellery. 2022. "E-voting: Results of the first independent examination available." 20 April, https://www.admin.ch/gov/en/start/documentation/media-releases.msg-id-88085.html.

Frey, C.B. 2019. *The Technology Trap*. Princeton, NJ: Princeton University Press.

Gabel, C. and N. Goodman. 2021. "Methodological and Academic Challenges in Canadian Political Science: The Value of a Socially Engaged Approach for Indigenous Research." *Politics, Groups, and Identities* 9 (2): 319–28.

Gabel, C., N. Goodman, K. Bird, and B. Budd. 2016. "Indigenous Adoption of Internet Voting: A Case Study of Whitefish River First Nation." *International Indigenous Policy Journal* 7 (3): 1–20.

Garnett, H.A., and M.V. Keir. 2022. "Where Regulation Counts: Provincial Regulation of Municipal Elections in Canada." *Canadian Public Administration* 65 (2): 333–51.

Garnett, H.A, and M. Pal. 2022. *Cyber Threats to Canadian Democracy*. Montreal and Kingston: McGill-Queens University Press.

Gerlach, J., and U. Gasser. 2009. "Three Case Studies from Switzerland: E-voting." *Berkman Center Research Publication No 3*. Cambridge, MA: Berkman Centre.

Germann, M. 2021. "Internet Voting Increases Expatriate Voter Turnout." *Government Information Quarterly* 38 (2): 1–10.

Germann, M., and U. Serdült. 2017. "Internet voting and turnout: Evidence from Switzerland." *Electoral Studies* 47 (1): 1–12.

Gidengil, E., A. Blais, N. Nevitte, and R. Nadeau. 2004. *Citizens*. Vancouver: UBC Press.

Good, K.R. 2016. "Municipal Political Parties: An Answer to Urbanization or an Affront to Traditions of Local Democracy?" In *Canadian Political Parties in Transition*, edited by A-G Gagnon and B. Tanguay, 432–64. Toronto: University of Toronto Press.

Goodman, N. 2014. "Internet Voting in a Local Election in Canada." In *Internet and Democracy in Global Perspective*, edited by B. Grofman, A. Trechsel, and M. Franklin. London: Springer Verla.

— 2017. *Online Voting: A Path Forward for Federal Elections*. Ottawa: Privy Council Office.

Goodman, N., and A. Essex. 2021. "Now is the Time to Regulate Voting Technologies in Canada." *Globe and Mail*. https://www.theglobeandmail.com/opinion/article-now-is-the-time-to-regulate-voting-technologies-in-canada/.

Goodman, N., and C. Gabel. 2020. "Internet Voting: Strengthening Canadian Democracy or Weakening It?." In *Digital Politics in Canada: Promises and Realities*, edited by T. Small and H. Jansen, 90–111. Toronto: University of Toronto Press.

Goodman, N., and J. Lucas. 2016. "Policy Priorities of Municipal Candidates in the 2014 Local Ontario Elections." *Canadian Journal of Urban Research* 25 (2): 35–47.

Goodman, N., R.M. McGregor, J. Couture, and S. Breux. 2018. "Another Digital Divide? Evidence that Elimination of Paper Voting could Lead to Digital Disenfranchisement." *Policy and Internet* 10 (2): 164–84.

Goodman, N., J.H. Pammett, and J. DeBardeleben. 2010. *A Comparative Assessment of Electronic Voting*. Prepared for Elections Canada. Ottawa: Elections Canada.

Goodman, N., and H. Pyman. 2016. "Understanding the effects of internet voting on elections: Results from the 2014 Ontario municipal elections." Technical Paper, Centre for e- Democracy. Toronto: Centre for E-Democracy.

Goodman, N., and R. Smith. 2016. "Internet Voting in Sub-national Elections: Policy Learning in Canada and Australia." In *Electronic Voting. E-Vote-ID 2016. Lecture Notes in Computer Science*, edited by R. Krimmer et al, 164–77. Cham: Springer International Publishing.

Goodman, N., and Z. Spicer. 2019. "Administering Elections in a Digital Age: Online Voting in Ontario Municipalities." *Canadian Public Administration* 62 (3): 369–92.

Goodman, N., and L.C. Stokes. 2020. "Reducing the Cost of Voting: An Evaluation of Internet Voting's Effect on Turnout." *British Journal of Political Science* 50 (3): 1155–67.

Gosling, S.D., P.J. Rentfrow, and W.B. Swann Jr. 2003. "A Very Brief Measure of the Big Five Personality Domains." *Journal of Research in Personality* 37: 504–28.

Graham, K. 2018. *Leading Canada's cities? A study of urban mayors. Dissertation: Western University*. https://ir.lib.uwo.ca/cgi/viewcontent.cgi?article=7704&context=etd.

— 2019. *Leading in chains? The role of Canada's mayors*. Prepared for the Annual Meeting of the Canadian Political Science Association. https://www.cpsa-acsp.ca/documents/conference/2019/511.Graham.pdf.

Gray, M., and M. Caul. 2000. "Declining Voter Turnout in Advanced Industrial Democracies, 1950 to 1997: The Effects of Declining Group Mobilization." *Comparative Political Studies* 33 (9): 1091–122.

Greenhalgh, S., S. Goodman, P. Rosenzweig, and J. Epstein. 2018. *Email and Internet Voting*. Washington, DC: US Policy and Election Technology Committee.

Grimmer, J., E. Hersh, M. Meredith, J. Mummolo, and C. Nall. 2018. "Obstacles to Estimating Voter ID Laws' Effect on Turnout." *The Journal of Politics* 80 (3): 1045–51.

Grofman, B., A. Trechsel, and M. Franklin. 2014. *The Internet and Democracy in Global Perspective: Voters, Candidates, Parties, and Social Movements*. London: Springer.

Gronke, P., E. Galanes-Rosenbaum, and P. Miller. 2007. "Early Voting and Turnout." *PS: Political Science and Politics* 40 (4): 639–45.

Gronke, P., E. Galanes-Rosenbaum, P.A. Miller, and D. Toffey. 2008. "Convenience Voting." *Annual Review of Political Science* 11: 437–55.

Gronke, P., and P. Miller. 2012. "Voting by Mail and Turnout in Oregon: Revisiting Southwell and Burchett." *American Politics Research* 40 (6): 976–97.

Hagar, D. 2014. "Campaigning Online: Social Media in the 2010 Niagara Municipal Elections." *Canadian Journal of Urban Research* 23 (1): 74–98.

Hajnal, Z.L., and P.G. Lewis. 2003. "Municipal Institutions and Voter Turnout in Local Elections." *Urban Affairs Review* 38 (5): 645–68.

Hall, T. 2015. "Internet voting: the state of the debate." In *Handbook of Digital Politics*, edited by S. Coleman and D. Freelon, 103–17. London: Edward Elgar Publishing.

Han, A., L. Laurian, and J. Dewald. 2020. "Plans versus Political Priorities. Lessons from Municipal Candidates' Social Media Communications." *Journal of the American Planning Association* 87 (2): 211–27.

Harmel, R., and K. Janda, K. 1994. "An Integrated Theory of Party Goals and Party Change." *Journal of Theoretical Politics* 6 (3): 259–87.

Hayes, H., N. Goodman, R.M. McGregor, Z. Spicer, and S. Pruysers. 2022. "The Effect of Exogenous Shocks on the Administration of Online Voting: Evidence from Ontario, Canada." Lecture Notes in Computer Science.

Heath, O. 2007. "Explaining Turnout Decline in Britain, 1964–2005: Party Identification and the Political Context." Political Behavior 29: 493–516.

Henry, S. 2003. "Can Remote Internet Voting Increase Turnout?" *Aslib Proceedings* 55 (4): 193–202.

Hertel-Fernandez, A., M. Mildenberger, L.C. Stokes. 2019. "Legislative Staff and Representation in Congress." *American Political Science Review* 113 (1): 1–18.

House of Commons. 2016. "Strengthening Democracy in Canada: Principles, Process and Public Engagement for Electoral Reform." https://www.ourcommons.ca/Content/Committee/421/ERRE/Reports/RP8655791/errerp03/errerp03-e.pdf.

International IDEA. 2011. "Introducing Electronic Voting, Essential Considerations: Policy Paper." The International Institute for Democracy and Electoral Assistance.

— 2023. ICTs in Elections Database. https://www.idea.int/data-tools/data/icts-elections-database.

Jackman, RW. 1987. "Political Institutions and Voter Turnout in Industrial Democracies." *American Political Science Review* 81 (2): 405–24.

Jaffe, A.M. 2021. *Energy's Digital Future*. New York: Columbia University Press.

James, T.S., and S. Alihodzic. 2020. "When is it Democratic to Postpone an Election? Elections During Natural Disasters, COVID-19, and Emergency Situations." *Election Law Journal: Rules, Politics, and Policy* 19 (3): 344–62.

Jamieson, K.H. 2018. *Cyberwar. How Russian Hackers and Trolls Helped Elect a President: What we Don't, Can't, and Do Know*. Oxford: Oxford University Press.

Javed, N. 2014. "Online Voting Clicks with Ajax Residents." *Toronto Star*. https://www.thestar.com/news/ajax/2014/11/11/online_voting_clicks_with_ajax_residents.html.

Jones, A. 2021. "Ontario Liberal Leader Steven Del Duca Pledges Ranked Ballots or He'll Quit." *Global News*. https://globalnews.ca/news/8271217/ontario-liberals-ranked-ballots/.

Jones, R.P. 2022. "How Will Toronto and Ottawa's New 'Strong Mayor' Powers Work?" *CBC News*. https://www.cbc.ca/news/canada/toronto/toronto-ottawa-strong-mayor-1.6597520.

Jones, Ryan Patrick. 2021. "Here's Why You Can't Vote Online in the 2021 Federal Election." *CBC News*. https://www.cbc.ca/news/politics/online-voting-federal-elections-1.6168106.

Kamenova, K., and N. Goodman. 2015. "Public Engagement with Internet Voting in Edmonton: Design, Outcomes, and Challenges to Deliberative Models." *Journal of Public Deliberation* 11 (2): 4.

Karp, J.A., and S.A. Banducci. 2000. "Going Postal: How All-Mail Elections Influence Turnout." *Political Behavior* 22 (3): 223–39.

Katz, R. S. 2005. "Why Are There So Many (or so Few) Electoral Reforms?" In *The Politics of Electoral Systems*, edited by M. Gallagher and P. Mitchell, 57–76. New York: Oxford University Press.

Kingdon, J.W. 1967. "Politicians' Beliefs about Voters." *American Political Science Review* 61 (1): 137–45.

Kiss, S. J., A.M. Perrella, and Z. Spicer. 2020. "Right-Wing Populism in a Metropolis: Personal Financial Stress, Conservative Attitudes, and Rob Ford's Toronto." *Journal of Urban Affairs* 42 (7): 1028–46.

Kostelka, F. and A. Blais. 2018. "The Chicken and Egg Question: Satisfaction with Democracy and Voter Turnout." PS: Political Science and Politics 51 (2): 370–6.

Kousser, T. and M. Mullin. 2007. "Does Voting by Mail Increase Participation? Using Matching to Analyze a Natural Experiment." Political Analysis 15(4): 428–45.

Krimmer, R., D. Duenas-Cid, and I. Krivonosova. 2021. "Debate: Safeguarding Democracy During Pandemics: Social Distancing, Postal, or Internet Voting – the Good, the Bad or the Ugly?" *Public Money & Management* 41 (1): 8–10.

Krivonosova, I., 2021. "The Forgotten Election Administrator of Internet Voting: Lessons from Estonia." *Policy Studies* 43 (6): 1254–76

Krook, M. 2006. "Reforming Representation: The Diffusion of Candidate Gender Quotas Worldwide." *Politics & Gender* 2 (3): 303–27.

Kushner, J.D. Siegel, and H. Stanwick. 1997. "Ontario Municipal Elections: Voting Trends and Determinants of Electoral Success in a Canadian Province." *Canadian Journal of Political Science* 30 (3): 539–53.

Ladner, A., and J. Pianzola. 2010. "Do Voting Advice Applications have an Effect on Electoral Participation and Voter Turnout? Evidence from the 2007 Swiss Federal Elections." In *Electronic Participation. ePart 2010. Lecture Notes in Computer Science*, 211–44. Berlin and Heidelberg: Springer.

Lagassé, P. 2017. "Institutional Change, Permanent Campaigning, and Canada's Fixed Election Date Law." In *Permanent Campaigning in Canada*, edited by A. Marland, T. Giasson, and A. Esselment, 167–83. Vancouver: UBC Press.

Landman, T., and L. Di Gennaro Splendore. 2020. "Pandemic Democracy: Elections and COVID-19." *Journal of Risk Research* 23 (7–8): 1060–6.

Larsen, R., and D. Buss. 2014. *Personality Psychology: Domains of Knowledge about Human Nature*. New York: McGraw Hill.

LeDuc, L. 2011. "Electoral Reform and Direct Democracy in Canada: When Citizens Become Involved." *West European Politics* 34 (3): 551–6.

LeRoux, K., F. Fusi, and A.G. Brown. 2020. "Assessing E-government Capacity to Increase Voter Participation: Evidence from the US." *Government Information Quarterly* 37 (3): 101–83.

Leuprecht, C. and J. McHugh, J. 2008. "Fixed Election Cycles: A Genuine Alternative to Responsible and Responsive Government?" *Commonwealth and Comparative Politics* 46 (4): 415–41.

Lewis-Beck, M.S., and M. Stegmaier. 2011. "Citizen Forecasting: Can UK Voters See the Future?" Electoral Studies 30 (2): 264–8.

Licht, N., D. Duenas-Cid, I. Krivonosova, and R. Krimmer. 2021. "To i-vote or Not to i-vote: Drivers and Barriers to the Implementation of Internet Voting." In *Electronic Voting. E-Vote-ID 2021. Lecture Notes in Computer Science*, edited by R. Krimmer et al, 91–105. Cham: Springer International Publishing.

Linos, K., 2011. "Diffusion Through Democracy." *American Journal of Political Science* 55 (3): 678–95.

Loeber, L. 2018. "The E-voting Readiness Index and the Netherlands." In Electronic Voting. E-Vote-ID 2018. Lecture Notes in Computer Science, edited by R. Krimmer et al, 146–59. Cham: Springer International Publishing.

Lucas, J. 2019. "The Size and Sources of Municipal Incumbency Advantage in Canada." *Urban Affairs Review,* 57 (2): 373–401.

Lucas, J., and R.M. McGregor. 2021. *Big City Elections in Canada*. Toronto: University of Toronto Press.

Lucas, J., R. Merrill, K. Blidook, S. Breux, L. Conrad, G. Eidelman, R. Koop, D. Marciano, Z. Taylor, and S. Vallette. 2021. "Women's Municipal Electoral Performance: An Introduction to the Canadian Municipal Elections Database." *Canadian Journal of Political Science* 54 (1): 125–33.

Lust, A. 2018. "I-Vote, Therefore I Am? Internet Voting in Switzerland and Estonia." *The SAIS Review of International Affairs* 38 (1): 65–79.

Madise, Ü., and T. Martens. 2006. "E-voting in Estonia 2005. The First Practice of Country-Wide Binding Internet Voting in the World." In Electronic Voting 2006–2nd International Workshop, Co-organized by Council of Europe, ESF TED, IFIP WG 8.6 and E-Voting. CC. Gesellschaft für Informatik eV.

Mauk, M. 2020. "Electoral Integrity Matters: How Electoral Process Conditions the Relationship Between Political Losing and Political Trust." *Qual Quant* 56 (3): 1709–28.

McCrae, R.R., and P.T. Costa Jr. 2003. *Personality in Adulthood: A Five-Factor Theory Perspective,* 2nd ed. New York: The Guilford Press.

McGregor, R.M., C.D Anderson, É. Bélanger, S. Breux, J. Lucas, J.S. Matthews, A. Mévellec, A.A. Moore, S. Pruysers, L.B. Stephenson, and E. Tolley. 2021. "The Canadian Municipal Election Study." *Frontiers in Political Science.* https://doi.org/10.3389/fpos.2021.745331.

McGregor, R.M., A. Moore, and L. Stephenson, L. 2016. "Political Attitudes and Behaviour in a Non-Partisan Environment: Toronto 2014." *Canadian Journal of Political Science* 49 (2): 311–33.

— 2021. *Electing a Mega-Mayor: Toronto 2014*. Toronto: University of Toronto Press.

McGregor, R.M., and S. Pruysers. 2022. "Post-Secondary Education and Canadian Political Behavior: How are the Level and Field of Study Related to Turnout and Partisanship?" *American Review of Canadian Studies* 52 (2): 139–62.

McGregor, R.M., S. Pruysers, N. Goodman, and Z. Spicer. 2020. "Survey Recruitment Messages and Reported Turnout – An Experimental Study." *Journal of Public Opinion, Elections, & Parties,* 32 (2): 322–38.

Mellon, J., T. Peixoto, and F.M. Sjoberg. 2017. "Does Online Voting Change the Outcome? Evidence from a Multi-Mode Public Policy Referendum." *Electoral Studies* 47: 13–24.

Mendez, F., and U. Serdült. 2017. "What Drives Fidelity to Internet Voting? Evidence from the Roll–Out of Internet Voting in Switzerland." *Government Information Quarterly* 34 (3): 511–23.

Meseguer, C., and F. Gilardi. 2009. "What is New in the Study of Policy Diffusion?" *Review of International Political Economy* 16 (3): 527–43.

Meyers, E.M., I. Erickson and R.V. Small. 2013. "Digital Literacy and Informal Learning Environments: An Introduction."Learning, Media and Technology 38 (4): 355–67.

Meyers, S., and D. Marquis. 1969. *Successful Industrial Innovations: A Study of Factors Underlying Innovation in Selected Firms*. Washington: National Science Foundation.

Miller, W.E., and D.E. Stokes. 1963. "Constituency Influence in Congress" *American Political Science Review* 57 (1): 45–56.

Milner, H. 1999. *Making Every Vote Count: Reassessing Canada's Electoral System*. Toronto: University of Toronto Press.

Miner, L. 2011. "The Unintended Consequences of Internet Diffusion: Evidence from Malaysia." https://personal.lse.ac.uk/miner/Research/MinerJobMarket.pdf.

Mondak, J.J., M.V. Hibbing, M.A. Seligson, and M.R. Anderson. 2010. "Personality and Civic Engagement: An Integrative Framework for the Study of Trait Effects on Political Behavior." *American Political Science Review* 104 (1): 1–26.

Moore, A., M. McGregor, and L. Stephenson. 2015. "Paying Attention and the Incumbency Effect: Voting Behaviour in the 2014 Toronto Municipal Election." *International Political Science Review* 38 (1): 85–98.

Morelli, M. 2004. "Party Formation and Policy Outcomes Under Different Electoral Systems." *The Review of Economic Studies* 71(3): 829–53.

Murr, A.E. 2011. "'Wisdom of Crowds'? A Decentralised Election Forecasting Model That Uses Citizens' Local Expectations." *Electoral Studies* 30 (4): 771–83.

Musiał-Karg, M., and I. Kapsa. 2020. "Attitudes of Polish Voters Towards Introduction of E-voting in the Context of Political Factors." In *E-Democracy – Safeguarding Democracy and Human Rights in the Digital Age. e-Democracy 2019. Communications in Computer and Information Science*, vol 1111, edited by S. Katsikas, and V. Zorkadis, 144–60. Cham: Springer.

Nadeau R., J.F. Daoust, and R. Dassonneville. 2021. "Winning, Losing, and the Quality of Democracy." *Political Studies* 71 (2): 483–500.

Norris, P. 1995. "The Politics of Electoral Reform in Britain." *International Political Science Review* 16 (1): 65–78.

— 1995. "Introduction: The Politics of Electoral Reform." *International Political Science Review* 16 (1): 3–8.

— 1997. "Choosing Electoral Systems: Proportional, Majoritarian and Mixed Systems." *International Political Science Review* 18 (3): 297–312.

— 2001. *A Digital Divide: Civic Engagement, Information Poverty and the Internet in Democratic Societies.* New York: Cambridge University Press.

— 2004. "Will New Technology Boost Turnout? Evaluating Experiments in UK Local Elections." In *Electronic Voting and Democracy*, edited by N. Kersting and H. Baldersheim, 193–225. New York: Palgrave Macmillan.

— 2005. "E-voting as the Magic Ballot for European Parliamentary Elections? Evaluating E-voting in the Light of Experiments in UK Local Elections." In *The European Union and E-voting*, edited by A.H. Trechsel and F. Mendez, 60–90. London: Routledge.

— 2011. "Cultural Explanations of Electoral Reform: A Policy Cycle Model." *West European Politics* 34 (3): 531–50.

— 2011. *Democratic Deficit: Critical Citizens Revisited.* Cambridge: Cambridge University Press.

OECD. 2022. *Building Trust to Reinforce Democracy: Main Findings from the 2021 OECD Survey on Drivers of Trust in Public Institutions.* Paris: OECD.

Oliver, J.E. 2012. *Local Elections and the Politics of Small-Scale Democracy*. Chicago: University of Chicago Press

Osborne, D., N. Satherley, and C.G. Sibley. 2021. "Personality and Ideology: A Meta-Analysis of the Reliable, but Non-Causal, Association Between Openness and Conservatism." In *Oxford Handbook on Behavioral Political Science*, edited by A. Mintz and L. Terris. Oxford: Oxford University Press. https://doi.org/10.1093/oxfordhb/9780190634131.013.35.

Palfrey, J.G., and U. Gasser. 2011. *Born Digital: Understanding the First Generation of Digital Natives*. ReadHowYouWant.com.

Pammett, J., and N. Goodman. 2013. "Consultation and Evaluation Practices in the Implementation of Internet Voting in Canada and Europe." Elections Canada. https://publications.gc.ca/collections/collection_2014/elections/SE7-2-2013-2-eng.pdf.

Pammett, J, and L. LeDuc. 2003. "Explaining the Turnout Decline in Canadian Federal Elections: A New Survey of Non-Voters." Elections Canada.

Panja, S., and B. Roy. 2021. "A Secure End-to-End Verifiable E-voting System Using Blockchain and Cloud Server." *Journal of Information Security and Applications* 59: 1–25.

Park, S., M. Specter, N. Narula, and R.L. Rivest. 2021. "Going from Bad to Worse: From Internet Voting to Blockchain Voting." *Journal of Cybersecurity* 7 (1): 1–15.

Patterson, T. 2002. "The Vanishing Voter: Why Are the Voting Booths So Empty?" *National Civic Review* 91 (4): 367–78.

Patterson, T.E. 2005. *Young voters and the 2004 election*. Retrieved from Joan Shorenstein Center on the Press, Politics, and Public Policy Vanishing Voter Project Web site: http://www.ksg.harvard.edu/presspol/vanishvoter.

Peterson, P. 1981. *City Limits*. Chicago: University of Chicago Press.

Petitpas, A., J.M. Jaquet, and P. Sciarini. 2021. "Does E-Voting Matter for Turnout, and to Whom?" *Electoral Studies* 71:102–45.

Phillips, J.A., and C. Wetherell. 1995. "The Great Reform Act of 1832 and the Political Modernization of England." *The American Historical Review* 100 (2): 411–36.

Phoenix Strategic Perspectives. 2011. "Survey of Candidates Following the 41st General Election." Report prepared for Elections Canada. https://www.elections.ca/res/rec/eval/pes2011/can/can_survey_e.pdf.

Picchio, M., and R. Santolini. 2022. "The Covid-19 Pandemic's Effects on Voter Turnout." *European Journal of Political Economy* 73: 102–61.

Pilon, D. 2013. *Wrestling with Democracy: Voting Systems as Politics in the 20th Century*. Toronto: University of Toronto Press.

Pomares, J., I. Levin, R.M Alvarez, G. Lopez Mirau, and T. Ovejero. 2014. "From Piloting to Roll-Out: Voting Experience and Trust in the First Full E-election in Argentina." In *2014 6th International Conference on Electronic Voting: Verifying the Vote (EVOTE)*, 1–10. Lochau/Bregenz, Austria.

Powell, A., C.K. Williams, D. Bock, T. Doellman, and J. Allen. 2012. "E-Voting Intent: A Comparison of Young and Elderly Voters." *Government Information Quarterly* 29 (3): 361–72.

Pruysers, S. 2020. "Personality and Attitudes Towards Refugees: Evidence from Canada." *Journal of Public Opinion, Elections & Parties*, 33 (4), 538–58.

— 2021. "A psychological predisposition towards populism?" *Contemporary Politics* 27 (1): 105–24.

Pruysers, S., and J. Blais. 2023. "Fair-Weather Voters: Personality and Vote Switching Intentions." Political Studies Review. Online First. https://doi.org/10.1177/14789299231174756.

Pruysers, S, J. Blais, and P.G Chen. 2019. "Who Makes a Good Citizen? The Role of Personality." *Personality and Individual Differences* 146 (1): 99–104.

Pruysers, S., and D. Stewart. 2018. "Federal-Provincial Variation in Leadership Selection: Processes and Participation." *Journal of Canadian Studies* 52 (3): 742–64.

Putnam, R.D., 2000. *Bowling Alone: The Collapse and Revival of American Community*. New York: Simon & Schuster.

Qureshi, A., D. Megias, and H Rifa-Pous. 2019. "SeVEP: Secure and Verifiable Electronic Polling System." *IEEE Access* 7: 19266–90.

Rainie, L,. and A. Perrin. 2019. "Key Findings about Americans' Declining Trust in Government and Each Other." Pew Research Center. https://www.pewresearch.org/fact-tank/2019/07/22/key-findings-about-americans-declining-trust-in-government-and-each-other/https://www.pewresearch.org/fact-tank/2019/07/22/key-findings-about-americans-declining-trust-in-government-and-each-other/.

Raynauld, V., and J. Greenberg. 2014. "Tweet, Click, Vote: Twitter and the 2010 Municipal Election." *Journal of Information Technology & Politics* 11 (4): 412–34.

Renaud, Jeff. 2021. "Online Voting Is Here, but Are We Ready? Research Shows Not Even Close." *Western News*. https://news.westernu.ca/2021/03/online-voting/.

Renwick, A. 2010. *The Politics of Electoral Reform: Changing the Rules of Democracy*. Cambridge: Cambridge University Press.

Renwick, A., C. Hanretty, and D. Hine. 2009. "Partisan Self-Interest and Electoral Reform: The New Italian Electoral Law of 2005." *Electoral Studies* 28: 437–47.

Report of the Special Committee on Electoral Reform. 2016. "Strengthening Democracy in Canada: Principles, Process and Public Engagement for Electoral Reform." https://www.ourcommons.ca/DocumentViewer/en/42-1/ERRE/report-3/page-ToC.

Richey, S. 2008. "Voting by Mail: Turnout and Institutional Reform in Oregon." *Social Science Quarterly* 89 (4): 902–15.

Riordan, M.H. 1992. "Regulation and Preemptive Technology Adoption." *The RAND Journal of Economics* 23 (3): 334–49.

Rodríguez-Pérez, A. 2022. "The Council of Europe's CM/Rec (2017) 5 on e-voting and secret suffrage: time for yet another update?." In Electronic Voting. E-Vote-ID 2022. Lecture Notes in Computer Science, edited by R. Krimmer et al, 90–105. Cham: Springer International Publishing.

Rogers, E.M. 2003. *Diffusion of Innovations*, 5th edition. New York: Free Press.

Rose, J. 2007. "The Ontario Citizens' Assembly on Electoral Reform." *Canadian Parliamentary Review* 30 (3): 9–16.

Roy, J., and C. Alcantara. 2012. "The Election Timing Advantage: Empirical Fact or Fiction?" *Electoral Studies* 31 (4): 774–81.

Sancton, A. 1983. "Conclusion: Canadian City Politics in Comparative Perspective." In *City Politics in Canada*, edited by W. Magnusson and A. Sancton, 291–317. Toronto: University of Toronto Press.

— 2011. *Canadian Local Government: An Urban Perspective*. Toronto: Oxford University Press.

Savoie, D. 2019. *Democracy in Canada. The Disintegration of our Institutions*. Montreal and Kingston: McGill-Queen's University Press.

Saxon, T. (2017). "Guelph City Council Deletes Online Voting for 2018 Municipal Election." *Guelph Today*. https://www.guelphtoday.com/local-news/guelph-city-council-deletes-online-voting-for-2018-municipal-election-596779. Accessed 7 April 2022.

Sayers, A. 1999. *Parties, Candidates, and Constituency Campaigns in Canada*. Vancouver: University of British Columbia Press.

Schumpeter, J. 1942. *Capitalism, Socialism and Democracy*. New York: Harper and Row.

Schwab, K. 2016. *The Fourth Industrial Revolution*. Massachusetts: MIT Press.

Sciarini, P., F. Cappelletti, A. Goldberg, A. Nai, and A. Tawfik.2013. "Étude du vote par Internet dans le canton de Genève." Rapport final à l'intention de la Commission externe d'évaluation des politiques publiques, Genève. http://ge.ch/vote-electronique/media/site_vote-electronique/files/imce/doc_rapports/rapport-final-sciarini-vote-par-internet.pdf.

Scott, C., and M. Medeiros. 2020. "Personality and Political Careers: What Personality Types Are Likely to Run for Office and get Elected?" *Personality and Individual Differences* 152 (1): 1–9.

Segaard, S.B, H. Baldersheim, and J. Saglie. 2016. "The Norwegian Trial with Internet Voting: Results and Challenges." In *El voto electrónico y sus dimensiones jurídicas: entre la ingenua complacencia y el rechazo precipitado*, edited by Jordi Barrat I Esteve, 189–218. Madrid: Iustel.

Sejnowski, T.J. 2018. *The Deep Learning Revolution*. Cambridge, MA: MIT Press.

Serdült, U., M. Germann, M. Harris, F. Mendez, and A. Portenier. 2015. "Who are the Internet Voters." In *Electronic Government and Electronic Participation*, edited by Efthimios Tambouris, Hans Jochen Scholl, Marjin Janssen, Maria A. Wimmer, Konstantinos Tarabanis, Mile Gasco, Bram Klievink, Ida Lindgren, Michela Milano, Panos Panagiotopoulos, Theresa A. Pardo, Peter Parycek, and Oystein Saebo, 90–105. Amsterdam: IOS Press.

Shipan, C.R. and C. Volden. 2014. "When the Smoke Clears: Expertise, Learning and Policy Diffusion." *Journal of Public Policy* 34 (3): 357–87.

Small, T.A., and H.J. Jansen, eds. 2020. *Digital Politics in Canada: Promises and Realities*. Toronto: University of Toronto Press.

Smartmatic. (2022). "Norwegian County Conducts Referendum Using Online Voting." Press release, February 2022. https://www.smartmatic.com/media/article/norwegian-county-conducts-referendum-using-online-voting/.

Solop, F.I. 2001. "Digital Democracy Comes of Age: Internet Voting and the 2000 Arizona Democratic Primary Election." *PS: Political Science & Politics* 34 (2): 289–93.

Solvak, M., and K. Vassil. 2018. "Could Internet Voting Halt Declining Electoral Turnout? New Evidence That E-Voting Is Habit Forming." *Policy & Internet* 10 (1): 4–21.

Southwell, P.L., and J.I. Burchett. 2000. "The Effect of All-Mail Elections on Voter Turnout. *American Politics Quarterly* 28(1): 72–9.

Spada, P., J. Mellon, T. Peixoto, and F.M. Sjoberg. 2016. "Effects of the Internet on Participation: Study of a Public Policy Referendum in Brazil." *Journal of Information Technology & Politics* 13 (3): 187–207.

Spicer, Z., M. McGregor, and C. Alcantara. 2017. "Political Opportunity Structures and the Representation of Women and Visible Minorities in Municipal Elections." *Electoral Studies* 48: 10–18.

Springall, D., T. Finkenauer, Z, Durumeric, J. Kitcat, H. Hursti, M. MacAlpine, and J.A. Halderman. 2014. "Security analysis of the Estonian internet voting system." In Proceedings of the 2014 ACM SIGSAC Conference on Computer and Communications Security, 703–15.

Stanwick, Hannah. 2000. "A Megamayor for all People? Voting Behaviour and Electoral Success in the 1997 Toronto Municipal Election." *Canadian Journal of Political Science* 33 (3): 549–68.

Stein, R.M. 2015. "Election Administration during Natural Disasters and Emergencies: Hurricane Sandy and the 2012 Election." *Election Law Journal* 14 (1): 66–73.

Stephenson, L.B; A. Harell, D. Rubenson, P.J. Loewen. 2020. 2019. "Canadian Election Study – Online Survey," https://doi.org/10.7910/DVN/DUS88V, Harvard Dataverse, V1.

Stevens, B.A., M.M. Islam, R. de Gues, J. Goldberg, J. R. McAndrews, A. Mierke-Zatwarnicki, P. Loewen, and D. Rubenson. 2018. "Local Candidate Effects in Canadian Elections." *Canadian Journal of Political Science* 52 (1): 1–14.

Stockemer, D. 2017. "What Affects Turnout? A Review Article/Meta-Analysis of Aggregate Research." *Government and Opposition* 52 (4): 698–722.

Strömbäck, J., C. Grandien, and K. Falasca. 2013. "Do Campaign Strategies and Tactics Matter? Exploring Party Elite Perceptions of What Matters When Explaining Election Outcomes." *Journal of Public Affairs* 13 (1): 41–52.

Taylor, Z., and Bradford, N. 2015. "The New localism: Urban Governance in the Twenty-first Century." In *Canadian Cities in Transition: Perspectives for an Urban Age*, edited by Pierre Filion, Markus Moos, Tara Vindrai, and Ryan Walker, 194–208. Toronto: Oxford University Press.

Taylor, Z., and S. McEleney. 2017. "Do Institutions and Rules Influence Electoral Accessibility and Competitiveness? Considering the 2014 Toronto Ward Elections." *Urban Affairs Review* 55 (1): 210–30.

Temporão, M., Y. Dufresne, J. Savoie, and C. van der Linden. 2019. "Crowdsourcing the Vote: New Horizons in Citizen Forecasting." *International Journal of Forecasting* 35 (1): 1–10.

Thomas, M., and M.A. Bodet. 2013. "Sacrificial Lambs, Women Candidates, and District Competitiveness in Canada." Electoral Studies 32(1): 153–66.

Thompson, D.M., J.A. Wu, J. Yoder, and A.B. Hall. 2020. "Universal Vote-by-Mail has no Impact on Partisan Turnout or Vote Share." Proceedings of the National Academy of Sciences, 117 (25): 14052–6.

Tilley, J., and G. Evans. 2014. "Ageing and Generational Effects on Vote Choice: Combining Cross-Sectional and Panel Data to Estimate APC Effects." *Electoral Studies* 33 (March 2014): 19–27.

Trechsel, A.H., and K. Vassil. 2010. "Internet Voting in Estonia. A Comparative Analysis of Five Elections since 2005: report for the Council of Europe." Strasbourg, Council of Europe. https://www.coe.int/t/dgap/goodgovernance/Activities/E-voting/CoE_Studies/GGIS(2010)15_Internet_voting%20_in%20_Estonia%202005-2009%20E.asp.

Trounstine, J. 2011. "Evidence of a Local Incumbency Advantage." *Legislative Studies Quarterly* 36 (2): 255–80.

Twizeyimana, J.D, and A. Andersson. 2019. "The public value of E-Government – A literature review." *Government Information Quarterly* 36 (2): 167–78.

Umberg, T., and J. Rivera Diaz. 2020. "Election Law Changes as a Result of COVID-19." *California Journal of Politics and Policy* 12 (1): 1–3.

United States Election Assistance Commission. 2005. "Voluntary Voting System Guidelines 1.0 Volume 1." https://www.eac.gov/sites/default/files/eac_assets/1/28/VVSG.1.0_Volume_1.PDF.

— 2005. "Voluntary Voting System Guidelines 1.0 Volume 2." https://www.eac.gov/sites/default/files/eac_assets/1/28/VVSG1.0Vol.2.PDF.

— 2021. "Requirements for the Voluntary Voting System Guidelines 2.0." https://www.eac.gov/sites/default/files/TestingCertification/Voluntary_Voting_System_Guidelines_Version_2_0.pdf.

— 2023. "Voluntary E-Poll Book Certification Requirements Version 0.9." https://www.eac.gov/sites/default/files/2023-06/EPB_Master_Requirements_DRAFT_January_19_2023.pdf.

Uslaner, E.M., and R.E. Weber. 1979. "US State Legislators' Opinions and Perceptions of Constituency Attitudes." *Legislative Studies Quarterly* 4 (4): 565–85.

Van Deursen, A., and J. Van Dijk. 2011. "Internet Skills and the Digital Divide." *New Media & Society* 13 (6): 893–911.

Vassil, K., M. Solvak, P. Vinkel, A.H. Trechsel, and R.M. Alvarez. 2016. "The Diffusion of Internet Voting. Usage Patterns of Internet Voting in Estonia Between 2005 and 2015." *Government Information Quarterly* 33 (3): 453–9.

Vassil, K., and T. Weber. 2011. "A Bottleneck Model of E-voting: Why Technology Fails to Boost Turnout." *New Media & Society* 13 (8): 1336–54.

Vox Pop. 2017. "MyDemocracy.ca: Online Digital Consultation and Engagement Platform. https://www.canada.ca/content/dam/pco-bcp/documents/pdfs/mydem/MyDemocracy.ca.PDF.

Wagner, A. 2016. "Candidate Orientation to ICTs in Canadian Municipal Elections." In *Citizen Participation and Political Communication in a Digital World*, edited by Alex Frame and Gilles Brachotte, 81–94. New York: Routledge.

Walter, R. 2018. "British Parliamentary By-elections During the First World War, 1914–18." *Parliamentary History* 37 (3): 415–34.

Warkentin, M., S. Sharma, D, Gefen, G,M. Rose, and P. Pavlou. 2018. "Social Identity and Trust in Internet-Based Voting Ddoption." *Government Information Quarterly* 35 (2): 195–209.

Warren M.E. 2009. "Citizen Participation and Democratic Deficits: Considerations from the Perspective of Democratic Theory." In *Activating the Citizen*, edited by J. DeBardeleben and J.H. Pammett, 17–40. Palgrave Macmillan, London.

Wattenberg, M. 2002. *Where Have All the Voters Gone?* Cambridge: Harvard University Press.

Wigginton, M.J., and D. Stockemer. Forthcoming. "Does the Introduction of Online Voting Create Diversity in Representation?" *Political Studies Review*.

Yard, M., ed. 2010. *Direct Democracy: Progress and Pitfalls of Election Technology*. Washington: International Foundation for Electoral Systems.

Zaller, J. 1992. *The Nature and Origins of Mass Opinion*. Cambridge: Cambridge University Press.

Index